AMERICAN INDIAN LIBERATION

A *Theology* of Sovereignty

George E. "Tink" Tinker

ORBIS BOOKS
Maryknoll, New York

Founded in 1970, Orbis Books endeavors to publish works that enlighten the mind, nourish the spirit, and challenge the conscience. The publishing arm of the Maryknoll Fathers and Brothers, Orbis seeks to explore the global dimensions of the Christian faith and mission, to invite dialogue with diverse cultures and religious traditions, and to serve the cause of reconciliation and peace. The books published reflect the views of their authors and do not represent the official position of the Maryknoll Society. To learn more about Maryknoll and Orbis Books, please visit our website at www.maryknoll.org.

Library of Congress Cataloging-in-Publication Data

Tinker, George E.
 American Indian liberation : a theology of sovereignty / George E. "Tink" Tinker.
    p. cm.
  ISBN 978-1-57075-805-8
  1. Indians of North America—Religion. 2. Indian cosmology—United States. 3. Indians of North America—Social conditions. 4. Liberation theology—United States. 5. Christianity and culture—United States. 6. Christianity and other religions—United States. 7. Racism—Religious aspects—Christianity. I. Title.
  E98.R3T54 2008
  299.7—dc22

                                            2008013933

This book is dedicated to the memory of the giant of all American Indian scholars and intellects, Professor Vine Deloria, Jr., who passed to the spirit world on November 13, 2005.

He was a mentor, a friend, a critic, and a constant source of encouragement to me and countless other younger Indian scholars.

ABOUT THE COVER

The cover painting depicts an Osage Inlonshka dancer. The Inlonshka, the most important traditional ceremonial occasion among the Osage, is danced by the men's society in the three districts of the Osage Reservation: Pawhuska, Hominy, and Grey Horse. The dances are held in each district for four days on three different weekends, usually in June. The traditional Osage ribbon-work in the painting was modeled after the actual ribbon-work worn for the dances by the author of this book.

The artist depicts the dancer without a face; this characteristic represents a questioning or loss of identity because of the effects of colonialism and oppression on Indian people. Yet, while the dancer may be searching for a fuller understanding of his identity, he continues with the traditions and values he has been given, such as this dance; and he will pass on these traditions to the future generations.

Alistair Bane, the artist, is a member of the Eastern Shawnee Nation and an important member of the Denver urban Indian community. Trained in art at the School of the Art Institute of Chicago, he is both a painter and a traditional beadworker.

Osage Inlonshka Dancer was commissioned for this particular book and was then photographed by another artist, Robert Maestas (indigenous Chicano), who shows work in the same gallery as Bane. Maestas's digital-painting images imprinted on ceramic tile are one of his most popular media.

Contents

Introduction

Historic Pain and the Political Present

Pointing to a Healthy Future

An American Indian theology must necessarily be a political theology, especially if we take political in its broadest sense to indicate the cultural life of
a community. Indian religious traditions are so thoroughly intertwined with
and infused in their cultures that we cannot conceive a theology that deals
only with "religion." Indian politics and spirituality are likewise wholly intertwined. This means that an American Indian theology must also reflect on the
deep connection between the culture and the religious traditions of Indian
peoples—both in all their diversity and in their underlying, foundational
similarity. It dare not, however, engage in the luxury of a mere insider description of Indian religious traditions in order to satisfy some White new-age lust
for the exotic other. As euro-western theologians have learned, often slowly
and particularly from Two-Thirds World writers, theological reflection cannot
be done in any healthy way without taking the social, cultural, political, and
general human context into account.[1] After five hundred years of conquest,

I want to acknowledge the consistent help of three people who worked on different parts
of the text, reading, critiquing, and suggesting textual emendations along the way. Two student
assistants read parts of or the whole of the text to help me improve it: Mark Freeland (Sault Ste
Marie Ojibwe) and Eric Larson. I received similar assistance from my wife, a Chicana indigenous person, Dr. Loring Abeyta, who always reads with a fine critical eye.

1. My use of the lower case for such adjectives as "english," "christian," "biblical," and so
on is intentional. While nouns naming religious groups might be capitalized out of respect for
each Christian—as for each Muslim or Buddhist—using the lower case "christian" or "biblical" for adjectives allows readers to avoid unnecessary normativizing or universalizing of
the principal institutional religious quotient of the euro-west. Likewise, I avoid capitalizing
such national or regional adjectives as american, amer-european, european, euro-western, and
so on. I also refer to north America. It is important to my argumentation that people recognize the historical artificiality of modern regional and nation-state social constructions. For
instance, who decides where the "continent" of Europe ends and that of Asia begins? Similarly,
who designates the western half of north America as a separate continent clearly divided by the
Mississippi River, or alternatively the Rocky Mountains? My initial reasoning extends to other

social destruction, and genocide, any useful commentary by American Indians speaking to the Indian context today must reflect on the political state of Indian affairs and the political hopes and visions for recovering the health and well-being of Indian communities.

Particularly since 1970, the most openly political branch of christian theology, called liberation theology, has emerged in Two-Thirds World circles and helped to generate organizations such as the Ecumenical Association of Third World Theologians (EATWOT). A contemporary Indian reflection can learn much from these Two-Thirds World theologians, even as we share some similarities in goals. Like these liberation theology advocates, American Indians must also see liberation, or freedom, as our principal goal, as indeed it was in the hearts of 1970s Indian activists, for instance, involved in the American Indian Movement and in the hearts of our ancestors who struggled with the immediacy of the colonial invasion. Yet, as indigenous communities, our notions of freedom and liberation will be necessarily different from the expressions of Christianity that have emerged, for example, from latin american liberation theologians during the last thirty or more years.

One critical difference, and one that is a correlative political issue, especially in the mind of the colonizer churches, Native American theologies may be identifiably christian or not. Indeed, they may be distinctly non-christian or even pronouncedly anti-christian. Even where an Indian theologian may want to identify as a part of the christian whole, the resulting theology may be quite distinct from the usual christian discourses and methodologies, preferring, for example, a variety of categories that have much more in common with traditional tribal thinking than with the usual established european categories. Politically, this simple difference is already a choice on the part of an Indian community or an Indian thinker that causes considerable discomfort in colonizer churches, especially when it comes to funding a denominational Indian church. The problem that emerges here in the relationship between Indians and the colonizer is that an Indian christian congregation may decide that their attention to their own culture and religious traditions means that they can no longer agree to behave themselves in terms of replicating denominational theology and doctrine. Denominations seem to have deeply invested themselves in a politics of replicating themselves in the colonized. The missionaries want nothing more

---

adjectival categories and even some nominal categories, such as euro, political designations such as the right and the left, and regional designations such as the west. Quite paradoxically, I know, I insist on capitalizing White (adjective or noun) to indicate a clear cultural pattern invested in Whiteness that is all too often overlooked or even denied by american Whites. Moreover, this brings parity to the insistence of african Americans on the capitalization of the word Black in reference to their own community (in contradistinction to the *New York Times* usage). Likewise, I always capitalize Indian and American Indian.

than to see themselves reflected back in the faith and language of their Indian wards. Yet, in the politics of freedom, a serious Indian theology dare not buy into denomination doctrine without offering its own cultural critique.

Because of our announced interest in American Indian freedom, this book may not and must not engage in the mere reporting of interesting American Indian spiritual or cultural traditions as merely an interest in the euro-exotic other. This would move us back into the politics of colonialism rather that toward a politics of freedom. Besides, there are plenty of other authors to which the reader can turn for that, although there are clearly problems associated with most of those texts, especially those written by non-Indian (and perforce, colonialist) authors. Both cultural anthropology and history of religions are tainted as disciplines by the cultural biases of the objective observer—whether conducted in the classic modality of detachment or in the more modern mode of participant-observer. New-age aficionados, on the other hand, continue to engage in the politics of colonial conquest in another way. They skim the surface structures of traditional Indian ceremonial life in order to commodify an illusion of exotic spirituality with the result that these fetishists have become the latest and most violent colonizers of Indian communities, all to serve the pecuniary purposes of the great american super-market of spirituality. This is not the book, however, to provide that sort of an anthropological or history-of-religions corrective to name more explicitly the egregious colonialism of the new agers. Rather, these essays reflect deeply on the contemporary state of Native America. The social and political context of modern Indian existence is critical for understanding who Indian people are today and how we begin to think through intellectual issues of survival and continuity with the traditions of our past.

Before we can move into the substance of the essays presented here, it would seem important to provide readers with some common foundational understanding of American Indian realities. While everyone in north America today knows something about American Indians, it seems that no one really knows much at all about Indians except Indians—and even much of what we know about ourselves is misinformation served up by public schools, would-be experts teaching about us in universities, new-age vultures commodifying Indian spirituality for capitalist gain, political pundits, and Hollywood, always Hollywood and its perjurious invention of truth.[2] It takes a great deal of intentional focus to break through the layers of colonial signification in order

---

2. See especially Ward Churchill, "Fantasies of the Master Race: The Stereotyping of American Indians in Film," in idem, *Fantasies of the Master Race: Literature, Cinema and the Colonization of American Indians*, rev. 2d ed. (San Francisco: City Lights Press, 1998), 167-224.

to begin to understand more accurately the contemporary situation for the aboriginal peoples of this continent.

Thus, it seems only fitting that this collection of essays begin with a basic primer of the fundamentals of contemporary Indian existence, including the history of colonialism and the political realities of cultural difference that sets Indian peoples apart. That is, this introduction attempts to provide a sketch of the basic information that anyone who lives in north America should know about American Indians and the basic information necessary to begin to make some sense of American Indian political theology. The material that follows cannot be exhaustive. Rather, it is a beginning outline of issues and concerns that are crucial for many contemporary Indian activists. This introduction will try to avoid the ahistorical romanticizing of so many White, amer-euro-pean histories of Indian peoples, just as it avoids reporting the stock-in-trade cultural (anthropology) items around tribal moiety structures or exoticized marriage and familial relationships. It is much more important for the reading of these essays to begin by putting the relationship of Indian nations and the european migrants into its proper historical, social, economic, and especially political context.

The question that is finally important is not "who are these exotic crea-tures who are so different from yourselves?" but rather, "how will we together (non-Indian and Indian) build the future differently than we have built the colonial past?" It should go without saying, of course, that creating a transfor-matively different future requires us necessarily to study the past, even when that history makes for very painful reading. In this way, an ethnographic study of American Indians is really insignificant—at least as insignificant as doing an ethnographic study of White America.[3] Hence, this brief introduction emphasizes the historical interrelationships between Indian and amer-euro-pean peoples rather than offering some romantic representation of Indians as an american exotic other.

It should be noted from the outset that the author is an American Indian by paternal heritage, enrolled in the Osage Nation, and thus writes as emic insider. That is to say, the following is written as much as possible from a native point of view rather than the usual dominant colonizer point of view, even when that is done by the most liberal and sensitive White interpreter. At the same time, the author is an Indian "mixed blood" who has a deep com-mitment to conversation with and healing of his mother's euro-western and amer-european peoples. I write with the hope that we will be able to initiate a symbiotic healing process whereby Indian poverty and devastation can find

---

3. With full apologies to Martin Mull ("The History of White People in America") and his analytical (comic) insight that "all White people love a good lawn."

healing even as White America begins to find healing from its ongoing history of violence and the resulting culture of violence that seems to have captured the north american present. Hence, this outline is a beginning point for a polyvalent understanding.

American Indians, the aboriginal residents of the Americas, entered european consciousness in 1492 with the columbian misadventure.[4] The subsequent european invasion of the Americas resulted in untold devastation to these indigenous residents and owners of the american territories. The intentional destruction of their cultures and massacres of their communities were often perpetrated in the name of the invaders' christian religious convictions and their attempts to impose their religion on those whose land they came to steal.[5] The laws invented in european and english legal discourse to permit the invasion and occupation of indigenous lands were deeply rooted in the canon law of the medieval church and in their ongoing manipulation of christian theology.[6] It should be noted from the outset that the european encounter with

---

4. Columbus engaged nearly immediately in kidnapping and enslaving Native peoples in the Caribbean. As governor of the Caribbean for some eight years, he was directly responsible for the murder and death of some seven million aboriginal inhabitants of the island of Hispaniola alone. See demographic research reported in George E. Tinker and Mark Freeland, "Thief, Slave-Trader, Murderer: Christopher Columbus and Caribbean Population Decline," unpublished manuscript; Sherburne F. Cook and Woodrow Borah, *Essays in Population History*, vol. 1, *Mexico and the Caribbean* (Berkeley: University of California Press, 1971); and Henry Dobryns, *Their Number Become Thinned: Native American Population Dynamics in Eastern North America* (Knoxville: University of Tennessee Press, 1983).

5. For example, within three years of his conquest of the Aztecas, Hernando Cortez brought in a cadre of Franciscan monks to begin the dual process of religious conversion and pacification of the countryside. For histories of the christian missionary participation in the projects of colonialism and conquest, see Luis N. Rivera-Pagán, *A Violent Evangelism: The Political and Religious Conquest of the Americas* (Louisville: John Knox Press, 1992); and George E. Tinker, *Missionary Conquest: The Gospel and Native American Genocide* (Minneapolis: Fortress Press, 1993).

6. One should note at a minimum the early legal scholarly writings of Francisco Vittoria, *De Indis Relectio Posterior, sive De Jure Belli Hispanorum in Barbaros* (1538), Hugo Grotius, *De jure bellis ac pacis* (1625), and Emmerich Vattel, *Le droit de gens; ou, Principes de la loi naturelle appliqués à la conduite et aux affaires des nations et des souverains* (1758). See the fine volume by Robert Williams, *American Indians and the Western Legal Tradition: The Discourses of Conquest* (New York: Oxford University Press, 1990). Williams traces the medieval and the early (european) modern roots of modern international law and the legal legitimizing of colonialism and conquest. For an analysis of the language of colonialism, see Glenn Morris's wonderful essay of the development of legal modes of conquest: "Vine Deloria, Jr. and the Development of a Decolonizing Critique of Indigenous Peoples and International Relations," in *Native Voices: American Indian Identity and Resistance*, ed. Richard Grounds, David Wilkins, and George E. Tinker (Lawrence: University of Kansas, 2003). Most recently, Lindsay G. Roberts, *Conquest by Law: How the Discovery of America Dispossessed Indigenous Peoples of Their Lands* (New York:

indigenous peoples was not the first european use of such violence. The european and english peoples had developed a long track record of combining religious sentiment and conquest (such as the *reconquista* of Iberia, the crusades, Lithuania, Ireland).[7]

When they first encountered european peoples, the indigenous peoples of the Americas must have numbered, according to current demographic research, well in excess of 100 million people.[8] These nations had very complex and diverse cultures with stable economies and political systems. Some had built incredible cities significantly larger than the largest cities in Europe; many had developed technologies (for example, Inca smelting and agriculture; Mayan and Aztecan mathematics) far in advance of Europe. Divided into thousands of different language communities derived from a large number of distinct language families, the aboriginal inhabitants of the Americas shared discrete and diverse cultures and religious traditions that were both related to one another and distinctly different from the cultures and religious traditions of their european invaders.

From the very beginnings of the european invasion and conquest of Indian peoples, the colonizers recognized the deep cultural differences and learned quickly how to exploit those differences politically to satisfy their own avarice and achieve their acquisitive purposes. Asserting their own culture to be superior, they codified laws based on fictive narratives that elevated themselves and insured that indigenous peoples were reduced to servitude or easily and legally removed from occupancy of prime lands of economic value. The more liberal-hearted among the colonizers devised "gentler" (Las Casas's word) methods for conquering the indigenous populations, hoping to destroy indigenous cultural structures in order to replace them with the european value system and cultural patterns of behavior. Missionaries of the gospel became the most efficient means of carrying out this aspect of the conquest.

Because of these fundamental cultural differences between Indians and the european colonizers and the radical imbalance of power, the very first missionary to enter any Indian community effectively initiated a political division

---

Oxford University Press, 2005), traces the U.S. Supreme Court's creation of the "Discovery Doctrine" language that was used not only in the United States but across the euro-colonized globe to enable and legitimize the theft of native lands by european colonizers, giving grand larceny a fictional history of legality that endures to this day as a legal "truth."

7. Again, see the historical analysis of Williams, *American Indians and the Western Legal Tradition*.

8. Dobyns, *Their Number Become Thinned*, argued for a total of 117 million people for the american hemisphere prior to the european invasion. He has since been revising his estimates upwards. For a recent assessment, see Charles Mann, *1491* (New York: Alfred A. Knopf, 2005).

of that community that proved genocidal. Since religion and culture are never separate in any Indian community, the arrival of the first missionary forced members of the community, for the first time in their lives, to make a choice between full participation in the culture of their community (including religious and ceremonial participation) and participation as an individual in the new religious tradition brought by the colonists. Forcing this choice was so successful as a part of the colonialist strategy in dividing communities and coercing compliance that missionization was further developed explicitly as a political strategy throughout the colonizing process to serve that purpose.[9]

I want to posit *four fundamental, deep structure cultural differences* between Indian people and the cultures that derive from european traditions that set American Indian cultures (including religious traditions, social structures, politics, and so forth) distinctly apart from amer-european cultures and religions. They are, briefly noted, spatiality as opposed to temporality; attachment to particular lands or territory; the priority of community over the individual; and a consistent notion of the interrelatedness of humans and the rest of creation. It should be added that language, while in a state of serious decay as a result of the colonial onslaught, also continues to be a cultural self-signifier for Indian communities.

First, these indigenous traditions are spatially based rather than temporally based. The euro-western world has a two-millennia history of a trajectory shifting decidedly away from any rootedness in spatiality toward an ever-increasing awareness of temporality. Whether in its capitalist or socialist (marxist?) guise,[10] history and temporality reign supreme in the euro-west, where time is money and "development," or progress, is the goal. On the other

---

9. In the new rogue nation called the United States, for instance, the Congress moved very early on to establish a "Civilization Fund" to reimburse certain missionary activities among Indian peoples. This, of course, was in clear contradiction to the freedom of religion touted in the Bill of Rights and its First Amendment non-establishment clause. Yet the missionaries continued to play a key role in the implementation of federal Indian policy into the twentieth century.

10. During the past couple of generations, these are the two possibilities argued most coherently for structuring modern political existence. Both are universalist systems, presumed suitable for all cultures and societies. Both are based on european philosophical structures. While the socialist solutions fit along a spectrum of various theories and policies, all modern socialist arguments have some rootedness in Marx and marxian critique. This was true of the arguments of latin american liberation theologians of the past generation even when, for political purposes, they denied any marxist connection. Today, many of these same theologians have despaired of marxist or socialist solutions and moved toward "civil society" arguments. For American Indian attitudes toward marxism, see Ward Churchill, "False Promises: An Indigenist Examination of Marxist Theory and Practice," in idem, *Acts of Rebellion: The Ward Churchill Reader* (New York: Routledge, 2003), 247-62.

hand, Native American spirituality, values, social and political structures, even ethics, are fundamentally rooted not in some temporal notion of history but in spatiality. This is perhaps the most dramatic (and largely unnoticed) cultural difference between Native American intellectual traditions and euro-western thought processes. The euro-western intellectual tradition is firmly rooted in the priority of temporal metaphors and modes of being. Native Americans think inherently spatially and not temporally.[11] The question is not whether time or space is missing in one culture or the other, but which of these metaphoric bases functions as the ordinary and which is the subordinate. Of course, Native Americans have a temporal awareness, but it is subordinate to our sense of spatiality. Likewise, the euro-western tradition has a spatial awareness, but spatiality lacks the priority of the temporal. Hence, progress, history, development, evolution, and process become key ideas and narratives that inform all academic discourse in the euro-west, from science and economics to philosophy and theology. History, thus, becomes the quintessential western intellectual device and gives rise to structures of cognition and modes of discourse that pay dutiful homage to the ascendancy of temporality.[12]

Second, American Indian indigenous cultures are communitarian by nature and do not share the euro-west's capitulation to the priority of the individual over against community.[13] Thus, for instance, spiritual involvement in the ceremonial life of a community is typically engaged in "for the sake of the people" and not for the sake of individual salvation or personal spiritual self-empowerment. This alone sets Indian cultures and spirituality radically apart from new-age seekers (which is radically individualist) and the whole european and amer-european genre of self-help. It also accounts for the extent to which euro-missionization, with its emphasis on personal decision making and the

---

11. See Vine Deloria, Jr., *God Is Red* (New York: Grosset & Dunlap, 1973); rev. ed., *God Is Red: A Native View of Religion* (Golden, Colo.: Fulcrum, 1992; 30th anniv. ed., 2002); idem, *The Metaphysics of Modern Existence* (New York: Harper & Row, 1979); and George E. Tinker, "American Indians and the Arts of the Land: Spatial Metaphors and Contemporary Existence," in *Voices from the Third World* 14, no. 2 (1991): 170-93.

12. If marxist thinking and the notion of a historical dialectic were finally to win the day, then American Indian people and all indigenous peoples would be surely doomed, just as we seem to be under the hegemony of globalized "democratic" capitalism. Our cultures and value systems, our spirituality, and even our social structures must soon give way to an emergent socialist structure that would impose a common notion of the good on all people regardless of ethnicity or culture.

13. Deloria, *God Is Red*; Jace Weaver, *That the People Might Live: Native American Literatures and Native American Community* (New York: Oxford University Press, 1997); George E. Tinker, "Spirituality, Native American Personhood, Sovereignty and Solidarity," in *Spirituality of the Third World: A Cry for Life*, ed. K. C. Abraham and Bernadette Mbuy-Beya (Maryknoll, N.Y.: Orbis Books, 1994), 119-32.

salvation of the individual soul, was so disruptive and destructive to indigenous communities. To remove individuals from the communitarian whole through the process of conversion affects the community whole and not just the individual, even though only the individual makes a self-conscious choice. Eventually the pressure of missionization destroyed the ceremonial life of the community, because so many Indian ceremonies require the participation of the whole community for their success.

Third, in the indigenous world there is a firmly established notion of the interrelatedness of all the created/natural world. This sense of interrelatedness means that there is a much larger community whole than the clan or village or band, and has enormous import for understanding the religious traditions of these peoples. Yet, this larger community is not the modern state but rather consists of animals (four-leggeds), birds, and all the living, moving things (including rocks, hills, trees, rivers, and so on), along with all the other sorts of two-leggeds (e.g., bears, humans of different colors) in the world. In Indian cultures, people live and experience themselves as a part of creation, for instance, rather than living as separate from creation with the freedom or even responsibility to consume it at will.

Finally, spatiality, a community-centered sense, and the notion of interrelatedness lend themselves to yet a fourth categorical difference between these indigenous cultures and the west. In native north America, indigenous peoples find their primary attachments in terms of particular lands and territory. Individual ownership, even group ownership, of land is a concept foreign to Indian peoples. Rather, there is a firm sense of group filial attachment to particular places that comes with a responsibility to relate to the land in those places with responsibility.

These four cultural identifiers are so interconnected that any damage to one cultural aspect extends the damaging effect to the other three. For instance, the primacy of the spatial metaphor among the indigenous peoples of the Americas is intimately linked to their experience of existence as deeply rooted in the land. This intimate interconnection between an Indian community and the spatiality of its territory explains why the history of our conquest and removal from our lands was so culturally and genocidally destructive to our tribes. Yet the removal of Indian peoples from their lands, the destruction of "joint tenure" as a cultural mode of territorial residence, and the teaching of private (individual) ownership of land became principal missionary strategies in the christianization and civilization of Indian peoples.[14]

---

14. See the collection of primary sources compiled, excerpted and edited by Francis Paul Prucha, *Americanizing the American Indian: Writings by the "Friends of the Indian," 1880-1900* (Omaha: University of Nebraska Press, 1973).

Perhaps the most precious gift that American Indians have to share with Amer-europeans is our perspective on the interrelatedness of all of creation and our deep sense of relationship to the land in particular. We are all relatives: from buffaloes and eagles to trees and rocks, mountains and lakes. Just as there is no category of the inanimate, there can be no conception of anything in the created world that does not share in the sacredness infused in the act of creation. Traditional stories relate dialogue and interaction between different animal relatives quite as if they were like us human beings. Indeed, they may have been in some earlier age—or rather we humans were like them. Many tribal traditions, then, include stories that try to account for the necessity, for the sake of the survival of one species, of violent acts, perpetuated in hunting. In many of these stories, the four-leggeds and wingeds engage in long debate that concludes with a consensus to permit hunting by two-leggeds—for their good, that is, survival—but establishes certain parameters that will always ensure respect for the sacredness of all life. This contrasts starkly with the traditional theological interpretation of the Genesis creation accounts by european and amer-european churches, capitalist entrepreneurs, and politicians. For example, those who occupied what became the United States used Genesis 1:26 as one of the theological foundations for the politico-religious doctrine of Manifest Destiny, a doctrine that still seems to fuel U.S. political action in the international arena today under the guise of the "new world order" or its gentler and kinder rearticulation as "globalization."[15]

These American Indian cultural characteristics manifest themselves repeatedly in the spiritual and ceremonial life of indigenous peoples in north America, and among a great variety of the world's indigenous peoples,[16] since the spiritual and ceremonial life is merely an extension of day-to-day existence, all parts of which are experienced within ceremonial parameters. Moreover, these traits remain deeply rooted, even where they have been eroded considerably for many in a community. So, in spite of the long-lived and ongoing colonial effort to reduce Indian difference to amer-european sameness, there continue to be qualitative differences between Indian and amer-european that apply even among Indian people who have converted to Christianity.

---

15. The post-Soviet triumphalist articulation of a new world order was, evidently, too raw a naming of the new relationship between the United States, as the only remaining world superpower, and its now global empire of dependencies. There was need for a defining word that held out hope of some market appeal, at least among the elites in the Third World.

16. For the similarity of cultural attachment to the particularity of a land base, note the Australian Aboriginal context. See Anne Pattel-Gray (aboriginal Australian), *The Great White Flood: Racism in Australia: Critically Appraised from an Aboriginal Historico-Theological Viewpoint* (American Academy of Religion Cultural Criticism Series 2; Atlanta: Scholars Press, 1998).

In the centuries of colonization and genocide following Columbus, the christianization of these indigenous populations became one key strategy for their conquest, that is, facilitating the exploitation of their labor and natural resources. The conquest was brutal from the beginning. In almost every context, the european invaders initiated a very quick 90 to 95 percent (or higher) death rate among native populations through programs of mass murder and enslavement, through brutal military repression, and through the introduction of disease epidemics to which the natives lacked resistance. The spanish invaders managed to kill nearly the entire population of more that seven million residents of the island Columbus named Hispaniola (his center of operations) within ten years (by 1502).[17] Within thirty years of the first invasion of Mexico, according to Bartolomé de Las Casas, the spanish had killed twenty million of the original twenty-five million native residents.

Many colonizers began to look toward missionization as a principal means of pacifying Indian resistance. Especially more squeamish (liberal) colonialists, for whom mass murder seemed opprobrious, turned to missionization and "civilization" as a principal means for both saving Indians from death by extermination and still allowing the settlers to steal Indian land and resources. Others, such as Hernando Cortez (c. 1521) in Mexico and John Winthrop in 1630s New England, shamelessly engaged in both strategies simultaneously. Winthrop, for example, provided official support for John Eliot's missionary efforts (beginning in 1643) on the one hand, but also, on the other, self-consciously arranged the mass murder of Pequots in 1637 as an effective way of dealing with two different Indian nations. Cortez, who also engaged in mass murder with few apparent conscience pangs, imported Franciscan friars immediately after his conquest of Tenochtitlan (Mexico City) to aid in the colonization (through pacification) of the countryside.

Bartolomé de Las Casas, the historic hero of liberal Christians during the 1992 columbian quincentenary, became one of those liberal colonialists who courageously described the barbarity of the spanish colonizers (*conquistadores*) in the Caribbean and on the mainland during the first half of the sixteenth century. He gives eyewitness descriptions of the widespread murdering in graphic detail in numerous tracts and books. In 1551 Las Casas engaged in a famous public debate before the spanish court in order to argue that the indigenous peoples of the Americas were also human beings, a position that was not patently obvious to the avarice of the spanish *conquistadores*. Yet, even Las Casas was in the final analysis thoroughly committed to european colonialism

---

17. Cook and Borah, *Mexico and the Caribbean*, argue the evidence very persuasively for an aboriginal population of eight million on the island of Hispaniola. Many scholars have been moving increasingly toward agreement with Cook and Borah.

and the exploitation of Indian lands and labor. His concession to his christian conscience was to promulgate "a gentler conquest" conducted by the church on behalf of his royal majesties in Spain. His plan for this gentler conquest involved a process of missionization that became the predominant structure used by Catholics in both south and north in the Americas and reproduced by Protestants in the north. The mission compound is still in use today by fundamentalist christian groups such as the Summer Institute of Linguistics (originally Wycliffe Bible Translators) in the southern hemisphere as a way of separating the converts from their families and home communities in order to ensure that their new religious and cultural commitment holds.

North America became a settler colony almost immediately, unlike south and central America where the settlers remained a minority of the population until the renewed european migrations during the nineteenth and early twentieth centuries changed demographics in many countries of the south. Hence, there was a more persistent and concerted effort in north America to deal in decisive ways with aboriginal landowners. The result was a persistent ethnic cleansing of the continental territory that became the United States. As the settlers grew in number and pushed farther and farther west, Indian people found themselves compressed into smaller and smaller enclaves, most often having been forced to move away from their homes to strange lands. Andrew Jackson ran for president in 1828 on a platform that explicitly promised to remove Indian peoples from their coveted lands in the southern states (especially Georgia) and carried out the plan in the 1830s in a project that has been forever remembered as the "Trail of Tears." While many northern churches (Congregationalists, northern Baptists) openly opposed the plan, many southern churches were either quietistic (for example, Moravian) or openly supported states' rights politics (Methodists) and the removal as a means of opening up Indian lands to White settlers.[18]

In the post–U.S. Civil War era, the western print media (in Kansas, Colorado, the Dakotas, and so on) consistently called for the extermination or removal of Indians from the western states as an inhuman infestation on lands they coveted for amer-european settler expansion. Eastern liberals, however, having long secured their own land base, magnanimously believed that Indian peoples were capable of being "civilized" and christianized.[19] At this late date in the colonization process, the debate of Las Casas over the humanness of Indian peoples remained unresolved for amer-european colonists as they con-

---

18. The best analysis of the wrestlings of conscience among the missionaries in Cherokee Territory during the late 1820s and early 1830s is in William Gerald McGloughlin, *Cherokees and Missionaries: 1789-1839* (New Haven: Yale University Press, 1984).

19. See my chapter on Bishop Henry Benjamin Whipple in Tinker, *Missionary Conquest*.

tinued to hold these two very different assessments of the humanity of Indian people—even if both sides held to different but equally genocidal solutions. The moral solutions offered called either for the justified extermination (murder) of Indian peoples who got in the way of U.S. Manifest Destiny or some imposed cultural transformation of Indian peoples to allow a more peaceful access to and appropriation of their lands. On the extermination side of the debate, Rev. John Chivington gave up his methodist pastorate in Denver to lead the attack of a Colorado territorial militia against a peaceful Cheyenne village, insisting on the killing of babies and children as well as the adults, reciting the adage to his captains the night before the attack, "Nits make lice." Their surprise attack at dawn in winter murdered some 1,600 Indian peoples, mostly civilians—women, children, and old people.[20]

The liberals eventually won the policy battle in the United States, and the "civilization" project began in earnest for Indian communities in the 1870s.[21] In order to ensure the success of the project and to succeed also in reducing Indian land holdings and increasing the land holdings of White settlers, the liberal reformers in the government and in the churches built a policy platform with a number of planks. They first called for teaching Indians the private ownership of property and breaking up the reservation land holdings. Second, they called for the evangelization and education of Indian children. Most important to their strategy was their insistence that Indian national communities relinquish their status as sovereign nations and come under direct U.S. governance as full citizens. This, of course, was the U.S. attempt to administer the coup de grace to Indian cultures, values, and religious traditions. Supported strongly by church leaders as well as by liberal politicians, this Indian affairs "reform" movement was yet another persistent (and self-conscious) attempt at Indian genocide. Indians today find themselves still battling to preserve their own identity as sovereign national communities.[22]

The constant pressure of amer-european settlers and their colonialist federal government worked to slowly erode much of the basic cultural structures and values of Indian nations as part of their strategy to erode the political and economic viability of Indian tribes. In the late nineteenth century, both gov-

---

20. The best book available is still Stan Hoig, *The Sand Creek Massacre* (Norman: Oklahoma University Press, 1961). See also Ward Churchill's critique of the failings of a couple of more recent attempts: "It Did Happen Here: Sand Creek, Scholarship, and the American Character," in idem, *Fantasies of the Master Race*, 19-26.

21. The so-called Peace Policy initiated by President U.S. Grant marks this period. Again, my chapter on Whipple in *Missionary Conquest* is a good starting point for understanding the politics of the time.

22. Note again Prucha's collection of excerpts from original sources that date from this reform movement in *Americanizing the American Indian*.

ernment schools and church missions shared the common task of substituting a new european cultural attachment for the ancient cultural traditions of Indian peoples.[23] This substituting of one culture for the other, these liberal, White american politicians and church leaders called "civilizing" Indians—as if Indians, being more animal than human, had no civilization of their own.

Resistance to colonialism and conquest continues to be strong among Indian communities both in north and south America. In the United States, the American Indian Movement (AIM), formed in 1968, has been one of the key organizations for Indian resistance. Other organizations, such as the National Indian Youth Council, also were important in developing Indian resistance during this period. Their proactive resistance during the 1970s especially gave many Indians a forum for discussing Indian justice issues and for creating strategies of resistance. They generated a renewed pride in being Indian and helped many to affirm Indian cultures, values, and religious traditions. AIM chapters continue to exist in many regions of the country and continue to press for justice and recognition of Indian justice issues. Colorado AIM, for instance, organized the largest protests of "columbus day" commemorations (celebratory parades) in the late 1980s to 1992, when the parade was stopped, and again since 2000, when a new consortium of organizers once again resuscitated the overtly racist parade and its celebration of mass murderer and infamous terrorist Christopher Columbus as the all-american hero.[24]

Today, there are some three million Indians in the United States, many of whom continue to maintain a connection with mission churches. At the same time, there has been a revival over the past quarter century of traditional Indian cultures and religious traditions, and many who might have formerly professed Christianity have today embraced these traditional religious structures and ceremonies. Indian activism over the past quarter century has also drawn attention to the negative impact of Christianity on Indian communities—politically, economically, spiritually, culturally, and in terms of mental health. Hence, there is growing criticism of Christianity and the churches in most Indian communities.

---

23. This is the period when both the U.S. government and church boarding schools began to supplement the schools already long established by missionaries for training well-behaved Indian subjects. See Ward Churchill, *Kill the Indian, Save the Man: The Genocidal Impact of American Indian Residential Schools* (San Francisco: City Lights Press, 2004). My preface to *Kill the Indian* ("Tracing a Contour of Colonialism: American Indians and the Trajectory of Educational Imperialism," xiii-xli) sketches the formation of U.S. policies in this regard, particularly in the context of the Lake Mohonk Conferences of the late-nineteenth and early-twentieth centuries.

24. See my essay "Columbus & Coyote: A Comparison of Culture Heroes in Paradox," *Apuntes* 12, no. 2 (Summer 1992): 78-88.

Likewise in the southern hemisphere, indigenous activists have carried the decolonization struggle a step further and now have named and challenged the christian churches of all denominations as complicit in the oppression of the native peoples of the hemisphere. As in north America, there has been a shift in allegiances away from Christianity and back to traditional indigenous ceremonial life. Even those who remain in the churches are more insistently taking control of their Christianity, insisting on interpreting the scriptures and the christian traditions in the light of their own traditional religious culture. Indians from both north and south have begun to work together toward public statements of their own theological interpretations both of the gospel and of tribal religious traditions. The problem for mainline european and amer-european Christians is that indigenous Christianity among Indians begins to look less and less like mainline european and amer-european Christianity as Indians determine for themselves how they will interpret the gospel.

This volume represents one contribution to this ongoing process of indigenous theological reflection. It intends to build on the history of pain and violence. At the same time, it hopes to point to a more balanced and healing future for all those who inhabit the continent today. Moreover, in their anticolonial resistance, American Indians continue to believe that they have clung to a set of cultural values that can prove salvific, not only for ourselves but for the very amer-european colonizer who has attempted unmercifully to destroy both Indian peoples and Indian cultures. These essays will attempt to express some of that spirit of resistance and the inherent optimism of Indian peoples, on the one hand, and to point to continuing problems of colonization on the other.

Chapter 1

Struggle, Resistance, Liberation, and Theological Methodology

Indigenous Peoples and the Two-Thirds World[1]

wakoⁿda moⁿshita! wakoⁿda uidseta! witzigoe ski ikoe! wiⁿachnoⁿ miⁿkshe.

Grandmother! Grandfather! Sacred One Above and Sacred One Below.
Thank you for this day, for life itself,
  and especially for this gathering of relatives in the struggle for
  liberation.

I am an American Indian, a member of the Osage Nation, *ni u koⁿ ska wazhazhe,* a nation surrounded by the United States—in more ways than one. For those of you who do not know much american history, Osages once controlled the southern mid-section of the north american continent, from the Mississippi River west and from the Missouri River south as far as the Arkansas River. In 1803 the United States bought our land from the french, in a bizarre act that was called the Louisiana Purchase. Osages, of course, are still trying to figure out how that was possible. Only five years later, we were forced also to cede a large chunk of our lands to the United States in return for a permanent territory to the west. "Permanent," it turns out, means in english "a few years," since we were forced to sign a series of treaties over about six decades, almost always ceding new pieces of territory. And each treaty forced the Osages to

---

1. An early version of this chapter was delivered as a plenary address to the Fifth General Assembly of EATWOT (the Ecumenical Association of Third World Theologians), December 1996, in Tagaytay City, Philippines, and was published as "EATWOT and Theological Methodology: Struggle, Resistance, Liberation and Indigenous Peoples," in *Search for a New Just World Order: Challenges to Theology,* Papers and Reflections from the Fourth Assembly of the Ecumenical Association of Third World Theologians, December, 1996, Tagaytay, Philippines, a Special Issue of *Voices from the Third World,* ed. K. C. Abrams (Bangalore, India: EATWOT, 1999), 59-78.

move again to smaller, unknown lands.[2] Generally today, Indian people are the poorest of all ethnic groups in the United States, suffering a 60 percent unemployment rate, the highest rates of alcoholism and teen suicide, and the highest rates of disease and death, still dying more than twenty years sooner than the U.S. average.[3] My comments here on theological methodology are deeply rooted in this history of pain and the ongoing struggle for survival of Indian peoples as peoples.

I would like to say something briefly about the words of prayer that begin this chapter. American Indian experiences of the "sacred" (?) Other ("god"?) were almost invariably a bi-gender, reciprocal duality of male and female. Colonization of language, however, has meant that even traditional speakers when speaking in the colonial language (english) will customarily reference the bi-gender *wako^{n}da* with male pronouns, "he," "his," and "him," although they would never do this in their native language. Yet when we pray in the traditional way, we still call upon that bi-gender duality of male and female, represented by Sky and Earth, the two great cosmic fructifying powers. Thus, my cautious precision with respect to gender here is self-conscious and intentional and has everything to do with how an American Indian would construct a theology.

This chapter is a discussion of theological methodology and hopes to speak to both the world of euro-church and the rest of us in the world of the global south, particularly including indigenous peoples around the globe. We should begin by acknowledging that methodology has been used as a most effective device for enhancing colonial intellectual control, including theological/religious control, even in this "post" era that is sometimes referred to as postcolonial. The intellectual and religious realms have been crucial to colonial political and economic domination of indigenous peoples. All too often the world of amer-european and euro-western academic theology can dispense with what the Two-Thirds World has to say about its own spiritual world by judging us somehow inferior on methodological grounds. It is not always a matter of blatant racist deprecation and disavowal by our colonizer colleagues. Colonial euro-science, of course, has a history of debunking indigenous knowledge using the disavowal of the primitive, savage, superstitious, and the like. Today's liberals among the colonizer more often dismiss our best

---

2. Louis F. Burns, *A History of the Osage People* (Fallbrook, Ca.: Ciga Press, 1989), discusses each of these treaties in some detail.

3. It should be noted that the case of the Osages includes an ironic twist. The early discovery of oil on the final Osage Reservation made them very wealthy for a short period of time. That made Osages a prime target for White european corruption beginning in the second decade of the last century. Moreover, as the oil has been depleted, that wealth has also shriveled, leaving unemployment and poverty in its wake.

intellectual reflection with the cursory judgment of "interesting," or even "excellent for our context." And always, it seems, our work is not "heard" even when it is read.[4] In the same way, the colonization of the mind is such that even we male scholars of the Two-Thirds World will say about our own female colleagues, in marginalizing words: "She is very good on gender issues."[5]

And yet, the most important gift we have to give back to our colonizer may be the foundational discursive modalities of the intellectual tradition of the oppressed. We have a different way of seeing the world and engaging in critical analysis of the world that is transformative and liberating. If this is true, then we need to focus our attention on the question of how we will do theology with increasing care and diligence, even in the face of a growing globalization that will insist that we speak in ways that conform to a more universal discourse in order to function more pragmatically within the present reality. The emergence of methodological discussions in Two-Thirds World discourses is anything but simplistic. It is as complex as it is powerful and liberating. But it must continue to be a methodology rooted in resistance to oppressive power and in the struggle for the freedom of each of our disparate and distinct peoples.

We cannot take time here to summarize the variety of methodological concerns and the complexities that have structured traditional Two-Thirds World liberation theologies: contextualization, grass roots participation, praxis, and the like. They are firmly established and continue to be vitally important to our theological enterprise. I propose here to add to the discussion by broadening those analytical tools and methodologies from the perspective of an indigenous, that is, American Indian, person. I hope that some of what I have to say will generate some controversy, controversy that will elicit honest, collegial dialogue that holds the promise of advancing the common cause for the freedom of our peoples and our sense of intercontinental unity with the global south.

It seems to me, in terms of methodology, that there are four critical aspects that call for our attention today as forms of resistance to colonizers' (now "globalizers") destructive intentions. The first has to do with the close connection between race and the politics of oppression that we have experienced as Two-Thirds World communities. The second has to do with the inappropriateness

---

4. See Gayatri Chakravorti Spivak, "Can the Subaltern Speak?" in *Marxism and the Interpretation of Culture,* ed. Cary Nelson and Lawrence Grossberg (Urbana: University of Illinois Press, 1988), 271-313; now significantly expanded and revised in Spivak, *Critique of Postcolonial Reason: Toward a History of the Vanishing Present* (Cambridge, Mass.: Harvard University Press, 1999).

5. For detailed discussion of the psychological effects of colonization on the colonized, see Linda Tuhiwai Smith, *Decolonizing Methodologies: Research and Indigenous Peoples* (London: Zed Books, 1999); and Albert Memmi, *The Colonizer and the Colonized* (Boston: Beacon Press, 1967).

of treating indigenous peoples as a part of a larger class of the poor that sur-round them, even though the indigenous are almost always the poorest of the poor. Then I will move the discussion to an analysis of the colonization of our language, the extent to which our use of language is shaped by the colonizer, even when we think we are doing our best work. Finally, we must begin to reflect critically in our theological constructions about the marginalization of women. I want especially to press Two-Thirds World men to ask ourselves plainly where our participation in the marginalization of women originated.

COLONIZATION AND THE RACIALIZATION OF POLITICS

In the United States we have experienced, consistently and persistently, a radi-cal racialization of all politics, whether civil politics or ecclesiastical, theologi-cal, or academic politics. From my reading of Two-Thirds World literature and discussions over the years with Two-Thirds World colleagues from other con-tinents, the racialization of politics characterizes colonial arrangements in all our parts of the world, especially under the globalization of capital; but let me address the issue from my own immediate experience. Our attention to this phenomenon is a crucial methodological link. Without the ability to identify and analyze the racialization of politics, within the United States and in the context of globalization, we will continue to pursue liberation without a full analysis of the power relationships that are the source of our peoples' oppres-sions.

While slave trading certainly existed in the ancient and classical worlds and the precolumbian Americas, it did so generally as a consequence or byproduct of conquest.[6] However, it only became explicitly racialized with the advent of the raiding for new sources of wealth along the coasts of West Africa by the Portuguese early in the fifteenth century. Columbus, who was a slave trader in both african and indigenous american bodies, participated in this portuguese slave trade in african bodies before his fateful invasion of the Americas; then on his second foray into the american hemisphere, he took five hundred American Indian natives back to Spain to be sold as slaves in Seville.[7] Thus was born the atlantic system of trade in human beings, which almost immediately was expanded to include American Indians as well as Africans.[8] Since Columbus, then, political racialization has always served a specific pur-

---

6. Howard Winant, *The World Is a Ghetto: Race and Democracy since World War II* (New York: Basic Books, 2001), 54.

7. See George E. Tinker and Mark Freeland, "Thief, Slave Trader, Murderer: Christopher Columbus and Caribbean Population Decline," *Wicazo Sa Review* 23, no. 1 (2008): 40-82.

8. Ibid.

pose, most certainly related to the economic aspirations of the colonizer, from the beginning of the european invasions of the Americas, Africa, and Asia. Of particular significance is the understanding that race was manifested as *both* cause and effect such that racializing was essential and fundamental to western Europe's projects of state building and political and economic expansion.[9] Our experiences ring with a certain similarity even if the colonial process of oppression and racialization has been played out differently depending on the context and the specific needs of the colonizer. For instance, african Americans were historically denied any integral participation in american life on the basis of their skin color even after slavery was officially abolished in the 1860s. The general rule was that a single drop of african (Black) blood was (and is) enough to contaminate the person with this disease of Blackness, and thus, even mixed-blood african Americans could not shed the stigma no matter how light their resulting skin color. With regard to American Indians, however, the U.S. government has concocted a scheme to determine exactly when, through the process of intermarriage, we *stop* being Indian and can be safely considered to be White. Both of these are racialized political responses to the world. The one strategy was intended to separate Black people from economic and political opportunity in general and to maintain a source of cheap labor within the United States; the other was intended to include Indian peoples so that our lands and economic resources could be more easily taken away from us without the specter of guilt ever looming over the process. Indeed, in the colonizing years prior to the mid-1820s, by virtue of the european invaders' claims to the legal right of local jurisdiction over "discovered" land, and subsequently, as the purview of the U.S. Congress, a number of programs were imposed on Indian peoples with the express purpose of forcing their assimilation into amer-european culture.

We can see how the racialization of politics is manipulated through government policy and is determined whether the colonizing power profits through cheap labor or the acquisition of the land and resources of the colonized. In the case of Africans and african Americans, there was and still is a persistent colonizer need to maintain a sizable and clearly defined poverty sector of the population that can be relied on for cheap labor. Hence, maintaining the stigma is critical to maintaining economic control of the system. In the case of the Indian, seemingly to the contrary, the legitimate and moral aboriginal claim to territory is so compelling that it is in the government's best interest to get rid of Indian peoples once and for all simply to clarify issues of land ownership.[10]

---

9. Ibid., 21.

10. This distinction in forms of oppression is noted by Englebert Mveng, "African Theology: A Methodological Approach," *Voices from the Third World* 18, no. 1 (1995): 108f.

Extermination is no longer a politically correct notion.[11] A subtler means is to marry us off to White Americans and move to disqualify us as Indians as quickly as possible. In Canada, for instance, until 1985, any Indian woman who married a non-native was automatically removed from the tribal rolls by canadian law and could never be readmitted to membership in the tribe even if she should divorce her husband. Birth certificates were regularly altered at the time of a woman's marriage, stamped boldly with the message "*No longer an Indian.*"[12] Thus are the ranks of aboriginal land claimants thinned in the economic interests of the colonizer. Of course, this is not to suggest that the actual treatment of Indian people is defined only by law, but to demonstrate that the racist deprecation of Indian people and other people of color extends even to legal discourse.[13] What we can add here is that no birth certificates were marked "No longer poor" or "No longer Black" or "No longer urban." The varieties of U.S. government policies included a not-so-subtle measure from 1954 until 1970 called *termination*, whereby the government took upon itself the responsibility to decide whether any particular tribe continued to be a tribe, and hence a separate people, or not. In the early years of the policy, dozens of tribes were determined to be ready for assimilation into the general population of Americans. The government thereby terminated their tribal existence and abrogated all treaty relationship with each terminated tribe, resulting in significantly reduced treaty-obligated financial expenditures by the government and the hope of fewer complications in terms of land rights and future acts of indigenous resistance. Thus, there are political and economic reasons rooted in the structures of colonialism that cause states to treat indigenous peoples differently and to create legal forms of oppression.

Quite aside from the political and economic abuse and exploitation of our peoples, it is abundantly evident that this subjugation has been characterized by an apparently inherent *genderizing* of the racialized subject in the form of sexual stereotyping, rape, and concubinage.[14] These are systemic issues of rac-

---

11. Extermination was the solid cry of the settler press in the western part of the United States in the 1860s and 1870s, over against the call for civilizing and christianizing Indian peoples largely voiced by the eastern establishment. See my chapter on Bishop Henry Benjamin Whipple in George E. Tinker, *Missionary Conquest: The Gospel and Indian Genocide* (Minneapolis: Fortress Press, 1993).

12. See Olive Patricia Dickason, *Canada's First Nations: A History of Founding Peoples from Earliest Times* (Norman: University of Oklahoma Press, 1992), 258-59 and 328-31; and Thomas Isaac, *Aboriginal Law: Cases, Materials and Commentary* (Saskatoon: Purich Publications, 1995), 399-406.

13. I recall here Rita Nakashima Brock's very-well-constructed response paper delivered at the EATWOT General Assembly on December 12, 1996, responding to Samir Amin's presentation on contemporary globalization.

14. Winant, *The World Is a Ghetto*, 61.

ism and oppression that call for resistance and struggle and generate our goal of liberation. The methodological question, of course, is this: how will our theologies identify systemic issues like the racialization of politics and then respond with hope for a liberated, transformed future?

CLASS ANALYSIS AND THE LIBERAL COLONIZER SOLUTION TO COLONIAL VIOLENCE

Our methodology must become much more open to categories of analysis other than the sort of class analysis that we have learned from marxist theory. As useful as the analytical tools of marxism have been over the past several decades, including our incorporation of it into liberation theologies, it may be time for theologians in the globalized Two-Thirds World to reckon with the europeanness of this mode of discourse and to see it as a liberal colonizer solution to colonizer violence, after the fact.[15] It may be time to look for new sorts of political discourse, new social visions of the future that can embrace all of us more satisfactorily in the Third (and Fourth) World. As Aruna Gnanadasan would remind us, class analysis can be helpful, but liberation involves much more than class struggles.[16] In fact, indigenous peoples are struggling with existence in ways that are not and probably cannot be addressed by class analysis at all. Our oppression and the resulting poverty are *not* primarily due to any class status. Rather, they are rooted in the economic need of the colonizer to quiet our claims to the land and to mute our moral judgment on the United States' long history of violence and conquest in north America.

What indigenous communities want most of all is to have our cultural differentness recognized and respected as signifying distinct political entities based on specific land territories. To reduce us to some notion of class is to obviate that differentness and to replace our community identity with participation in a general class struggle for mere economic sufficiency. Such a movement must eventually impose notions of value, ethics, and aesthetics on indigenous communities, just as the colonizer governments and missionaries have always done. Only this time, the imposition is from a more liberal side of the colonizer with the "good intention" of building solidarity among a presumed class for the sake of the economic well-being and even survival of the class as a whole. Thus, our land will still not be ours but would enter into the collective possession of a much larger colonizer proletariat who are also foreign to our

---

15. For American Indian attitudes toward marxism, see Ward Churchill, "False Promises: An Indigenist Examination of Marxist Theory and Practice," in idem, *Acts of Rebellion: The Ward Churchill Reader* (New York: Routledge, 2003), 247-62.

16. "Asian Theological Methodology: An Overview," *Voices from the Third World* 18, no. 1 (1995): 88f.

land and who must be considered invaders.[17] The need to embrace "difference" will be more critical as we move forward into the future of liberation.[18]

Indigenous peoples want something very different. We want our lives back, our ways of being—rooted, of course, in connection to the land itself. We want back the sovereignty that was ours before the invasion of european colonizers. Class analysis presumes the validity of the modern state as much as democratic capitalism does. The difference is that class analysis usually has some vision of exerting influence or control of the state in order to mitigate the oppression of the identified class. American Indians who are most engaged in struggle and resistance refuse to acknowledge the validity or legality of the United States' claim for the occupation and governance of north America; nor do they recognize the right of the United States to any claim on our lands or on our peoples as subjects.[19] Socialist ideology wants to take over and transform the state into a more egalitarian whole; indigenous ideologies want to challenge the very legitimacy of the idea of state and claim our freedom from these larger, artificial and imposed political entities that were born out of euro-western colonization and the will to empire.

Until now there has been no discourse or language in the international arena—legal, international relations, political theory, or human rights theory—to account for the existence of indigenous peoples. States of all varieties have a vested interest in resisting any development of this sort of language. There has been scant mention in the United States of the sixty years of armed struggle for sovereignty and autonomy by the Naga peoples against the nation-state of India. We know now that the situation was no better in the former Eastern Bloc than it is in democratic capitalist states. Indigenous nations in Siberia, for instance, were (and are yet today under the hegemony of Russia, e.g., Chechnya) oppressed and marginalized. Likewise, indigenous national communities in China have had their identity denied and even destroyed. Tibet is only the most celebrated example. And in January 1994, at the beginning of the Chiapas uprising, the U.S. press insisted for several days that the irruption was some sort of "peasant" revolt in southern Mexico. Only after several days of letters to the editor did the press begin to correctly identify the event as an "Indian" uprising of ancient, aboriginal Mayan communities that had been too long oppressed by the state that presumed territorial and governance rights over their lands. Both socialist and democratic capitalist states

---

17. See Churchill, "False Promises," 247-62.

18. Ada María Isasi-Díaz, "The Present-Future of EATWOT: A Mujerista Perspective," *Voices from the Third World* 19, no. 1 (1996): 98ff.

19. See, for instance, Ward Churchill, "The US Right to Occupancy in North America," in *Since Predator Came: Notes from the Struggle for American Indian Liberation* (Littleton, Colo.: Aigis, 1995).

have a vested interest in the continued oppression of indigenous communities in all parts of the world.

We must be clear about this one thing: states *must necessarily* oppress indigenous peoples, must destroy our self-identity, our cultures, and our religious and spiritual traditions. States have no choice but to oppress and suppress precisely because our ancient claim to the land is a constant and persistent challenge to the legitimacy and coherence of the state and its claim by virtue of discovery (read conquest) of our territories. Vandana Shiva argues that, according to western economic and political doctrine, any and all indigenous people who demand the return of their rights, such as their traditional lands and resources, are "regarded as thieves."[20]

Our analysis and the resulting theologies we write must now begin to seriously consider indigenous issues as relating to the poorest of the poor in virtually every region of the world. Those who suffer such continuing violence suffer not because of their class affiliation but because of their cultural identification and ancient relationship to particular lands coveted by the modern states that claim jurisdiction over their people and their territories.

THE COLONIZATION OF LANGUAGE AND CATEGORIES OF ANALYSIS

Colonizers' control of the colonized means that the colonized are forced to accede to the colonizer's language, social structures, economic structures, and political structures. In the church, for example—which is one of the colonizers' main instruments for enforcing the colonizing arrangements—the same sort of imposition has always been critical to colonizing missionary control. If we are serious about the continued emergence of theologies of liberation, our methodologies must begin to seriously challenge the very categories of analysis and modes of discourse that have been imposed on us as normative by the euro-western and amer-european church structures with which so many indigenous and Third World peoples are affiliated.

For instance, as long as we continue to accept uncritically the western notion of God as the apex of a male hierarchy, we will not be whole or liberated.[21] This male image of God was a metaphor that may have worked in the

---

20. Vandana Shiva, *Biopiracy: The Plunder of Nature and Knowledge* (Boston: South End Press, 1997), 3.

21. Women members of EATWOT, of course, will continue to name God-language as a key piece of the cross-gender theological dialogue that needs to take place in EATWOT. See Mercy Amba Oduyoye, "The Impact of Women's Theology on the Development of Dialogue in EATWOT," in *Voices from the Third World* 19, no. 1 (1996): 29. It is Oduyoye who also argues for the use of "cross-gender dialogue" as signifying an "intentional conversation of women and men on the challenge of gender as a construct" (33).

judeo-christian world of the first christian century. From an American Indian perspective, I want to argue that it is fatally flawed for our vision of liberation today. The problem is that the churches (all mainline denominations) have made God's maleness a doctrine rather than understanding it in a literary sense as a metaphor. If it is a doctrine, then the language cannot be changed. If it is a metaphor, then we have an absolute responsibility to translate the metaphor in ways that our people can understand and claim as their own. It is like the *basileia tou theou* (the so-called kingdom of God). Proclaimed by Jesus, the metaphor worked in that culture at that time. Today, quite apart from the inherent sexism of the english literal translation, the concept is incomprehensible except as religious language. There are no longer very many peoples in the world who continue to have experiential knowledge of kings (or even queens, for that matter), especially those who actually rule. Thus, the metaphor must be translated to be understood.

If the churches are to insist that the maleness of God is doctrine and not metaphor, then we need to pursue a much deeper understanding of this doctrine. Do we really want to anthropomorphize God as male to such a full extent? Do we really imagine God as a male in our own image? For instance, does God's maleness not require us with utter consistency to imagine God as a fully complete male with the correct biological appendage that would identify God as a male? And if so, what would be the purpose of such an appendage and how would it function in our theology?

If these sorts of questions embarrass you or are an affront, then we need to ask again, what does it mean to call upon God as "he"? If it is the parenting metaphor that is at stake, then why not allow God to be referenced as "mother," or at least as "parent"? Do we also not risk believing in and calling on a God that has been so minimized and restricted by our obsession to identify and define that both our faith and our God will be ineffectual? Or if we are serious about our own liberation, why not allow each region or national community to look at their own world of experience and symbols to translate the metaphor in ways that speak more directly to that community rather than imposing a metaphor from some other language and culture?[22] Can we not begin at least to discuss alternatives for this fundamental theological act of signifying God?[23]

---

22. See George E. Tinker, "An American Indian Theological Response to Ecojustice," in *Defending Mother Earth: Native American Perspectives on Environmental Justice*, ed. Jace Weaver (Maryknoll, N.Y.: Orbis Books, 2003), 155-57.

23. See Mary John Mananzan, "Gender Dialogue in EATWOT—An Asian Perspective," *Voices from the Third World* 19, no. 1 (1996): 57-83, especially the discussion beginning on pp. 61ff. Also, Teresa Okure, "An African Historical Perspective on EATWOT Christologies and Popular Religion," *Voices from the Third World* 18, no. 2 (1995): 88-98; and Charles Nyamiti, "The African Sense of God's Motherhood in the light of Christian Faith," *African Ecclesial Review* 23, no. 5 (1981): 269-74.

One of our most spiritually rich elders among American Indians more than a quarter century ago taught me much about our indigenous American Indian notions of the sacred.[24] At my invitation this revered medicine person spoke to a large audience at the Graduate Theological Union in Berkeley. In accord with this teacher's request, I had placed a small table holding a fist-sized rock next to the podium. At one point in the lecture, this elder asked the assembled crowd, "I understand that you are all theologians or studying to be theologians. Do you mind if I take this opportunity to ask you something I have always wanted to know? What does God look like?"

Receiving only silence from the audience, the elder finally conceded that it had been a trick question. No one knows what God looks like, of course. But then, this elder picked up the rock and asked, "If you do not know what God looks like, can you tell me absolutely, without a doubt, that this rock is not God?" Again, there was silence as this theological audience mulled over the logical possibilities for an absolutely certain answer.

Finally, after tossing the rock gently to me, the elder asked the most telling question. "I, too, do not believe that this rock is God. But tell me, if you cannot describe God to me and cannot tell me with absolute certainty that this rock is not God, how is it that your missionary ancestors told Indian people that they were worshiping a false god when we pray to the sun? The sun is the most powerful physical presence in our lives. Without it we could not live and our world would perish. Yet our reverence for it was considered idolatry.

> But your missionary ancestors misunderstood even that much, because we never worshipped the sun. We merely saw in it the reflection of the sacred, the creator, and used its image to focus our prayers of thanksgiving for Creator's life-giving power. It is, for us, a constant reminder of the creative power of God, as we greet the sun in the morning when we first arise and again in the evening. In between, as we go about our day, we constantly will see our shadow on the ground and will be reminded again of God's creative goodness. We can stop, look up, and say a short prayer whenever this happens.

This unschooled elder went on to teach about the American Indian understanding of the Sacred Other in a way that is very complex and sophisticated, although the missionaries have taught us—all too well—that our ways were simplistic and childish, at best. *wako^{n}da*, to paraphrase this elder, has no sexual gender identity. Rather, *wako^{n}da* is unknown and unknowable until *wako^{n}da* decides to reveal *wako^{n}da*'s self. Only then does *wako^{n}da* take on characteristics that can help us to image *wako^{n}da* as a tangible reality. But *wako^{n}da* is never limited to a single manifestation but makes itself manifest in a variety

---

24. The elder was Muskogee medicine man Philip Deere.

of ways to help different people at different times. It is in this context that the elder noticed that the first manifestation and most important manifestation of *wako^nda* was as a duality of reciprocal completion, as the Sacred Above and the Sacred Below, as male and female, as Sky and Earth (again as representations or mirrors of *wako^nda* Above and Below). We must not confuse these manifested forms with the euro-western concept of duality as a *binary opposition*. Love and hate, dark and light are dualities, but they are not intrinsically reciprocal. This duality is reciprocal because the two parts of *wako^nda* are necessary for there to be a sense of wholeness or completion.

When we pray at Four Winds American Indian Council, we always begin our prayers with this image of *wako^nda* in mind, as Grandfather and Grandmother. For us the notion of hierarchy is shattered: politically, spiritually, socially, and sexually. I am not suggesting this image of God to you for your consumption, as a new commodity. That would be wrong. But I am suggesting this as a paradigm for taking the missionary, colonizing categories and deconstructing them in order to replace them with categories from our own cultural worlds of experience that can speak to our peoples with a new liberating voice. I am convinced, however, that our American Indian image of the sacred can have potent and liberating political and social consequences, just as much as the colonizers' image of God has served historically to constantly reinforce and undergird the colonizers' control and domination in the world.

COLONIZATION AND THE MARGINALIZATION OF WOMEN: KNOWING OUR OWN PAST

History, we are told, is written by the victors. Yet this is the very notion that we must resist. Any methodology for a liberation theology must begin by remembering who we are as the colonized, an activity that the colonizer has a vested interest in stopping. As the conquerors, the colonizers would always prefer to substitute their own telling of our histories. The truly destructive consequence that proceeds from the project of coopting a people's history occurs as they are forced to learn this revised history and expected to accept it as their own. Dipesh Chakrabarty explains that the experience in India with british/european hegemony has shown "the deep collusion between 'history' and the modernizing narrative(s) . . . ," and concludes by declaring, "'history' as a knowledge system is firmly embedded in institutional practices that invoke the nation-state at every step. . . ."[25] Their scholars become the *de facto* experts

---

25. Dipesh Chakrabarty, "Postcoloniality and the Artifice of History," in *The Postcolonial Studies Reader*, ed. Bill Ashcroft, Gareth Griffiths, and Helen Tiffin (New York: Routledge, 1995), 384.

about us. Their scholars are the ones trusted and used in courts of law to testify on issues that affect us. And eventually, even we have to turn to their books and their expertise to learn about ourselves. This is an important colonizer methodology designed to enforce the colonization of our minds. To break this cycle of intellectual dependency, we must become even more critical and analytical than the presumed scholarly status of the colonizers' academic specialists. I would like to offer an example of how deeply we must engage this critical task as a foundational methodology for our theological reflection.

I fully agree with EATWOT women who call us to confession and repentance with regard to sexism within our organization.[26]

Whether American Indian or others in the global south, we must pay attention to gender concerns in a deeply analytical way. Male scholars in the global south must be willing to challenge ourselves in terms of sexist patterns of behavior that have marginalized women in our own communities. Our self-criticism must be vigilant even as we evaluate our participation in aspects of our societies that are dysfunctional or oppressive. We cannot call for liberation unless we ourselves are open to a critique of behavior that can fall into oppressive patterns. I am deeply touched by women's stories of violence, and not just the systemic violence generated from outside of our communities, but the violence perpetrated by men in our societies themselves.[27] I am touched by the continuing stories of structural exclusion and oppression women have experienced within our liberation movements. Our theological methodology must begin with a commitment to listen to our own people, those out of whose midst we do our theological construction. This means listening, as well, to those in our own midst who experience us as participants in oppressive acts.

Yet we must, I argue, carefully distinguish between the cultures lived by our ancestors and the continuation of those cultures as we live them today, as dysfunctional residuals of what we once were when we were still free peoples. We must vigorously reclaim the best of our past even as we engage in self-criticism in the present. Even as I am touched by our women's stories of cultural and social structures that marginalize them, even as I witness the marginalization of our brightest and ablest women right here at the General Assembly, I am not convinced by the occasional feminist pronouncement that women

---

26. See Oduyoye, "The Impact of Women's Theology." She develops there the notion of conversion, requiring confession and repentance, as the initial process that will move EATWOT men beyond our sexism toward a genuine interaction with women's theological experiences and ideas.

27. See the important collection of essays edited by Mercy Amba Oduyoye and Musimbi R. A. Kanyoro, *The Will to Arise: Women, Tradition, and the Church in Africa* (Maryknoll, N.Y.: Orbis Books, 1992).

have always and everywhere been oppressed and marginalized by men. This cannot be, lest there be no hope for the future.[28]

I understand the sentiment when I hear these things spoken by White feminists, because they have a gendered vested interest in trying to coopt women's pain in the Third and Fourth World. At the same time they have a racially vested interest in arguing that other cultures are just as vicious toward women as their own culture, because it excuses them from taking liberation seriously. It allows them to continue to enjoy the comfort and wealth of their own culture—and of White privilege—guilt free, as it were, because they have successfully reduced the other to their own level. Like male White scholars, these White feminists have resorted to a presumption of expertise that allows them to define and describe Indian traditional cultures in ways that play the game of blaming the victim.

I am more concerned when we engage in speaking these sorts of disparagements about ourselves in uncritical and unreflected ways.[29] Let me repeat what I have already indicated above: this is in no way to deny the experiences of our women to which we men *must* pay attention, both socially and theologically, unless we intend to liberate only men, bringing the women along for good measure like the Ronald Reagan trickle-down theory of economics. (If we can only liberate the men, perhaps the women will receive some benefit as well?)

My concern here is that we be clear that our cultures are experiencing the results of some five hundred years of colonizing pressures continuing today in the neocolonial garb of capitalist globalization. As a result, what we have today, even when we call it traditional culture, is far from what we were. For instance, many American Indian men were surprised to discover that they were supposed to be the head of the household, when until the missionaries came to them they had not even owned the houses in which they lived. The net effect of a couple hundred years of missionary and government schooling has destroyed the old social arrangements that affected the balance of power between genders. Those schools were training centers, not educational

---

28. As an American Indian, I am not an evolutionist and do not concede that there is either a natural or a divine process toward future progress or improvement. I rather believe that the future is up to us as people of faith committed to political and social transformation as a natural part of our spiritual practice. See Vine Deloria, Jr., *Evolution, Creationism, and Other Modern Myths: A Critical Inquiry* (Golden, Colo.: Fulcrum, 2002), for an articulation of the possibilities of a future that takes seriously the perspectives and knowledge of American Indian peoples. Deloria rigorously critiques both evolution and creationism, including its "intelligent design" variant.

29. See Devon Abbott Mihesuah, *Indigenous American Women: Decolonization, Empowerment, Activism* (Omaha: University of Nebraska Press, 2003), particularly chap. 12, "Feminists, Tribalists, or Activists?"

centers, and their self-identified task was to destroy the Indian culture and replace it with the colonizer's own value system and social structures.[30] Young Indian men were trained to become agricultural hired help to be hired out to White farmers and ranchers; young women were trained to become household maids to serve the wives of White businessmen. The extended kinship family arrangement was willfully and intentionally destroyed in the vain hope of teaching Indians to adopt european nuclear family arrangements. The sense of community that gave us life had to be destroyed in favor of european radical individualism. As one commissioner of Indian Affairs in the mid-nineteenth century proclaimed, "We must teach the savage to say, 'This is mine,' instead of 'This is ours.'" Or as General William T. Sherman reported with dismay in a letter from the frontier to the War Department in 1869, "It will take a lot longer than I thought to civilize these Indians. For they know no greed, and until they know greed, they will not understand the private ownership of property."

These historic colonizing pressures cannot have left us unaffected. Indeed, it is remarkable that American Indians have survived at all. It should not be surprising that our communities are in considerable disarray and in serious poverty in the United States today. Still, there are pieces of our cultures that we are able to reclaim and begin to live. And it is this process of reclaiming ourselves and living out of that reclaiming that will bring health and well-being to our communities. Among other cultural treasures, we American Indians are trying very hard to reclaim something of those social arrangements that made for greater gender balance in our ancient communities, and we are finding that our women have not forgotten those arrangements and are perfectly willing to remind the men of their obligation in those arrangements. This means that we are trying to reclaim women's participation in decision making, political leadership, and participation in our intellectual development and liberative praxis.

Our American Indian societies were unashamedly cosmic or "axial," to borrow John Hick's language,[31] and non-hierarchic in their worldview and

---

30. The development of these missionary and government boarding schools largely coincides with the insight of T. B. Macaulay with respect to the needs of the British Empire to train natives in the colonies in order to enhance British control and government throughout the empire: "We must at present do our best to form a class who may be interpreters between us and the millions whom we govern; a class of persons, Indian in blood and color, but english in taste, in opinion, in morals, and in intellect." From the conclusion of Macaulay's "Minute on Education," reprinted in Wm. Theodore De Bary, *Sources of Indian Tradition*, vol. 2 (New York: Columbia University Press, 1958), 49. See now especially Ward Churchill, *Kill the Indian, Save the Man: The Genocidal Impact of American Indian Residential Schools* (San Francisco: City Lights Press, 2004); and also K. Tsianina Lomawaima, *They Called It Prairie Light: The Story of Chilocco Indian School* (Omaha: University of Nebraska Press, 1994).

31. Or is it pre-post-axial? In any case, "axial/post-axial" language is the newest, most

praxis. Neither were they patriarchal in the oppressive sense that we have come to identify.[32] To the contrary, many of them would have and still qualify as matriarchal. Today in many Iroquoian tribes in the United States and Canada, each male chief is appointed to this responsibility by his clan mother. He serves at her pleasure, and no decision can be made in council without final ratification of the clan mothers.[33] In a great many other tribes, the home itself was characteristically owned by the women: that is, women were responsible for the home and were the authority figures for all the household activities involved in keeping the home. Indeed, in most plains societies women actually manufactured the home itself. In general, there existed specific and intentional social devices for balancing gender power relationships within native societies.[34] M. Annette Jaimes Guererro has argued that political decision making in aboriginal north America was predicated on a domestic base, that is, on the smallest social unit of the female-controlled home, rather than hierarchically from some ruling council, from the top down.[35]

The contemporary problem is that we American Indians seem to have forgotten much of this, having been taught our history by colonizer scholars and missionaries who were either unprepared to recognize the intentional and inherent empowerment of women in our social structures or had a vested interest in destroying that reality and replacing it with the colonizer's own value

---

politically correct way to refer to indigenous peoples as "primitive" and as somehow "less than" modern, more rational, post-axial capitalists and marxists. It has become the easiest way to dispense with the political and economic concerns of "tribal" peoples without taking them seriously. See the use of the term in John H. Hick, *Philosophy of Religion*, 4th ed. (New York: Prentice-Hall, 1990), 3, where he uses this terminology to disparage all indigenous religious traditions as axial and to rationalize the superiority of Christianity and its *post-axial* or *meta-cosmic* world religion competitors. A liberal theologian, Hick wants to open dialogue between Christianity and its world religion counterparts such as Islam, Hinduism, Buddhism, and so forth. But in the process he explicitly or implicitly moves to exclude entirely Fourth World traditions as somehow too primitive to be of use in a modern or postmodern world. See also Makau Mutua, "Returning to My Roots: African 'Religions' and the State," in *Human Rights and Religion: A Reader*, ed. Liam Gearon (Brighton: Sussex Academic Press, 2002), 228. Mutua discusses the continued persistence and prevalence of the need by some to denigrate traditional African beliefs and spiritual cosmology as "primitive" and not evolved when compared to monotheistic traditions.

32. See the suggestive but all-too-short comment by Mveng, "African Theology," 114f.

33. See especially Barbara Mann's discussion of Iroquois worldview and practice in *Iroquois Women: The Gantowisas* (New York: Peter Lang, 2000).

34. Thus, many American Indian nations were matrilineal and/or matrilocal. Oduyoye notes that the Asante of Ghana were matrilineal: "Violence Against Women: Window on Africa," *Voices from the Third World* 18, no. 1 (1995): 172.

35. In a public lecture, August 1994. See also M. Annette Jaimes and Theresa Halsey, "American Indian Women," in *The State of Native America: Genocide, Colonization and Resistance*, ed. M. Annette Jaimes (Cambridge, Mass.: South End Press, 1992), 311-44.

system, invested in hierarchical and patriarchal structures from the home all the way to the statewide governing institutions.[36]

We have to admit that the colonizer has been largely successful, although the conquest is not yet complete.[37] First of all, no matter how oppressed American Indian peoples are as a group, we men can count on some benefit from the inherent male privileging of the White colonizer society. Even historically, anthropologists and U.S. government officials have always preferred to talk with our men (thus empowering them, in that strange, codependent, colonizing way) and even ignored our women. Even White female anthropologists did this. The missionaries, on the other hand, were far more explicit in actually teaching male privilege to Indian peoples, as were the schools (mission and government run) that were designed especially for "civilizing" the children of Indian savages.

I know that many of these experiences resonate with other indigenous (tribal) peoples around the world. Africa, of course, comes quickly to mind in this regard. Ultimately, I want to ask about all of our cultures. What was the aboriginal gender relationship and how can we begin to reclaim a better past as we set our eyes on a liberated future? Yes, there will be enormous colonial baggage that many of us will have to unload to discover that past. Others will have to go back even further in time, before the birth of male hegemonic structures of control in order to discover what the people were. Yet this process of critical excavation of ourselves is important for understanding the economic relationships of hegemony and oppression that we hope our theologies will liberate us from.

CONCLUSION

Indigenous peoples and folk from the global south can no longer afford the luxury of constructing our theologies in isolation from one another any more

---

36. I use the word "statewide" here rather than "national." I refuse to concede nation status to the modern state, which is, after all, not really a nation but an artificial political construct designed for controlling and ruling diverse nations. See Glenn Morris, "International Law and Politics," in Jaimes, ed., *State of Native America*, 55-86; and Rebecca L. Robins, "Self-Determination and Subordination," in Jaimes, ed., *State of Native America*, 87-122.

37. Robert A. Williams, Jr., *American Indians in Western Legal Thought: The Discourses of Conquest* (New York: Oxford University Press, 1990), argues that colonization generates a pressure to complete a conquest totally, not just militarily but legally, culturally, in all ways, similarly to Mveng's explanation of "anthropological poverty" as including cultural, political, economic, militarized, technical, moral, and spiritual pauperization (Mveng, "African Theology," 109f.). This, argues Williams, explains the continuing oppression of American Indian peoples today: the conquest is not yet complete. It also counts for the continuing movements of resistance among the colonized; see particularly Williams for the continuing resistance among American Indian peoples.

than we can isolate ourselves from the experiences of our own peoples. The long-presumed division between the liberation theologies of latin America and the inculturation/cultural analysis/africanization theologies of Africa dare not separate us for long, lest the colonizer find a wedge to drive in the crevice. Divide and conquer has long been a colonizing strategy that has worked all too well both in colonizing political and economic arrangements and in the subsequent ecclesial arrangements of mission church structures. American Indian peoples have a particularly burning need to connect with allies in the struggle for freedom around the world because we are so outnumbered today by our colonizer.

At the same time, as James Cone has noted, there are enormous pressures on theologians in each region to dialogue more directly with the dominant theologies of the north rather than with one another.[38] Those pressures have not stopped us from talking to one another within our regions, but it has hampered the intercontinental dialogue. I should add that this insistent pressure that we focus on dialogue with the theologies of dominance in the north affects religious thinkers of color in the United States even more persistently than it does the rest of the Two-Thirds World. Whether we teach in church schools of theology or university religion faculties in the United States, we function in institutions dominated by White amer-european scholars who constantly, both implicitly and explicitly, challenge us to speak their language, use their discourses, and force our arguments into their methodological frameworks.

Two-Thirds World theologies are theologies of liberation and begin from a focus on people's experiences of oppression, conquest, and colonization. Indeed, these theologies have defined the category of liberation theology since the 1960s and especially since the seminal and defining work of Gustavo Gutiérrez in latin american liberation theology in 1971.[39] They have been characteristically theologies of resistance and struggle and have engaged the colonizer's missionary theology by way of challenge and deconstruction. It must be emphasized that Two-Thirds World theologians discovered the principles

---

38. James H. Cone, "Editorial Report: First EATWOT Inter-Continental Dialogue," *Voices from the Third World* 18, no. 1 (1995): 7-16.

39. Gutiérrez's work was defining in the sense of a starting point: *Teología de la Liberación* (Lima: CEP, 1971); Eng. trans., *A Theology of Liberation: History, Politics, and Salvation,* trans. and ed. Sister Caridad Inda and John Eagleson (Maryknoll, N.Y.: Orbis Books, 1973). James Cone plays the same role in the United States for african Americans with *Black Theology and Black Power* (New York: Harper & Row, 1969). And in a very different manner Vine Deloria, Jr., did this for American Indians in a series of titles from the same era: *Custer Died for Your Sins: An Indian Manifesto* (New York: Macmillan, 1969); *We Talk, You Listen: New Tribes, New Turf* (New York: Macmillan, 1970); and *God Is Red* (New York: Grosset & Dunlap, 1973); rev. ed.: *God Is Red: A Native View of Religion* (Golden, Colo.: Fulcrum, 1992).

involved in deconstruction long before we discovered Jacques Derrida.[40] This commitment to a theological methodology that speaks "from the underside of history"[41] is precisely what holds theological thinkers from the global south together in precarious unity.

I want to emphasize that my call for cultural analysis is not a call to abandon socio-economic and political analysis, the hallmark of global south theologies for nearly forty years, but rather to enhance it, to give it new power. As Kwok Pui-Lan said at the Nairobi General Assembly of EATWOT (1992), what we need is *more* analysis. I am arguing for deepening our analysis and enlarging our assortment of analytical tools for shaping our vision and praxis of liberation. I am certainly not suggesting that we completely abandon what we have learned from marxist analysis itself. Yet what we learned in that endeavor must now be significantly augmented by bringing culture and gender issues into the analysis. Never should we abandon our hope for the "new just world order" called for at the 1996 EATWOT General Assembly in the Philippines, especially a world order that is inclusive of female voices and leadership and inclusive of a concern for justice for indigenous peoples as the poorest of the poor.

It must be clearly said, at this point, that the values and cultural structures of indigenous peoples may help point the way to the social and political transformation of the world in ways that are unexpected. Our ancient cultures already celebrated a much greater gender balance and a more egalitarian social structure. And yet today, indigenous peoples stand in opposition to the globalization of the new world order of late technocratic capitalism, against mass consumption, against the exploitation of our lands, against ecological devastation that particularly affects poor communities and communities of color, against the devaluation of women, and against the devaluation and exploitation of any human being. Indigenous cultures present us with the beginnings of a new, critical paradigm that could generate a liberative force in the world today.

---

40. Jacques Derrida, of course, is french-algerian. His work, however, unlike that of his french colleague Michel Foucault, shows less persistent interest in the structures of political power to which Third World theological reflection must persistently respond.

41. Note the title of the volume edited by Sergio Torres and Virginia Fabella, *The Emergent Gospel: Theology from the Underside of History* (Maryknoll, N.Y.: Orbis Books, 1978). While I have criticized the use of "history" as a european (and now amer-european) category of cognition that does not fit with American Indian intellectual traditions, which are predicated on spatiality rather than temporality, it is also clear to me that the United States functions politically and socially in the world as an ahistorical amnesiac. For the United States, the violence of its past is always forgotten in the self-righteous necessity for perpetrating ever new acts of violence in the world.

Chapter 2

Creation, Justice, and Peace

Indians, Christianity, and Trinitarian Theologies

We live in a very dangerous moment, and not just because of the global threat of terrorist violence and what seems like a perpetual state of war in Iraq and Afghanistan. In the midst of the rush to globalize euro-western political ideologies, religious ideas, and economic structures, we in the northern hemisphere are making decisions and acting in ways that are devastating to our ecohabitat just as readily as we are enforcing poverty on most of the southern hemisphere. We are using up the world and its resources;[1] we are destroying the natural world at an alarming rate, polluting the earth's waters and air, and at the same time inventing ever new and ever more brutal ways to oppress greater and greater portions of the earth's human population, ways more devastating than ever known before. Megacities of millions and tens of millions of desperately poor people are emerging throughout the south to satisfy the need for cheap labor to produce the north's growing appetite for cheap consumer goods. Some 10 percent of the world's rain forest is being destroyed, cut, cleared every year, and indigenous jungle societies are being removed to make way for agriculture.[2] Within a few years this regenerative source of the earth's oxygen supply could be completely destroyed. And even as this craziness continues, it has precipitated a new oppression of Indian tribal people

---

1. Six percent of the world's population, all living in the United States, possesses 59 percent of the entire world's wealth. Twenty percent of the world's population, including the United States, Canada, and Europe, uses 80 percent of the world's available energy resources.

2. "Amazon Forest Nearly Halved by 2050," Reuters News Service, March 22, 2006, cited from http://www.msnbc.msn.com/id/11961547/; Monte Reel, "Crops cutting into Amazon rain forest: Agricultural boom threatens habitat," *Washington Post*, June 26, 2005. Cited from *The Boston Globe*, http://www.boston.com/news/world/latinamerica/articles/2005/06/26/crops_cutting_into_amazon_rain_forest/; Charles J. Hanley, "Amazon Deforestation Adds to Warming Trend," Associated Press, February 16, 2005; Scott Morrison, "The Brazilian Tropical Forest: Deforestation and Human Rights," *International Journal of Politics and Ethics* 1 (2001): accessed online at Questia.com; Oliver T. Coomes and Bradford L. Barham, "Rain Forest Extraction and Conservation in Amazonia," *Geographical Journal* 163 (1997): accessed on-line at Questia.com.

in the jungles of Brazil and elsewhere over the past couple of decades, from whence reports of massacres and genocide continue to come. As if that were not enough, we live with the constant terror of violence and war. This chapter is one response to these threats. It is an American Indian's response to contemporary Christianity, speaking out my own *wazhazhe* Nation values and traditions. I propose these Indian thoughts as a way of finding some middle ground culturally between euro-western Christianity and indigenous peoples worldwide.

Two decades ago, the World Council of Churches (WCC) initiated a conciliar process intended to address many of these issues as they were emerging at that time, a process they labeled "Justice, Peace, and the Integrity of Creation" (JPIC).[3] It seems to me in retrospect that the process was systemically flawed from the outset by a use of language that was and is deeply bogged down in the particularities of the intellectual development of the euro-west. Instead of offering a genuinely new and creative solution, the process ironically tended to continue the churches' participation in the global problematic, even as it tried to identify a breadth of concerns. In particular, I want to argue that the failure of the WCC to take its own historic trinitarian theology seriously left the process with a much less powerful means for envisioning global harmony and balance, the only serious American Indian goal for all of life and spiritual involvement, whether personal or communal.

A genuine trinitarian analysis of the global predicament would take creation seriously as the starting point for theology rather than treat it merely as an add-on to concerns for justice and peace. That would have given the churches a whole new perspective on how to achieve lasting global balance, justice, and peace. Indeed, I will argue, the process should have been engaged as "creation, justice, and peace," with the word "creation" beginning the title. The wording and the word order, then, are both important in my own analysis. Moreover, the theological perspectives of traditional American Indian communities on creation and the order of reality become a key paradigm in the analysis. American Indian peoples have never been inclined toward trinitarian thinking but rather have been, as San Juan *Tewa* anthropologist Alfonso Ortiz put it succinctly, "relentlessly tetradic."[4] Yet it seems important, from my indigenous perspective, to push the churches of the WCC to reclaim its

---

3. See Preman Niles, *Between the Flood and the Rainbow: Interpreting the Conciliar Process of Mutual Commitment, Covenant to Justice, Peace and the Integrity of Creation* (Geneva: World Council of Churches, 1992).

4. This is American Indian common-sense knowledge, readily demonstrated with fairly simple analysis. I first heard Ortiz articulate it using the language of "relentlessly tetradic" during a lecture at the University of California Berkeley in 1986 in a postdoctoral seminar in which he and I shared leadership.

own trinitarian doctrinal structures to better achieve its goal of world justice, peace, and environmental security. Whether we look at the world through the tetradic spiritual insights of traditional American Indians or the trinitarian theology of euro-Christianity, a clear and deep-structure understanding of creation must be the starting point.

The World Council of Churches is an organization of mainline Christianity that includes almost all of the historic denominations in Europe, the United States, and other places around the world where the religion has been long established, along with emerging denominations of many Third World countries, where conversion came historically in the wake of the colonial invasion via the euro-western colonial missionary movement. While the WCC does not include the Roman Catholic Church as a member or many of what are called "evangelical" churches, it is a large and influential segment of world Christianity. Committed to world peace after the end of World War II and the beginning of the Cold War, and having begun to address concerns for global justice at its General Assemblies in 1968 and 1975, the WCC turned to ecojustice with its decision to initiate the JPIC Process in 1983. The name of the initiative seemed deficient to me at the time, and in retrospect it continues to demand a corrective from the perspective of indigenous peoples and their particular theological insights, one that would, with some sense of irony, push these christian communities back toward their own historic roots in early Christianity. To do this, we need to recall the early creeds of the christian churches, sometimes called the ecumenical creeds, and the trinitarian notion of deity as father, son, and spirit, which was developed in and along with the creeds.

An adequate theology of creation becomes the indispensable foundation for the pursuit of justice and peace. Moreover, an adequate theology of creation must include a theology of nature, the very point where indigenous cultural values and theological notions become helpful. That is, this new theology must address the sacredness of all in the world and our relation as human beings to that all. If we human beings could agree to affirm the sacredness of the natural world, if we could begin to live that affirmation, if we could begin to experience the world, including one another, as sacred, then "God's" (*theos*, in the greek text of the christian Bible) demand for justice would become a vital and consuming concern. And God's desire for peace built on justice would become the human community's passion as well.

The restoration of trinitarian balance in euro-christian theology requires a strong and well-articulated affirmation of the priority of the first articles of the ecumenical creeds. In the first place, a proper prioritizing of first-article/ creation concerns of the ecumenical creeds would enable the churches of the euro-west to appreciate and value the inherent spiritual gifts that many cultures, especially indigenous, tribal, Fourth World cultures, might bring to Christianity. More than that, it would reestablish the churches' own spiritual base for pursuing justice and peace. Second, this new appreciation for the spiritual insights of indigenous peoples can lead the churches back to a stronger affirmation of the priority of creation in the oldest confessions and on to a new understanding of how that confession can function for healing and reintegration in a modern, disintegrating world. We will discover that respect for creation can become the spiritual and theological basis for justice and peace just as it is the spiritual and theological basis for God's reconciling act in Christ Jesus and the ongoing life of sanctification in the Holy Spirit.

I want to begin my discussion of American Indian theological values with an image: As the community gathers to cut down the tree marked for use in the center of a Sun Dance, the community members collect their thoughts so that the people might have a single heart and a single mind among themselves. The ceremony is, after all, about and for the community as much as it is a ceremony for maintaining the life of the world around us.[5]

On the fourth and last day of the purification, the people process out from their village to gather at the base of the tree selected to serve as the center of their Sun Dance. Because of their theological understanding of the relationship of all people in the world (both human and non-human), there is no possibility that the people could simply cut down the tree and bring it back for the dance. Rather, this act requires a ceremony of its own, an attention to spiritual detail. So the tree is approached in a sacred way, with words of explanation to the tree and thanksgiving for its gift of its life for the people. To engage in an act of violence, to take the life of the tree, requires some means for maintaining the harmony and balance of the world. Indeed, the Sun Dance is about harmony and balance; it would be an inconceivable paradox, a violent contradiction, to violate it at the very beginning and to hope for balance as a result.

Out of their love and respect for this relative, they do not allow the tree to fall to the ground as they cut it, but the men catch it in its fall. After trimming the tree carefully, the men carry it back to the place designated for the dance. When the tree is carefully set into the hole prepared in advance to hold it, the people begin to approach the tree wrapping strings of colorful prayer offerings around the trunk, each prepared by an individual or a family. With his or her string of offerings, the person talks again to the tree explaining why she or he had made the offerings and what expectation they had for help during the next four days of the dance. Many would speak to the tree, speaking consoling

---

5. See George E. Tinker, "Sundance," in *The Encyclopedia of Religion*, Lindsay Jones, editor in chief (2nd ed.; Detroit: Macmillan Reference, 2005), 13:8848-49.

words of apology, gratitude, purpose and promise. They are grateful for the life of the tree and its gift to the people in this ceremony colloquially called Sun Dance in english.

There is a real cultural value being exposed in this gathering. The ceremony is dismissed as animism in many of the colonial anthropology discussions, but Indian people know (this is not a mere *belief* among us) that everything around us in the created world has its own life and thus is marked by a particular spirit. Hence, we realize that in cutting down a tree for our dance, we are necessarily taking a life, an act of violence, and that act requires special spiritual attention on our part. There is here an attitude toward creation and all that is created that sets American Indians apart from Amer-europeans and other euro-westerners. Yet this spiritual attention to creation is characteristic of a great many of the world's indigenous peoples and represents a set of cultural values that perseveres even in those indigenous communities that have been converted to Christianity. Perhaps an outsider would describe the attitude of these Indians as one of awe or wonderment. We American Indians think of it as neither, but would prefer to call it "respect," the appropriate attitude of respect necessary to fulfill our responsibility as part of the created whole, necessary to help maintain the harmony and balance, the interdependence and interrelationship of all things in our world. Indigenous peoples tend to think of themselves as part of creation rather than somehow set apart from the created whole as a species with special and particular privilege over against the rest of creation. We are a part of creation and in relationship with every other part of the created whole rather than apart from it and free to use the rest of the world up as our private resource bank.

The key word then, for the American Indian cultural context, is respect, respect for a tree. Just as important theologically is the underlying corollary, namely, the notion of reciprocity. The prayers and the offering of tobacco are reciprocal acts of giving something back to the earth and to all of creation in order to maintain balance even as we disrupt the balance by cutting down this tree. In the same way, there were specific ceremonies that were performed prior to the hunting and killing of buffalos for the food to sustain a village of people. Osages and other plains Indian peoples lived a close sibling relationship with the buffalo. Typically, the oral traditions of plains tribes recalled how the buffalo agreed at some point in the long-ago historical past to give up their lives for human beings. The agreement between humans and buffalos, however, called on human beings to engage in their hunting activities with the appropriate respect and to perform the ceremonies necessary to restore life to the buffalo nation.

Inherent in these traditions is a key question Indian cultures pose to christian peoples, especially those of Europe and north America: How can respect for a tree or rock, animals, or even other human beings find any place in the industrial-commercial world that has emerged out of modernity and now threatens all of creation with postmodern extinction? And what sort of reciprocity do we engage in, will we engage in; what do we return to the earth when we clear-cut a forest or gouge out a strip mine leaving miles upon miles of earth totally bare? Perhaps more painfully, the same question can be put in terms of human justice: Where is the reciprocity, the maintaining of cosmic balance, with respect to those who are suffering varieties of oppression in our modern world? Blacks in southern Africa, non-Jews in Palestine, Tamils in Sri Lanka, or tribal peoples in latin America?

"Justice, Peace and the Integrity of Creation" resulted in an exciting and innovative moment which seemed at the time to push the churches of the WCC more decisively toward what I have described as the American Indian foundation of respect.[6] It initiated a crucial discussion that began to move the christian churches in the right direction. In spite of the historical tendencies of most of our churches and the explicit sequence of words in the title, which puts creation at the end, the "Final Document" of the JPIC World Convocation bites the bullet and puts concern for creation ahead of justice in its priority. I say this with a certain satisfaction, even though I sense a danger here. Like many other Third and Fourth World peoples, I, too, have worried that the growing concern for and awareness of the ecological crisis facing all of creation might and often has distracted people of genuine conscience from their awareness of and commitment to issues of justice and liberation in the Two-Thirds World. The concern for the survival of fish in mountain lakes polluted by acid rain, for instance, is surely noble. However, when that concern distracts the attention of christian peoples in the north from the daily suffering of Blacks in Africa (from the economic distresses of globalization, from AIDS and other diseases, from the dictatorships that are the residual result of euro-western colonialism), then the churches become an actual participant in the oppression imposed on those human sisters and brothers.

For my part, I must constantly remind euro-christian people in north America of the continued oppression of American Indians—of our 60 percent unemployment rate, the destruction of our cultures, the theft of our lands, and our greater victimization by disease and dysfunctionality resulting in a horrible life expectancy of only forty-six years.[7] The need for justice, for

---

6. "Final Document: Entering into Covenant Solidarity for Justice, Peace and the Integrity of Creation," in *The Final Document and Other Texts from the World Convocation on Justice, Peace and the Integrity of Creation, Seoul, Republic of Korea, 5-12 March, 1990* (Geneva: WCC, 1990).

7. See the summary of contemporary conditions of Indian communities in Tex G. Hall's op-ed piece, written in the wake of the unfolding Jack Abramoff scandal. Hall was the

churches that will proclaim some "good news to the poor and oppressed," is indeed real, even in the midst of north America's wealth. American Indians continue to suffer from the effects of conquest by european immigrants over the past five centuries—an ongoing and pervasive sense of community-wide post-traumatic stress disorder.[8] We live with the ongoing stigma of defeated peoples who have endured genocide, the intentional dismantling of cultural values, forced confinement on less desirable lands called "reservations," intentionally nurtured dependency on the federal government, and conversion by missionaries who imposed a new culture on us as readily as they preached the gospel.[9] All this has resulted in a current situation, which is marked by a dreadful poverty not usually associated with the United States in the minds of the international community.

More to the point, the pervasive result is a depreciated level of self-esteem that all too readily internalizes any missionary preaching that intends first to convict people of their sin. This American Indian context of poverty and history of conquest means that christian mission efforts can have a particularly devastating consequence on many Indian peoples, given the usual modus operandi of euro-western churches and their message of fall and redemption. Unfortunately, by the time the preacher gets to the "good news" of the gospel, people are so bogged down in the reification of their experience and in the internalization of brokenness and lack of self-worth that too often they never quite hear the proclamation of "good news" in any actualized, existential sense. Both in terms of intrinsic Native American values, then, and in terms of Native American sociological and psychological realities, a starting point of fall and redemption is singularly unhelpful, while a first-article/creation starting point would form a natural bond with indigenous cultural roots. To put it bluntly,

---

tribal chair of the Mandan, Hidatsa, Arikara Nation in North Dakota and past president of the National Congress of American Indians ("American Indians and the Abramoff Scandal: You don't know Jack," *San Francisco Chronicle* [Friday, January 27, 2006], B-13; accessed online at http://sfgate.com/cgi-bin/article.cgi?file=/chronicle/archive/2006/01/27/EDGT 0GTK471.DTL.

8. See Ward Churchill's lengthy preface to the collection of his late wife's writings: Leah Renae Kelly, *In My Own Voice: Explorations in the Sociopolitical Context of Art and Cinema* (Winnipeg: Arbeiter Ring, 2001), 9-58. Churchill discusses aspects of post-traumatic stress disorder (PTSD), especially as it affects American Indian communities mired in the residual effects of colonialism and conquest. Churchill's volume on the infamous Indian boarding schools underscores one of the important root causes for the cycle of PTSD that continues to plague our reservation and urban Indian communities (*Kill the Indian, Save the Man: The Genocidal Impact of American Indian Residential Schools* [San Francisco: City Lights Press, 2004]).

9. Ward Churchill, *A Little Matter of Genocide: Holocaust and Denial in the Americas* (San Francisco: City Lights Press, 1995, 2002); George E. Tinker, *Missionary Conquest: The Gospel and Native American Genocide* (Minneapolis: Fortress Press, 1993).

an American Indian spiritual proclamation must begin with the affirmation that all of life is sacred, and therefore I am sacred as a part of the created whole. That is, I begin by affirming myself and all of life, especially every other human being, as a sacred and good part of creation rather than beginning by succumbing to the acute euro-missionary pressure to admit culpability as a sinful being. I begin with goodness and not with evil or sin.

Not only do I want to argue that respect for creation must be our starting point for theological reflection in our endangered world, but, more explicitly, I would argue, from an American Indian perspective, that justice and peace would flow as a natural result from a genuine and appropriate concern for creation. Hence, the "integrity of creation," in the WCC's jargon, must be understood as much more than a concern for ecological disintegration. At a theological level, the sequence of words in the title "Justice, Peace and the Integrity of Creation" was and is problematic for Native Americans, and I expect for other Fourth World indigenous peoples. For us as for the early ecumenical creeds of the christian church, respect for the act of creation and my role as part of continuation of creation must come first.

The World Council of Churches made the shift over the past four decades away from "peace and justice" language to language of "justice and peace." Justice must logically precede peace, the argument was. Thus, the word order of JPIC is more than just a curiosity. It reflects a definite prioritization, not so much in terms of importance but in terms of an appropriate sequencing of the whole agenda. This sensitivity of the churches is indeed a response to the voices of marginalized peoples all over this world. Third and Fourth World peoples have been almost univocal that their primary need—whether within their own country or in the international community—has been for a measure of real justice and that peace in our context has first to do with justice. We have been equally clear that any sudden emergence of international peace in the world as we know it today would fall far short of satisfying the pervasive need for justice. Indeed, it might function, quite to the contrary, to institutionalize further the injustices suffered, just as many peace movements have often functioned to steal peoples' energies away from some of the more immediate struggles for justice.

Just as concerned christian people have begun to learn that true peace can only be realized through the establishment of justice and that peace is a consequence of justice, so now we must begin to learn that justice and then peace flow naturally out of a deep respect for all of creation. Thus, for Native Americans and other indigenous peoples, a much more theologically intact title would be "Creation, Justice and Peace." It already seemed clear to many of us two decades ago that the "Integrity of Creation" was merely a tacked-on First World concern for environmental issues, tacked on to the end of the sequence so as not to impede the insistence on justice voiced by poor Two-Thirds World churches in the global south.

While concern for ecojustice as a concern for human habitat has a certain usefulness in the context of today's global devastation of the ecosystem, it fails to capture the indigenous notion of balance, respect, and reciprocity. Indeed, it continues the overwhelming anthropocentrism of euro-western thought and euro-western Christianity. So, we might ask, what hinders the euro-west from making creation its spiritual and theological starting point? It would seem that the very insistence on differentiating the christian belief system from all others has made for a very different theological priority. Along with that need to differentiate, the euro-west has equally used its religious structures to help define the sort of racialized sense of superiority that created the imperialist colonial ventures that became definitive of the european global posture after 1492. To differentiate european religious identity, the notion of christomonism began to assume central importance in christian theology and practice.

The First Shall Be Last: Christomonism and the Loss of Creation

In the more respectable form of the varieties of fall/redemption theologies of the different historic communions, christomonism (Christ alone) appears to be the dominant heresy of this contemporary age, if I can be permitted a less pejorative and more neutrally descriptive use of the word "heresy."[10] It certainly is the dominant theology, in practice at least, of most mainline denominations in the United States, and it provides us with a metaphoric language of salvation with which Amer-europeans and many others have become most comfortable. It is, indeed, fealty to Jesus that distinguishes Christianity from other religious communities, so it should not be surprising that some expression of this doctrinal commitment should be the beginning of any christian church's proclamation of its purposes. Christomonism, however, moves the doctrinal posture one step further than simply differentiating Christianity from other expressions of faith. In one manner or another, it announces the proclamation

---

10. From the greek word *haeresis*, which Liddell and Scott define broadly as taking choice, election, purpose, condition, and, more narrowly, as a "system of philosophical principles, or those who profess such principles, sect, school" (H. G. Liddell, R. Scott, and H. S. Jones, *A Greek-English Lexicon*, 9th ed., with revised supplement [Oxford: Oxford University Press, 1996]). This differs from Webster's definition of the english word: "an opinion contrary to the orthodox opinion." In light of the work of Walter Bauer (*Rechtglaubigkeit und Ketzerei im ältesten Christentum* [Tübingen: Mohr, 1934]), and the rise of the ecumenical movement in the last one hundred years, we might be well advised to recover this more ancient use of the word as "school of thought."

in a universalizing voice and then voices the theological/doctrinal rationale that underscores the global need for a confession of Christ predicated on a theological worldview that universalizes human sin. Using a particular interpretation of an ancient middle-eastern oral tradition (textualized in Genesis 3), the churches predicate a primal fall from grace that taints all human beings from birth and becomes the prima facie logic for a presumed need of salvation. The Jesus event then becomes, for these churches, the salvific solution in their fall-and-redemption proclamation, and that schematic in turn becomes the major impetus for the colonial and imperial missionary outreach of the nineteenth and twentieth centuries. Yet, I want to argue, making the Christ event, fall and redemption, the starting point in the christomonic theological scheme, at least in practice, has completely obviated the first article of the ancient christian ecumenical creeds. The story of humanity's primal fall from grace, as european christian folk have interpreted it, has blunted any variety of more complex theological developments of theologies of creation or theologies of nature. Moreover, the fall/redemption schematic has proven to be painfully damaging to fragile Indian communities.

While the stated purposes of new evangelical churches tend to emphasize the health and spiritual well-being of the individual (also a quintessential development that derives directly from european cultures), the purpose statements of the historic mainline denominations in our contemporary moment tend to be rather wonderful laundry lists that include that church's concern for justice and peace. They name concern for the poor and oppressed, as well as concerns for the spiritual nurturing of one another and for evangelical outreach to others in the world. It is, however, the first item on each list to which I wish to draw attention. No matter how good or long or inclusive the list becomes, it is always the first item that implicitly predicates the foundation for the rest of the list. It becomes the starting point for understanding the whole mission of that church, the starting point for that church's theological understanding.

For example, as the Evangelical Lutheran Church in America came into being nearly two decades ago, the participating factions wrestled to create a new purpose statement satisfying to all. From the first draft until the next to the last (the final version merely inserted a pro forma one-line affirmation of trinity), as the list of purposes grew more and more inclusive of a great variety of concerns, the top of the list always began, "the purpose of this church shall be: A. To proclaim God's reconciling act in Christ Jesus." Now, folk may quibble from denomination to denomination over the wording of this affirmation, but surely few adherents would question the importance of this christocentric proclamation to the self-identity of Christianity and as the unique contribution of Christianity to the salvation of the world. At least in some degree it begins to articulate what is perhaps the central doctrine of Christianity for most churches. In one way or another it is the centrality of Christ's reconciling death and resurrection that marks each church as christian and binds them together in ecumenical dialogue and ministry in the World Council of Churches.[11]

Yet it is still appropriate, at both theological and sociological levels, to challenge the propriety of even so central a doctrine, and especially so when we are challenging not so much the doctrine itself but its relationship to other teachings and the systematic framework into which it has been placed. For even so central a doctrine does not live a life of its own but necessarily functions in a variety of ways depending on the larger structure of which it is a part. The immediate question before us is not *whether* christian churches will affirm such a proclamation as significant or its centrality to their understanding of the christian faith. The question is whether this is the appropriate *starting place* for any church's theological reflection. Concomitant questions will ask how the proclamation thus functions, how it might best be nuanced, and how it might otherwise function.

The argument put forth here for discussion is as follows: any structuring of theology that *begins* with "God's reconciling act in Christ Jesus" violates the traditional trinitarian confession of Christianity and hence depreciates the significance of doctrines of creation. At an obvious level, to make the Christ event the starting point is to circumvent the first article of the ancient ecumenical creeds and to begin with the second article. To some extent it could be argued that creation/first-article concerns are not necessarily ignored but merely delayed in their consideration in favor of emphasizing the more central and more unique aspect of christian faith. Certainly all churches voice theological assent to the first article of the creeds, even those who customarily disavow creeds; and all give theological support to the doctrines of creation embedded there. The point here is how those concerns are addressed and with what priority. It should become clear that first-article/creation concerns are indeed devalued when their priority is deferred in favor of more immediate, first-place consideration of a fall-and-redemption category. One could go a step further and suggest that christian denominations tend to devalue that which they have in common with many other religious faiths in favor of overvaluing that which distinguishes them. It was a small move, then, for these

---

11. For a structurally similar prioritizing of second-article proclamation, see the Preamble (paragraph 2) of "The Constitution of the United Church of Christ," 1984 edition. It begins: "The United Church of Christ acknowledges as its sole Head, Jesus Christ, Son of God and Saviour." So much for trinitarian confession or the priority of first-article/creation proclamation. The U.S. Presbyterian constitution likewise begins with a section proclaiming the headship of Jesus Christ: "The Head of the Church" (*The Constitution: Presbyterian Church (USA), Part II: Book of Order*, 1983-1985 [New York: Offices of the General Assembly, 1981], ch. I:1, p. 13).

churches to succumb to euro-colonial notions of colonizer superiority in their missionary endeavors.

So euro-western Christians have characteristically overvalued Jesus in their self-identification. In that process, the colonial missionary effort made "accepting" Jesus a universal boundary marker between good and evil, civilized and savage, saved and condemned. As this functioned to undergird the political and economic efforts of colonial conquest, it put the churches directly in the wake of the euro-colonial governmental structures—even when they occasionally protested a policy of some kind. As a result, not only did euro-western Christians lose sight of a theology of creation, but they failed to critique their own growing nepotistic relationship with the social whole that emerged out of an empire-driven culture. Likewise, on this continent, Amereuropeans were blinded by their own relationship to colonial structures to any appreciation of cultural difference they met in indigenous people, consigning the aboriginal population they met to savagery and primitiveness. The failure to learn from the colonial other made euro-western Christianity complicit in the growing environmental destruction we see today and complicit in the devastating destruction of aboriginal peoples—on this continent and around the globe. It is essential today that we all learn to live in better balance with all of creation. It is incumbent on Christians to create their own theologies of creation and nature; American Indian peoples have a great deal to say on the topic from which others might well learn.

THE CIRCLE AND *MITAKUYE OYASIN*

American Indians and other indigenous peoples have a long-standing confidence that they have much to teach european and north american peoples about the world and human relationships in the world. They are confident in the spiritual foundations of their insights, confident that those foundations can become a source of healing and reconciliation for all human beings and ultimately for all of creation. Let me use a couple of simple examples from an Indian perspective.

My Indian ancestors had a relationship with *wako^n da* as creator, the fructifying force of the cosmos, that was healthy and responsible long before they knew of or considered a confession of the gospel of Jesus Christ. They had a relationship with the Creator that was solidified in the stories they told around the campfires in each of our tribes, in their prayers, and especially in their ceremonies. This relationship began with the recognition of the Sacred Other as the Creator, the creative force behind all things that exist, and long predated the coming of the missionaries. In that relationship, the people saw themselves as participants within creation as a whole, as a part of creation, and they celebrated the balance and harmony of the whole of the universe in all that they did together.

In all that they did our Indian ancestors acknowledged the goodness of the Creator and of all creation, including themselves. That was the point of the stories, the focus of their prayers, and the purpose of the ceremonies. They recognized the balance and harmony that characterized all of the created universe: winter and summer were held in balance with each other. So also were hunting and planting, sky and earth, hot and cold, sun and moon, female and male, women and men. Our ancestors recognized all this as good, just as does "God" at the end of the sixth day in the opening chapter of the hebrew Bible (Gen 1:31).

All American Indian spiritual insights, and hence Indian theology, begin necessarily with creation, and this is reflected in the basic liturgical/ceremonial posture of Indians in many north american tribes. Our prayers are most often said with the community assembled into some form of circle. In fact, the circle is a key symbol for self-understanding in these tribes, representing the whole of the universe and our part in it. We see ourselves as coequal participants in the circle standing neither above nor below anything else in the created world. There is no hierarchy in our cultural context, even of species, because the circle has no beginning or end. Hence, all the createds participate together, each in their own way, to preserve the wholeness of the circle.

So when a group of Indians forms a circle to pray, all know that the prayers have already begun with the representation of a circle. No words have yet been spoken, and in some ceremonies no words need be spoken; but the intentional physicality of our formation has already expressed our prayer and deep concern for the wholeness of all of creation. It should be noted in this context that Indians do not hold hands when they pray thus, unless they have been tainted by the piety of a White missionary. There is no need to hold hands because we know it is enough to stand in the circle already joined together, inextricably bound, through the earth which lies firm beneath our feet, the earth who is, after all, the true mother of each of us and of all creation.

The Lakota and Dakota peoples have a phrase used in all their prayers that aptly illustrates the Native American sense of the centrality and wholeness of creation. In prayers, the phrase *mitakuye oyasin* functions structurally somewhat like the word "amen" in european and american Christianity. As such, it is used to end every prayer, and often it is in itself a whole prayer, being the only phrase spoken when a person has nothing else she or he desires to speak aloud. The usual translation offered is, "For all my relations." Yet, like most Native symbols, *mitakuye oyasin* is polyvalent in its meaning. Certainly, one is praying for one's close kin, aunts, cousins, children, grandparents, and so forth. And "relations" can be understood as fellow tribal members or even all

Indian people. At the same time, the phrase includes all human beings, all two-leggeds as relatives of one another, and the ever-expanding circle does not stop there. Every Lakota who prays this prayer knows that our relatives necessarily include the four-leggeds, the wingeds, and all the living-moving things on Mother Earth. One Lakota teacher has suggested that a better translation of *mitakuye oyasin* would read, "For all the above me and below me and around me things: that is, for all my relations." Perhaps one can begin to understand the extensive image of interrelatedness and interdependence symbolized by the circle and the importance of reciprocity and respect for one another for maintaining the wholeness of the circle. The American Indian concern for starting theology with creation is a need to acknowledge the goodness and inherent worth of all God's creatures. We experience evil or sin as disruptions in that delicate balance, disruptions that negate the intrinsic worth of any of our relatives.

The Circle as Symbolic Cosmos of Interrelationship

As Alfonso Ortiz articulated it two decades ago,[12] one of the most precious gifts that American Indian peoples have to share with our colonizer-settler relatives on this continent is our firm sense of the interrelationship of all life and all of creation. The anthropocentrism of the euro-west has no place among us or among any indigenous peoples. All of life consists of our relatives, from buffalos to rocks. Thus, there can be no conception of anything in the created world that does not share in the sacredness infused in the *wako^{n}da's* creative action. Traditional stories relate dialogue and interaction between different animal relatives quite as if they were like us human beings, which, indeed, they may have been in some earlier age. Many tribal traditions then include stories that try to account for the necessity, for the sake of the survival of one species, of violent acts, perpetuated in hunting. In many of these stories, the four-legged and winged engage in a long debate that concludes with a consensus to permit hunting by two-leggeds—for their good, that is, survival—but establishes certain ceremonial parameters that will always ensure respect for the sacredness of all life.

As I have argued elsewhere, the Indian understanding of creation as sacred, of Mother Earth as the source of all life, goes far beyond the notion of such western counter-institutions as the Sierra Club or Greenpeace. It embraces

---

12. This is American Indian common-sense knowledge, readily demonstrated with fairly simple analysis. As noted above, I first heard Ortiz articulate it using the language of "relentlessly tetradic" during a lecture at the University of California Berkeley in 1986 in a postdoctoral seminar in which he and I shared leadership.

far more than concern for harp seals, snail darters, or the Alaskan National Wildlife Refuge. Rather, it is life affirming in all of its wholeness, embracing all of life from trees and animals to international relations. This sense of respect for life in turn informs all of a community's actions, from ceremonial dances to writing grant proposals, from hunting to engagement in military battles. It especially concerns itself with the way we all live together. Perforce, it has to do with issues of justice and fairness.

Creation and Kingdom

In the remainder of this essay I want to pursue this American Indian image of creation in terms of the important biblical image of *basilea*, the so-called kingdom of God. In particular I want to suggest the benefits to western Christianity of a Native American reading of the kingdom. I would like to do this with special attention to Mark 1:15 and the conjunction of the nearness of the kingdom and the need for repentance.[13] But first we must make some decisions about the nature of the *basilea* or kingdom.

If the Indian image of creation is at all compelling, then it might be equally compelling for the churches to come to a new (or perhaps very old) understanding of creation in their denominational theologies, one that begins to image creation as an ongoing eschatological act and not just God's initiatory act. I want to argue that christian theology must begin to see creation as the eschatological basis even for the Christ event itself. If this is difficult, it may, indeed, be so because the cultures in which the gospel has come to find a home in the west are so fundamentally oriented toward temporality and so disoriented toward spatiality. As a result, the very categories of existence and all the categories of knowledge in the western intellectual tradition function out of a temporal base and pervade our understanding of all reality.[14] This then characterizes our theologies and especially our interpretation of key biblical themes and texts.

Since the emergence of eschatology as a central aspect of the interpretation of especially the gospels in western biblical criticism in the work of Johannes

---

13. What follows borrows heavily from "Indian Culture and Interpreting the Christian Bible," a chapter in George E. Tinker, *Spirit and Resistance: Political Theology and American Indian Liberation* (Minneapolis: Fortress Press, 2004), 88-99.

14. So argues Robert A. Nisbet, *Social Change and History: Aspects of the Western Theory of Development* (New York: Oxford University Press: 1969). While Nisbet rightly sees temporality as important for understanding all western culture, he finds this aspect to be wholly positive. I, of course, find it problematic.

Weiss and Albert Schweitzer,[15] until very recently the kingdom of God has been given over completely to a temporal interpretation.[16] That is, the only appropriate question to ask about the kingdom has been *when?* It is not that scholars did not consider other possibilities. In fact, the question *where?* has been consistently disallowed. Norman Perrin spoke for some seventy years of scholarly dialogue in Europe and north America when he wrote in 1967: "[the kingdom] is not a place or community ruled by God."[17] From Weiss and Schweitzer to Perrin and beyond, the question had been: When will the kingdom of God happen? When will it appear? In the course of the dialogue, a wide variety of answers have been argued, each of them generating a new *terminus technicus* (latin for "jargon") to label the theory. So we have argued between realized eschatology, actualized eschatology, immanent eschatology, or future eschatology, ringing all the changes on those themes.

This emphasis on time fails to make sense of the clear linguistic connotation implied in the notion of monarchy, the underlying metaphor in the biblical text, or in the word "kingdom," which seems to clearly imply a realm, a place where the monarch rules. At least, for American Indians, who have no historical experience of monarchy prior to the european invasion and colonization but who culturally prioritize spatiality over temporality, the question of where the act of hegemony occurs seems most natural, but such an interpretation requires a cultural move away from the superimportance of the european emphasis on temporality to a renewed sense of prioritizing spatiality.

Curiously enough, it was Norman Perrin and his student Werner Kelber who in the mid-1970s announced a major shift in interpretation of *basilea*. Kelber first put forth arguments for a consistent spatial understanding of the kingdom in the Gospel of Mark, linking its meaning to expanding territorial/geographical developments in that gospel.[18] Perrin decisively articulated the metaphoric nature of *basilea* language, distinguishing between "steno" and "tensive" symbols and identifying *basilea* as the latter. So, we now can begin to understand the kingdom of God as a "symbol," which Perrin defines with Philip Ellis Wheelwright as "a relatively stable and repeatable element of per-

---

15. Johannes Weiss, *Die Predigt Jesu von Reich Gottes* (Göttingen: Vandenhoeck & Ruprecht, 1892); Albert Schweitzer, *Das Abendmahl in Zusammenhang mit dem Leben Jesu und der Geschichte des Urchristentums* (Tübingen: Mohr, 1901); and Albert Schweitzer, *Von Reimarus zu Wrede: Eine Geschichte der Leben-Jesu-Forschung* (Tübingen: Mohr, 1906).

16. See Bruce Chilton, ed., *The Kingdom of God in the Teaching of Jesus* (Philadelphia: Fortress Press, 1984); and Wendell Willis, ed., *The Kingdom of God in 20th Century Interpretation* (Peabody, Mass.: Hendrickson Publishers, 1987).

17. *Rediscovering the Teaching of Jesus* (Harper & Row, 1967), 55.

18. Werner Kelber, *The Kingdom in Mark: A New Place and a New Time* (Philadelphia: Fortress Press, 1974).

ceptual experience, standing for some larger meaning or set of meanings which cannot be given, or not fully given in perceptual experience itself."[19]

It seems obvious enough that spatial categories do not necessarily exclude the temporal, nor vice versa. Yet the orientation assumed by the interpreter becomes crucial. Like Boring, I do not see how temporality can be excised from Mark's proclamation of the kingdom, yet I certainly disagree with his assumption that the kingdom of God sayings in Mark must be read in terms of an "overwhelming temporal orientation."[20] To the contrary, I want to argue for the possibility of spatial priority in language of the kingdom of God, perhaps in Mark particularly. The possibility becomes pronounced in any Native American reading of the text, because the Indian world is as decidedly spatial in its orientation as the modern western world is temporal.[21] In fact, any Indian reader of Mark or the synoptics is bound to think first of all in terms of the question *"where?"* with regard to *basilea*. And it is in this context that I want to pursue the discussion.

It seems safe to suggest that the image represents a symbolic value and that the parameters of the symbol might be filled in as follows: (a) The gospels seem to view the divine hegemony as something that is in process. It is drawing near, it is emerging (Mark 1:15). Yet it is also "among us," in our midst (Luke 17). It is something that can be experienced by the faithful here and now, even if only proleptically. Its full emergence is still in the future. (b) The symbolic value captured by the imagery in no small part includes a view of an ideal world. And (c) the structural definition of that ideal world is, above all else, relational.

I am convinced that the imagery of divine rule is essentially creation imagery, that the ideal world symbolically represented in the image builds on the divine origin of the cosmos as an ideal past and an ideal future. It is relational, first of all, because it implies a relationship between the created order of things and its creator, and, second, because it implies a relationship between all of the things created by the Creator. As the creator of all, God is perforce the rightful ruler of all. And the ideal world to which Jesus points in the gospels is precisely the realization of that proper relationship between the Creator and the created.

---

19. Norman Perrin, *Jesus and the Language of the Kingdom: Symbol and Metaphor in New Testament Interpretation* (Philadelphia: Fortress Press, 1976), 30; and Philip Ellis Wheelwright, *Metaphor and Reality* (Bloomington: Indiana University Press, 1962), 92.

20. M. Eugene Boring, "The Kingdom of God in Mark," in *The Kingdom of God in 20th Century Interpretation*, ed. Wendell Willis (Peabody, Mass.: Hendrickson Publishers, 1987), 140.

21. See Vine Deloria, Jr., *God Is Red* (New York: Dell, 1973); idem, *The Metaphysics of Modern Existence* (New York: Harper & Row, 1979); George E. Tinker, "Native Americans and the Land: The End of Living and the Beginning of Survival," *Word and World* 6 (1986): 66-74; idem, "American Indians and the Land: Spatial Metaphors and Contemporary Existence," in *Voices from the Third World: 1990* (New York: Scribners, 1991), 170-94.

Human beings may have been created as the last of all the created (Gen 1), or perhaps a human being was created first (Gen 2). That is really inconsequential. What is really at stake is that the harmony and balance of the created order was good. While that order has been somewhat shaken by the human createds, it is still the ideal state toward which we all look forward in Christ Jesus. The process is going on now, and all of creation is a part of the process. As Paul says, all of creation groans in travail, that is, in childbirth (Rom 8:22).

Repentance as Return

Now, to return to Mark 1:15, we need not discuss at length the nature of the word for "time." It is enough to suggest the cyclical seasonal nature of *kairos* here over against the more linear concept of *chronos*. In any case, the mention of a time element should not distract us from a spatial, now creational, understanding. Nor at this point would it prove fruitful to pursue the verb *engizo* ("has drawn near").

More important for my case is an understanding of the imperative *metanoete* ("repent!"). And here I want to argue for the underlying aramaic sense of *shub* as "return" rather than the greek notion of *metanoete* as "change of mind." Repentance is key to the establishment of divine hegemony because it involves a "return," namely, a return to God. Feeling sorry for one's sins is not a part of repentance at all though it may be the initial act of confession. Even in the most "greek" of the new testament writings, in Luke's Acts of the Apostles, repentance is not a penitential emotion but instead carries the hebrew sense of "return." In Acts 2:37f, people feel penitential emotion as a result of Peter's sermon and come to him to ask what they must do. His response is to say to them in the depth of their penitential emotion: "Repent and be baptized." They already feel sorry for their sins. That's not what he requires of them. The hebrew notion of repentance really involves calling on God's people to recognize the divine hegemony, to return to God, to return to the ideal relationship between creator and the created.

The establishment of any ecclesiastical structure should be then an attempt to actualize as much as possible (proleptically) this ideal. A "church" ought to be an attempt on the part of a community of people to respond to God's call to relationship, first of all, to relationship with God as creator, and, second, with one another as fellow createds. A church should be a response to Jesus' vision of an ideal world characterized by love of God and love of one's neighbor as one's self. But this ideal world can be actualized only through repentance, that is, by "returning" to God as creator and rightful *hegemon* of all of creation. Hence, church is a vehicle of repentance or "return." Moreover, this ideal world, which exists only within the divine hegemony, is "good"; it is marked by divine balance and harmony.

Confession, Return, and the Integrity of Creation

It is my hope that the theological imagination of Native Americans, rooted as it is in the dynamic, generating power of creation, can help show new direction for the trinitarian theology of christian churches. It should be clearly noted here again that the theological priority of creation is not a priority for environmental concern, but rather is a firm foundation for *justice* and a vision for *peace*. If we can begin with a first article affirmation of God as creator and ourselves as created, then perhaps there is hope for a spiritual transformation that can bring us all closer to recognizing the *basileia* of God in our midst (Luke 17:21). Then, perhaps, we can acknowledge our humanness in new and more significant ways, understanding that confession precedes return, and that both become the base for living in harmony and balance with God and all creation. Besides confessing our individual humanness, this means confessing the humanness of our churches, the humanness of our theologies, and the humanness of the world economic order in which we participate. Then it is possible to make our repentance, our returning, our going back from whence we came, that is, going back to the Creator in whom we, like all of creation, "live and move and have our being" (Acts 17:28). We must go back to a proper relationship with the Creator, confessing our human inclination to put ourselves in the Creator's place, renewing our understanding of ourselves and our institutions as mere creatures. We must go back to a recognition of ourselves as a part of and integrally related to all of creation.

Harmony and Balance: Reimaging Creation

The American Indian is concerned for the wholeness and balance of creation. In his poem "Mid-America Prayer," Acoma Pueblo poet Simon Ortiz pens driving verse that presses repeatedly a concern that all things be done "for the sake of the land and all the people." He pictures the people standing together with the ancestors,

> as sisters and brothers, mothers and fathers,
> daughters and sons, grandmothers and grandfathers—
> the past and present generations of our people. . . .

More to the point, in consistent Indian fashion, he envisions human beings standing in solidarity with all of the creation and participating in the act of balancing all things:

> Standing again
> with and among all items of life,
> the land, rivers, the mountains, plants, animals,
> all life that is around us
> that we are included with. . . .

Indeed, Ortiz knows that we humans have a distinct responsibility for helping to maintain the balance of the whole, a whole that includes all of creation. And Indian people, when we are rooted in the traditions of our cultures, are acutely aware of an ever-unfolding duty to the earth:

> to be in relationship that is responsible
> and proper, that is loving and compassionate,
> for the sake of the land and all people. . . .[22]

The need for humans to be participants in maintaining balance and harmony then focuses all of life's activity. Acts of violence against any relative disrupt the balance and are inexcusable—even those that become necessary. But balance can be restored if we stay within established boundaries. Animal relatives can be killed for food, shelter, tools, and the like, but only if balance is insured by performing the appropriate ceremonies. Quite often, prayers need to be spoken or sung and even words of respect spoken to the animal itself, perhaps words of explanation telling the purpose of this act of hunting and apologizing for it. Likewise, most tribes engaged in elaborate ceremonies before going to war with another tribe. Even one's enemies must be respected. No killing was to be random. A tribe's survival or territorial integrity might be at risk. Nevertheless, maintaining balance, respect for all one's relatives, meant that from four to twelve days of ceremony might be necessary before battle could be engaged.[23]

---

22. From a poem titled "Mid-America Prayer" by Simon J. Ortiz (Acoma Pueblo) in his book of poetry *Fight Back: For the Sake of the People, For the Sake of the Land* (Albuquerque: Institute for Native American Development, University of New Mexico, 1980), 1.

23. Such was the custom in my tribe, for instance. See Francis La Flesche, "*Wa-sha'-be A-thi*", or War Ceremony," in *War Ceremony and Peace Ceremony of the Osage Indians* (Bureau of American Ethnology, Bulletin 101; Washington, D.C.: U.S. Government Printing Office, 1939), 3-198.

If our theology—and hence our human communities—can begin to wrestle seriously with the necessity of balance and harmony in all of creation, then our self-image as a part of creation must also be deeply affected. As our self-perception and self-understanding begin to be self-consciously centered in respect for all creation, we will begin to participate actively not in the exploitation of the earth but in the establishment of balance and harmony. Our participation in the balance and harmony of all creation will then most naturally include other individuals and communities of human beings. And justice and then genuine peace will flow out of our concern for one another and all creation.

The churches of the WCC, especially those churches in the north, in Europe and north America, must move to rediscover their historical spiritual rootedness in the first article of their ecumenical creeds as a clear biblical image and allow that spiritual foundation to generate decisive action for justice and peace. And it may be that the inherent spirituality of American Indians, Pacific Islanders, tribal Africans, aboriginal Australians, and other indigenous peoples may help point in the right direction. While the climactic WCC Consultation (1990 in Seoul) could not agree to change the formal name of the program, it remains important to debate the issues involved. "Justice, Peace and the Integrity of Creation" logically and theologically should have been "Creation, Justice and Peace."

Yes, Indian peoples have experienced and continue to experience endless oppression as a result of what some would call the barbaric invasion of America. And we certainly suspect that the oppression we have experienced is intimately linked to the way the immigrants pray and how they understand creation and their relationship to creation and the Creator. Moreover, we suspect that the greed that motivated the displacement of all indigenous peoples from their lands of spiritual rootedness is the same greed that threatens the destruction of the earth and the continued oppression of so many peoples and ultimately the destruction of our White relatives. Whether it is the stories the settlers tell or the theologies they develop to interpret those stories, something appears wrong to Indian people. But not only do Indians continue to tell the stories, sing the songs, speak the prayers, and perform the ceremonies that root themselves deeply in Mother Earth; they are actually audacious enough to think that their stories and their ways of reverencing creation will some day win over our White settler relatives and transform them. Optimism and enduring patience seem to run in the life blood of Native American peoples.

May justice, followed by genuine peace, flow out of our concern for one another and all creation.

Chapter 3

Ecojustice and American Indian Sovereignty[1]

It is an enduring irony that those who have the deepest cultural connection to american soil have been among those most deeply affected by the modern, technological devastation of the land, whether the issues are land tenure, water, hydroelectric damming, mining, or toxic waste deposit sites.[2] Yet it is the painful truth that ecological devastation, while it eventually affects the well-being of everyone, initially and most particularly affects American Indians and people of color on this continent and Two-Thirds World people in general more directly and adversely than it affects White Americans, especially those of the middle and upper classes.[3] As Ward Churchill implies, genocide seems all too often to accompany ecocide.[4]

---

1. An earlier version of this essay was published as "An American Indian Theological Response to Ecojustice," in *Defending Mother Earth: Native American Perspectives on Environmental Justice*, ed. Jace Weaver (Maryknoll, N.Y.: Orbis Books, 1996), 153-76. The essays in that volume continue to raise some of the significant concerns for environmental justice from an Indian perspective.

2. Donald A. Grinde and Bruce E. Johansen, *Ecocide of Native America: Environmental Destruction of Indian Lands and Peoples* (Santa Fe: Clear Light Books, 1995). In a world full of profound and sometimes cruel ironies, one stands out: Native Americans, who held the lands of the western hemisphere in a living trust for thousands of years, have been afflicted by some of the worst pollution in an environmental crisis that has reached planet-wide proportions (p. 1). See also Winona LaDuke, *All Our Relations: Native Struggles for Land and Life* (Boston: South End Press, 1999), for a useful and well-written survey of American Indian ecojustice concerns on a variety of reservations in the United States and Canada; and her more recent volume, *Recovering the Sacred: The Power of Naming and Claiming* (Boston: South End Press, 2005).

3. Benjamin F. Chavis, Jr., and Charles Lee, eds., *Toxic Wastes and Race in the United States: A National Report on the Racial and Socio-Economic Characteristics of Communities with Hazardous Waste Sites* (New York: Commission for Racial Justice, United Church of Christ, 1987); and Benjamin A. Goldman and Laura Fitton, *Toxic Wastes and Race Revisited: An Update of the 1987 Report on the Racial and Socioeconomic Characteristics of Communities with Hazardous Waste Sites* (Washington, D.C.: Center for Policy Alternatives, 1994). I find Gregg Easterbrook's popular news essay on Two-Thirds World pollution particularly problematic, especially in what I see as a short-sighted and typically simplistic proposal for resolving Two-Thirds World ecojustice concerns. See Easterbrook, "Forget PCB's. Radon. Alar: The World's Greatest Environmental Dangers Are Dung Smoke and Dirty Water," *The New York Times Magazine* (September 11, 1995), 60-63.

4. Ward Churchill, *Struggle for the Land: Indigenous Resistance to Genocide, Ecocide and Expropriation in Contemporary North America* (Monroe, Me.: Common Courage Press, 1993);

To consider the effects of environmental destruction on indigenous communities, one need only think of the long history of uranium mining in the United States and its devastating consequences on Indian lands, devastation severe enough to cause U.S. government policy thinkers to write off certain Indian nations' lands, their reservation territories, as "national sacrifice areas."[5] As Winona LaDuke reminds us, all U.S. nuclear testing has occurred on the lands of indigenous peoples, with some six hundred detonations on western Shoshone land alone. Add to this the burgeoning problem of toxic nuclear waste and the emerging reality of the attempt to locate nuclear waste and other toxic waste facilities on Indian lands. Indian nations are currently hosts for fifteen of eighteen monitored, retrievable nuclear storage facilities.[6] The clear racism here is that we are too poor and too demoralized and dysfunctional from generations of colonization to be able to say no to offers of what seems like sizable income from these waste storage projects.

Moreover, ecological devastation is equally pervasive in the southern american hemisphere along with its destruction of Native cultures and their lands with the usual negative effect on the economic sustainability, health, and lives of indigenous peoples. The reports of destruction caused by oil explo-

---

Mark Zannis, *The Genocide Machine in Canada: The Pacification of the North* (Montreal: Black Rose Books, 1973). Also see Grinde and Johansen, *Ecocide of Native America.*

5. This term seems to have been coined in a study commissioned by the National Academy of Science on resource development on Indian lands. It was submitted to the Nixon administration in 1972 as input toward a national Indian policy. See Thadis Box et al., *Rehabilitation Potential for Western Coal Lands* (Cambridge, Mass.: Ballanger, 1974), for the published version of the study. Also, Churchill, *Struggle for the Land,* 54, 333, 367; and Russell Means, "The Same Old Song," in *Marxism and Native Americans,* ed. Ward Churchill (Cambridge, Mass.: South End Press, 1983), 25; and Churchill and Winona LaDuke, "Native America: The Political Economy of Radioactive Colonialism," in *The State of Native America: Genocide, Colonization and Resistance,* ed. M. Annette Jaimes (Cambridge, Mass.: South End Press, 1992), 241-66.

6. Winona LaDuke, "Foreword: A Society Based on Conquest Cannot Be Sustained," in *The New Resource Wars: Native and Environmental Struggles against Multinational Corporations,* ed. Al Gedick (Boston: South End Press, 1993), xiii. Note most recently the developments with regard to the Skull Valley Goshutes in the state of Utah, where the lingering postcolonial poverty of the tribe has resulted in the political and economic victimization by Private Fuel Storage, a limited liability company that was formed by eight large utilities to find places to temporarily store nuclear waste. The environmental racism involved here is to offer the poverty-ridden tribe so much money that it cannot afford not to trade the long-term medical health of its people for the immediacy of a short-term cash infusion. See Laura Hancock, "Work with Goshutes, USU Historian Says," *Deseret Morning News* (March 7, 2006), http://deseretnews.com/dn/view/0%2C1249%2C635189890%2C00.html; also Anna Chang-Yen, "Waste Raises Questions of Tribes' Sovereignty," *Daily Herald* (March 7, 2006), D-1, http://www.heraldextra.com/content/view/168694/4/. LaDuke also has two titles that should be noted: *Recovering the Sacred* and *All Our Relations* (see n. 2, above). LaDuke offers detailed descriptions of several Indian communities in north America who are affected by ongoing environmental disaster.

ration and extraction in Bolivia, Brazil, Ecuador, Colombia, and Peru are astounding. Yet central (state) governments there seem bent on increased oil and gas development at whatever ecological cost to the lives of peoples as the only possible solution to the state's increasing economic problems.[7] In Ecuador, for instance, oil extraction has made its way into the previously impenetrable lands of the Huaorani. Exxon, Conoco, Texaco, and Petro Ecuador have transected Huaorani lands with miles of one-hundred-yard-wide swaths spaced at one mile intervals. The resulting pollution caused by land erosion makes jungle waterways uninhabitable for many species that have long been a sustainable part of the Huaorani economy. Compounding the pollution from erosion is the constantly recurring problem of oil leaks from wells and pipelines, hundreds or thousands of gallons at a time, which again devastate both land and waterways. The annual spillage of crude oil in Huarani territory of the "Oriente" of Equador exceeds the infamous incident in Alaska of the accidental (one-time) spillage of the oil tanker Valdez.[8]

These examples represent only the tip of the iceberg, as it were; yet they are significant enough to press us toward the natural response of What can we do? What can Indian peoples do to insure their own survival—cultural and sociopolitical survival? What can religious communities of moral conviction and good will do to call the systemic whole to accountability for its participation in both ecocide and genocide? What can the churches, or your church, do to impact creatively and positively this course of destruction? At one level, the easy (non-)solution is what is called, in alcohol and drug addictions, denial. The colonizer tends either to lionize the colonized as an overly romanticized and exoticized other who somehow represents the colonized ideal but unachievable self or the colonizer continues the now ancient colonial process of signifying the colonized as a wholly demonic other, which ultimately serves inherently to rationalize the colonizer's self and the long history of colonial violence that has given rise to the presumed comfort of the colonizer.

On the one hand, there are those in the world today who would regularly espouse an environmental consciousness predicated on their presumption of

---

7. See "Increased Oil Development Rejected in the Amazon," *Abya Yala News: Journal of the South and Meso American Indian Information Center* 8 (Summer 1994): 31-33.

8. Two very enlightening articles on the struggle of resistance being waged in Ecuador's Oriente region by the Huaorani against the combined forces of state government and multinational petroleum corporations, particularly Chevron Texaco, Conoco, Exxon, and Petro Equador, are Joe Kane, "With Spears from All Sides," *New Yorker* (September 27, 1993), 54-79; and "Moi Goes to Washington," *New Yorker* (May 2, 1994), 74-81. More recently, see http://www.earthrights. org/irtk/conoco.shtml, the Web site for Earth Rights International: "Case Study, Conoco," last updated May 5, 2003. See also "Ecuadorean activists berate ChevronTexaco: Protesters claim oil company based in San Ramon has induced an environmental crisis," *Climate Ark—Climate Change Portal* (December 2002), http://climateark.org/articles/reader.asp?linkid=18550.

an American Indian belief system, summoning images of a simpler existence with a built-in concern for the whole of creation. This common notion that American Indian peoples and other indigenous peoples have some spiritual and mystical insight on the environmental issues confronting the world today is usually an instinctive if unstudied recognition of the differentness of those cultures. It thus tends to be a relatively intuitive truth claim based on little research and an overabundance of romanticization. Even those who have had the opportunity to witness the poverty of our poorest reservations, evidenced by the rusting hulks of worn-out automobiles parked in various states of abandonment around reservation homes, continue to recite their own facile version of Native spirituality and romanticized Native concern for the environment. At the same time, their own habits of consumption strangely parallel the bulk of american society. First of all, our starting point ought to be an awareness of how difficult it is to maintain any traditional Indian perspective on the environment when the community suffers from widespread PTSD associated with colonization and is so poor that heads of household wonder constantly how they might possibly succeed in taking care of their children.

On the other hand, there are others who have a more openly racist concern for protecting the privilege of White power and discourse in north America and who find ways to use their position and prestige to deprecate American Indian environmental consciousness. Sometimes this perspective is packaged in the clothing of modern academic research, typically by White scholars who use "Native American Studies," as Gerald Vizenor would remind us, as a "trope to power."[9] Namely, many White scholars who specialize in Native American studies feel so threatened by the emergence of Native scholars, who engage scholarly discourse as emic insiders and write from a Native perspective, that they write aggressively anti-Indian essays out of a deep defensiveness. They use their academic positions and their manipulation of the discourse more to empower themselves and their settler class than in any real quest for truth. Other commentators, largely in the White liberal ecology movement, seem to have their own racist power agenda. Namely, there seems to be a lingering self-defense (or defensiveness) among many in the more reactionary environmentalist set, such as *Earth First!*, that other peoples have also abused the natural world—they just lacked the resources and technology to do it as exhaustively as european and amer-european people have done.[10]

---

9. Gerald Vizenor, *Manifest Manners: Postindian Warriors of Survivance* (Hanover, N.H.: Wesleyan University Press, 1994).

10. This rather absurd and patently "euro-supremicist" hypothesis is argued, for instance, by George Weurthner, who ultimately reduces precontact Indian peoples to environmental pillagers ("An Ecological View of the Indian," *Earth First!* 7 [1987]). For an Indian critique of the position, see Ward Churchill, *Struggle for the Land*, 420, 447ff.; and M. Annette Jaimes, "The

The truth of the Native world is far more complex and sophisticated than either of these sides would allow. Even this essay is an attempt to begin a process of theological reflection that must finally be inclusive of many more voices (particularly Indian voices) than that of this author alone. The immediate need is to begin to delineate some of the complexity and sophistication of Indian beliefs in general, while paying attention to the specifics of different tribes along the way. What follows, then, is one Indian scholar's attempt to reflect theologically on the relationship between American Indian peoples and what western theologians would call "creation" and the contemporary ecological devastation of that creation. The original occasion for this essay was the continuing program of the World Council of Churches' program unit called "Justice, Peace and the Integrity of Creation" (JPIC, see chapter 2 of this volume) and the particular case study designed by the JPIC unit around the topic "Creation as Beloved of God." This was one attempt of the larger christian community to address the systemic concerns of ecological devastation and the attempt to involve indigenous peoples (including American Indians) in the process. It was around this assigned topic that we assembled for conversion nearly two dozen Indian spokespeople from nearly as many tribes in May 1995.

I want to move beyond the mere reporting on how ecojustice issues uniquely impact the indigenous peoples of the western hemisphere. Rather, I want to suggest that these examples are indicative of a systemic problem that is pervasively political and intellectual. The modern "world system" is driven by the economics and politics of domination inherent in the globalization of capital functions primarily on the basis of maximizing profits with only minimal regard for environmental concerns. In turn, this world system and its new eruption of empire are sustained intellectually in no small part by the prevailing theologies of the powerful churches of Europe and north America and the philosophies taught in their universities. If the european and amer-european churches do not pay particular attention to these philosophical and theological foundations that underlie modern technology, economics, and international politics, and their resulting contexts of ethno-ecojustice, then the political realities of interethnic and international injustice and ecological devastation have little chance of changing for the better.

"CREATION AS BELOVED OF GOD"

The first step in this theological reflection has to do with language and culture, and with the inappropriateness of typical euro-christian cultural language for

---

Stone Age Revisited: An Indigenist View of Primitivism, Industrialism and the Labor Process," *Wicazo Sa Review* 7, no. 2 (Autumn 1991): 34-48.

referencing American Indian cultural realities. As the heading of this section already implies, there are three words in the assigned program title that the World Council of Churches imposed on the discussions convened around the world without regard to the linguistic cultures of non-european peoples. The language poses significant problems for Indian peoples linguistically, culturally, and theologically—namely, the nouns and the adjective. If euro-Christianity is to make any legitimate claim to universality, it must struggle to overcome the cultural limitations of its traditional categories of theological analysis in order to better accommodate peoples with radically different cultures and languages. Otherwise, the christian enterprise is forever condemned to perpetrate imperialist acts of colonization and conquest.

"Beloved"

"Creation as beloved of God" is indeed very strange language for an American Indian community to consider. Of course, it makes sense in the largely euro-context of the World Council of Churches, especially given the scriptural tradition that understands God as typified by love in terms of the new testament understanding of the greek word *agape*. But this is a relatively technical linguistic-cultural phenomenon that only works universally for Christianity with careful translation from the greek and the ongoing education of english speakers for whom the greek distinction is entirely a mystery. In a cultural world that has been consistently abused by Christianity,[11] and one that has also struggled to maintain its own cultural and spiritual identity, the technicality of the greek language translation is almost completely irrelevant or even antagonistic.

This imposition of meaning is then heightened by the fact that no Indian community I know of refers to God's relationship with creation as characterized by "love." Of course, Indian peoples have nouns and verbs to describe emotive-bonding relationships between people, but we do not, as a rule, impute these same human emotive states, such as love, to the Sacred Other. *wako^{n}da* and the spiritual realm can be characterized as happy or upset with things that humans do (to succumb to the anthropomorphic); they even have expectations for our continued participation in the maintaining of balance in the world. There is no sense, however, that God or the spiritual realm has any different regard for human beings than for the rest of creation, and there is certainly no notion of God's relationship with the whole of creation as marked by the human emotion of love.

---

11. See George E. Tinker, *Missionary Conquest: The Gospel and Native American Cultural Genocide* (Minneapolis: Fortress Press, 1993).

This is in sharp contrast with euro-Christianity and its consistent inter-pretation of its sacred text. For instance, most commentators on the Gospel of John insist that God's love for the world (John 3:16: "God so loved the world") must be understood as love for human beings.[12] The greek word *kosmos,* trans-lated as "world," must refer in this context only to the world of human beings. God's salvific act in Christ Jesus is thought of as efficacious only for human beings; and, hence, God's salvific love for the world must imply logically that the world is limited only to those who are most privileged in creation and are the proper object of God's affections. The danger of such a privileging of human beings should be obvious. It runs the risk of generating human arro-gance that too easily sees the world in terms of hierarchies of existence, all of which are ultimately subservient to the needs and whims of humans.

In any case, the imposition of the word "beloved" functions necessarily to negate or at least falsify the traditional Indian understanding of the Sacred Other and its relationship to creation. If we are to insist that *agape* actually refers to "acting in the best interests of another," rather than to the emotion of love, then we need to inquire seriously about the effectiveness of translat-ing a greek word such as *agape* into a european language such as english and then having to translate the translation before sense can be made of the origi-nal. Thus, if one wants to affirm that God always "acts in the best interests" of human beings and of the whole of creation, why must we use the emotive word love as the only suitable language for articulating the relatively unemo-tive greek concept, especially when that new, emotive translation proves to be foreign to specific cultural communities?

"God"

"God" is yet another problem for Indian people, except to the extent that we have already been colonized by past missionaries to assume that the word is an adequate gloss for our own naming of the Sacred Other. To begin with, the word "God" is a difficult word in modern euro-western theological and philosophical discourse.[13] The givenness of its meaning for european and

---

12. So opines Raymond E. Brown, *The Gospel of John,* Anchor Bible, vols. 29 and 29A (New York: Doubleday, 1966-70).

13. For a sampling of the discourse over the past thirty-five years, see Philip Clayton, *The Problem of God in Modern Thought* (Grand Rapids: Eerdmans, 2003); Gordon Michaelson, *Kant and the Problem of God* (New York: Blackwell, 1999); Karen Armstrong, *The History of God* (New York: Knopf-Random House, 1993); Gordon Kaufman, *The Problem of God* (Cambridge, Mass.: Harvard University Press, 1972); Langdon Gilkey, *Naming the Whirlwind: The Renewal of God Language* (Indianapolis: Bobbs-Merrill, 1969); David Tracy, *Blessed Rage for Order* (New York: Seabury, 1975).

amer-european folk engaged in the professional discourse has long since given way to a modernist and postmodernist angst that leaves the word without an immediately agreed-upon sense among scholars. Much more important in this context, there is a facile popular assumption that languages are merely codes for one another and that a simple translation settles all difficulties. Hence, the question too often asked of Indian peoples is What is the word for God in your language?

Christianity and its sacred texts (the hebrew and greek testaments) regularly impute to God attributes that are intrinsically humanlike, even if these attributes are seen as somehow more than human in God's case. Hence, God is indeed identified not only as having emotions such as love and anger, but God is identified as the personification of love itself. The intense sophistication of Indian tribal spiritualities takes a different tack. Namely, what Christians would refer to as God is understood as a spiritual force or energy that permeates the whole of the world and is manifest in countless ways in the world around us at any given moment and especially in any given place.[14] *Wako^nda*, who is ultimately an unknowable mystery that is knowable only in particular manifestations, makes itself manifest first of all, but not exclusively, as Above and Below, *wako^nda mo^nshita* and *wako^nda udseta*, symbolized as Sky and Earth, and called upon as Grandfather and Grandmother, he and she. *Wako^nda*, which has no inherent or ultimate gender, is knowable only in the necessary reciprocal dualism of male and female. Thus, to assume that the simplistic gloss "God" somehow is adequate to translate and classify *wako^nda* (or *wakan tanka*, *gitchy manitou*, and so on) in english immediately falsifies the internal, cultural meaning of *wako^nda* for Osage peoples (or Lakota or Ojibwe, in the case of the other examples). Indeed, one of the destructive residual effects of generations of extensive colonization and missionization is that Indian people who would never do so in their own language have become perfectly comfortable in referring to the Sacred Other as "he" in english.

"Creation"

Finally, the word "creation" presents problems insofar as it assumes either the judeo-christian creation story or something like it. I am certainly aware of the irony of my comment here, having just stressed the important of reclaiming a theology of creation for our euro-western christian relatives in the previous chapter, but it needs to be said at this point that the word itself and the idea it names are basically euro-western. While every tribe has several creation

---

14. This sense is much more than Paul Tillich's notion of panentheism.

stories (sometimes even clan-specific variants), they are simply not valorized the way the judeo-christian accounts are in euro-Christianity. To begin with, the word is not commonly used in many tribes, and when it is used it almost always represents a convenient english signifier that has no immediate referent in the speaker's own language. Moreover, when the word is used in a christian context, it seems to Indian peoples to connote a heavy dose of reification that is completely lacking in any Indian intellectual tradition. That is, in the amer-european context, creation is objictified as something that is quite apart from human beings and to which humans relate from the outside. Most often, humans relate to creation as end-users, free to use creation and even use it up, perhaps. Increasingly, euro-western theologies, in their sudden new concern for an ethics of ecology, have tried to reduce creation to the status of being a ward of humans; humans are responsible for creation and its well-being, perhaps as stewards. The hebrew Bible's charge to human beings to exercise dominion over all things (Gen 1:26, 28) has now become a charge of steward-ship. But humans are still in charge. In an Indian understanding of the world, humans are certainly not in charge. We are merely a part of the whole, like any other species, and most often humans are traditionally perceived to be the least of all the species.

Another pronounced difference between amer-european and Indian tra-ditions is the usual assumption in the Indian of the preexistence of the world in some form. Thus, most Indian story-telling begins with the givenness of the world of which we are an integral part. Rather than conceiving of an initial cre-ation that was long ago and has little continuing relevance in a world in which only human redemption is in process, Indian intellectual traditions conceive of the world in a constant creative process that requires our continual partici-pation—just as it requires that of trees, for instance, and buffalos continually fulfilling their prescribed part.

If the words "creation" and even "createds" have a distinctly borrowed fla-vor in an Indian context, there is no easy alternative for articulating "what is," or "that which we are a part of." Some sense of what is at stake is apparent in the Lakota phrase that we discussed in the previous chapter. Remember that *mita-kouye oyasin* can be translated as a prayer "for all my relations" and includes much more than immediate family. Eventually, it calls for the well-being of the whole of a tribe or nation, of all the nations of two-leggeds in the world, and particularly of all the nations other than two-leggeds—the four-leggeds, the wingeds, and the living-moving things. As we have already argued, it is this interrelatedness that best captures what might symbolize for Indian peoples what Amer-europeans would call "creation." It is this understanding of inter-relatedness, of balance and mutual respect of the different species in the world, that Alphonso Ortiz called Indian peoples' greatest gift to amer-european people and, I would add, to the amer-european understanding of creation, especially at this time of such ecological crisis in the world.

HUMAN PRIVILEGE AND COMMUNITIES OF RESPECT

In the biblical creation story and in the ensuing christian tradition, human beings are significantly privileged over the rest of creation. Indeed, the relationship as it is explicitly stipulated at the beginning of the book of Genesis and as it is too commonly interpreted by amer-european readers is one of subjection and domination:

> And God said to them [the humans], "Be fruitful and multiply, and fill the earth and subdue it; and have dominion over the fish of the sea and over the birds of the air and over every living thing that moves upon the earth." (Gen 1:28)

In American Indian cultures there is no similar privileging of human beings in the scheme of things in the world. Neither is there any sense in which somehow humans are external to the rest of the world and its functions. To the contrary, humans are seen as simply part of a balanced whole rather than somehow a separate privileged category, a predator as it were, free to consume the rest at will. Yet there are expectations of human beings. We have particular responsibilities in the scheme of things, but, then, so do all our other relatives in the created realm: from bears and squirrels to eagles and sparrows, trees, ants, rocks, and mountains. In fact, many elders in Indian communities are quick to add that of all the createds, of all our relations, it is only we two-leggeds alone who seem to be confused as to our responsibility toward the whole and who are constantly engaged in seeking out the meanings of our lives.

I have long suspected that european Christianity has undergone a millennia-long transformation that has consistently put humans in increasing opposition to the rest of creation.[15] At the very least, this is signified in the

---

15. Veronica Strang argues that as euro-western Christianity postured human beings "hierarchically between God and Nature, with dominion over the latter," God became "no longer located in Nature, but in a 'far away' Heaven." This, she goes on to say, is quite opposed to indigenous cosmologies that are deeply rooted in nature (Veronica Strang, *Uncommon Ground: Cultural Landscapes and Environmental Values* [Oxford/New York: Berg, 1997], 264). See also Kenneth M. Morrison, "The Cosmos as Intersubjective: Native American Other-than-Human Persons," in *Indigenous Religions: A Companion*, ed. Graham Harvey (London: Cassell, 2000), 23-36.

theological, philosophical, scientific, and economic struggle for control over the world, its environment, and its "resources." This may have begun as early as the time of Aristotle, with the birth of so-called objective observation and description, an incipient scientific method. It continued its development during the european Renaissance with its neo-aristotelian project of emerging taxonomic systems and the control over the world that seems to come from naming and categorizing. The philosophical and scientific basis for control of nature was initially rooted in the acts of naming. Perhaps the modern amereuropean need for exerting control over the world was most explicitly founded by René Descartes in a logical extension of both Aristotle and the Renaissance. Descartes most clearly announced the ultimate knowability of the world and the human responsibility to do the knowing (and hence, exerting control).

This philosophical movement toward greater and greater human control over the environment was paralleled by an ever-increasing importance granted philosophically and theologically to the individual in european cultures. This shift toward the ascendency of the individual necessarily included a concomitant displacing of community values. I would argue that this shift meant not only the displacing of the importance of human communities, implicitly devaluing notions of the common good, but also the displacing of any lingering sense of the importance of a community inclusive of non-human entities in the created realm. In the Indian intellectual tradition and in cultural practice, human beings are not privileged over the rest of the world, nor are individuals privileged over the good of the whole community.

BALANCING THE WORLD FOR LIFE

If we allow for a broader understanding of the euro-christian, cultural-linguistic metaphor of "creation," then an extremely important Indian notion of the world emerges. Namely, what is clear to all American Indian peoples is that respect for creation, that is, for the whole of the created realm, or for all our relations, is vitally important to the well-being of our communities. While respect for all our relations in this world is critical for all Indian education, it is perhaps most readily apparent in the general philosophy of balance and harmony, a notion adhered to by all Indian communities in one form or another. Respect for "creation" emerges out of our perceived need for maintaining balance in the world around us. Thus, Indian spirituality is characteristically oriented toward both the everyday and the ceremonial balancing of the world and our participation in it. When the balance of existence is disturbed, whole communities pay a price that is measured in some lack of communal well-being.

Once we have clarified the place of human beings in the ongoing processes of world balancing and world renewal, there are two aspects of what might be considered a general Indian theology that Christians and other Amer-euro-peans might do well to note. They can be initially categorized as reciprocity and spatiality. My contention will be that attention to these two important spiritual aspects of Indian cultures and what I am calling Indian theology can become radically transformative for the amer-european system of values and structures of social behavior.

RECIPROCITY: A FOUNDATION FOR BALANCE

The general American Indian notion of reciprocity is fundamental to the human participation in world balancing and harmony. Reciprocity involves first of all a spiritual understanding of the cosmos and the place of humans in the processes of the cosmic whole. It begins with an understanding that everything that humans do has an effect on the rest of the world around us. Even when we cannot clearly know what that effect is in any particular act, we know that there is an effect. Thus, Indian peoples, in different places and in different cultural configurations, have always struggled to know how to act appropriately in the world. Knowing that every action has its unique effect has always meant that there had to be some sort of built-in compensation for human actions, some act of reciprocity.

The necessity for reciprocity becomes most apparent where violence is concerned, especially when such violence is an apparent necessity, as in hunt-ing or harvesting. Violence cannot be perpetrated, a life taken, in a Native American society, without some spiritual means for mitigating the violence and restoring balance around us. This calls for an act of reciprocation. I am so much a part of the whole of creation and its balance that any act of violence, anything I do that disrupts balance, even when it is necessary for our own survival, must be accompanied by an act of spiritual reciprocation intended to restore the balance of existence. It must be remembered that violence as a technical category must extend to all one's "relatives." Thus, a ceremony of reciprocity must accompany the harvesting of vegetable foods such as corn or the harvesting of medicinals such as cedar, even when only part of a plant is taken. The ceremony may be relatively simple, involving a prayer or song and perhaps a reciprocal offering of tobacco. Many tribes maintained very exten-sive and complex ceremonies of reciprocation to insure continuing balance and plentiful harvests. Likewise, there is a tradition of etiological stories that accompany such ceremonies and function to provide the theoretical founda-tion for the ceremonies. Ultimately, all of these stories function to ensure the continuing respect of the communities who tell the stories for all the parts of the created world, all the relatives, upon which the people depend for their own well-being. Even (or rather, especially) gathering rocks for a purification ceremony (the so-called sweat lodge ceremony) calls for care and respect, prayers, and reciprocation.

Ceremonies involving self-sacrifice (typically called "self-torture" or "self-mutilation" by the missionaries and early ethnographers) also come under this general category of reciprocation. In the Rite of Vigil (the so-called vision quest), which is very widespread among Indian peoples of north America, as well as in the Sun Dance, the suffering the supplicant takes upon him- or herself is usually thought of as vicarious and as some sort of reciprocation. Since all of one's so-called possessions are ultimately not possessions but relatives that live with someone, an individual is not giving away a possession when he or she gives a gift to someone else. In actuality, the only thing a person really owns and can sacrifice is one's own flesh. Thus, these ceremonies of self-sacrifice tend to be the most significant ceremonies of a people. While missionaries typically thought of these ceremonies as vain human attempts to placate some angry deity, Indian communities know that these ceremonies are more complex than that. Rather, they are thought of as vicarious sacrifices engaged in for the sake of the whole community's well-being. Moreover, they are thought of as ceremonies that came to the community as a gift from the Sacred Mystery in order to help the community take care of itself and its world. Thus, the Sun Dance is a ceremony in which two-leggeds participate with the Sacred in order to help maintain life, that is, to maintain the harmony and balance of the whole.

Hunting and war typically involved a complex ceremonial preparation—a preparation for a violence that will disrupt the balance of the community and of the world around them—before a contingent of warriors left their home. The Osage War Ceremony, for instance, involved a twelve-day ritual, allowing enough time to affirm the sacredness of life, to consecrate the lives that would be lost in war, and to offer prayers in reciprocation for those potentially lost lives.[16] In the hunt, most Indian nations report specified prayers of reciprocation, involving apologies and words of thanksgiving to the animal itself and the animal's spirit nation. Usually, this ceremonial act is in compliance with the request of the animals themselves, which the people remembered from the primordial negotiations in mythological stories. Thus, formal and informal ceremonies of reciprocation are a day-to-day mythic activity that has its origin in mythological stories in which human beings were given permission by the animal nations to hunt themselves for food. The resulting covenant, however,

---

16. See Francis La Flesche, *The War and Peace Ceremony of the Osage Indians*, Bureau of American Ethnography, Bulletin 101 (1939).

calls on human beings to assume responsibility for the perpetration of violence against four-legged relatives. Even after the hunt or battle, those who
participated must invariably go through a ceremonial cleansing before reen-
tering their own village. Not to do this would bring right into the middle of
national life a disruption of the sacred caused by the perpetration of violence
and put all people at risk.[17]

Animals, birds, crops, and medicines are all living relatives and must be
treated with respect if they are to be genuinely efficacious for people. The ideal
of harmony and balance requires that all share a respect for all other existent
things, a respect for life and the avoidance of gratuitous or unthinking acts of
violence. Maintaining harmony and balance requires that even necessary acts
of violence be done "in a sacred way." Thus, nothing is taken from the earth
without prayer and offering. When the tree is cut down for the Sun Dance, for
instance, something must be offered, returned to the spirit world, for the life
of that tree. The people not only ceremonially and prayerfully ask the tree's
permission but also ask for its cooperation and help during the four days of the
dance itself.

No model of "development," involving modern western technologies, as
far as I know, embodies or incorporates the indigenous ethic of reciprocity as
it is found in Indian communities. It is not enough to replant a few trees or to
add nutrients to the soil. These are superficial acts to treat the negative symptoms of development. The value of reciprocity, which is a hallmark of Indian
ceremonies, goes to the heart of issues of sustainability, which is maintaining
a balance and tempering the negative effects of basic human survival tech-
niques. Moreover, as far as I know, there is no ceremony for clear-cutting an
entire forest.

SPATIALITY: PLACE vs. TIME

That there is and has been historically a fundamental difference between amer-
european and American Indian worldviews emerging from different priorities
of space and time has been long recognized by American Indian observers of
amer-european cultures, even if it has not been regularly noticed or granted
by the academic specialists, the amer-european observers of Indian cultures.
These American Indian observations were first codified by Vine Deloria, Jr.,

---

17. Leslie Silko's famous novel *Ceremony* (New York: Viking, 1977) is precisely about such
a situation. The novel deals with the healing and cleansing of a World War II veteran for whom
a new ceremony had to be devised. The social and spiritual complexities of disintegration and
alienation had made it much more difficult for the Laguna people and for himself. Thus, his healing has to do with the healing of the whole community and not just of himself.

the late dean of American Indian academics, in his 1973 milestone book *God Is Red*.[18] As I have also argued,[19] it is not a case of one culture being marked by temporality and the other by spatiality. Rather, it appears to be the case that space or time have become primary categories of existence in one culture or the other around which all other categories are arranged. For amer-european peoples, temporality has been a primary category for many centuries, while space has been a secondary category of existence, subordinate in all respects to temporality. The sacred is measured in temporality with a seven-day cycle requiring the repetition of a ceremonial event (mass or liturgies of worship), most typically on the first day of the cycle, the cycle itself being a relatively arbitrary, human designation. For American Indians, however, spatiality has been the primary category and temporality the secondary.

In amer-european (and european) philosophical and theological history it is most common to see intellectual reflections on the meaning of time, while it is far less common to see intellectual reflections on space. Hence, progress, history, development, evolution, and process become key notions that invade all academic discourse in the west, from science and economics to philosophy and theology. Thus, the western worldview has an inherent blind spot that prevents any comprehensive or deep understanding of the scope of ecological devastation, which is, in fact, accelerating despite our best efforts at "sustainable development." To do no more than propose "solutions," such as reforestation projects, without acknowledging this blind spot, is only to address the superficial symptoms of maldevelopment.

In contrast, cultural values, social and political structures in Indian communities are rooted in a worldview shaped by reciprocity and spatiality. Indian ceremonial existence, for instance, is inevitably spatially configured with place taking precedence over the question of when a ceremony will happen. Even in the case of annual or periodic ceremonial cycles, spatial configurations involving spatial relationships between sun or moon and the earth are determinative. Hence, the spatial relationship between the community and the sun at solstice or equinox and the spatial appearance or non-appearance of the full or new moon are more important than calendar dates and Julian months.

This foundational metaphor of spatiality in Indian cultures also begins to

---

18. (Grosset & Dunlap, 1973); significantly revised and republished as *God Is Red: A Native View of Religion* (Golden, Colo.: Fulcrum, 1992; 30th anniv. ed., 2002).

19. George E. Tinker, "Spirituality and Native American Personhood; Sovereignty and Solidarity," in *Spirituality of the Third World*, ed. K. C. Abraham and Bernadette Mbuy-Beya (Maryknoll, N.Y.: Orbis Books, 1994), 119-32; "Indian Culture and Interpreting the Christian Bible," in *Spirit and Resistance: Political Theology and American Indian Liberation* (Minneapolis: Fortress Press, 2004), 88-99; and "Native Americans and the Land: The End of Living and the Beginning of Survival," *Word and World* 6 (1986): 66-75.

clarify the extent to which Indian spirituality and Indian existence are deeply rooted in our attachment to the land and to specific territories. Each nation has some understanding that they were placed into a relationship with a particular territory by spiritual forces outside of themselves and thus have an enduring responsibility for that territory just as the earth, especially the earth in that particular place, has a filial responsibility toward the people who live there. Likewise, the two-legged people in that place also have a spatially related responsibility toward all people who share that place with them, including animals, birds, plants, rocks, rivers, mountains, and the like. With such extensive kinship ties, including a kinship tie to the land itself, it should be less surprising that Indian peoples have always resisted colonial pressure to relocate them to different territories, to sell their territories to the invaders, or to allow the destruction of their lands for the sake of accessing natural resources. Conquest and removal from our lands, historically, and contemporary ecological destruction of our lands have been and continue to be culturally and genocidally destructive to Indian peoples as peoples.

There is, however, a more subtle level to this sense of spatiality and rootedness in the land. It shows up in nearly all aspects of our existence, in our ceremonial structures, our symbols, our architecture, and in the symbolic parameters of a tribe's universe. Hence, the land and spatiality are the basic metaphor for existence and determine much of a community's life. In my own tribe, for instance, every detail of social structure—even the geographic orientation of the old villages—reflected a reciprocal duality of all that is necessary for sustaining life. Thus, the *hu*ⁿ*ka*, or earth moiety, situated to the south of the village, and the *tzisho*, or sky moiety, situated to the north, represented female and male, matter and spirit, war and peace; but they only functioned fully because they were together, and together represented wholeness. Spirit without matter is motion without substance; matter without spirit is motionless and meaningless. Once again we see reciprocity in a symbiotic dualism, this time clearly configured spatially.

We should not think here of the oppositional dualism of good and evil that we have learned to identify as typical euro-western (which is to say ancient middle-eastern and mediterranean) dualism. American Indian duality is a necessary reciprocity, not oppositional. It involves different manifestations of the *same wako*ⁿ*da*, not of two *wako*ⁿ*da*, even though they carry personality specificity just as traditional christian trinitarian doctrine would assert. While the dualism involves manifestations of the same *wako*ⁿ*da*, they are different manifestations, both of which are necessary in order to have some balanced understanding of the Otherness that is the Sacred Mystery. Indeed, *wako*ⁿ*da* has manifested itself in a great many other ways, all of which help our people to better understand the Mystery, our world, ourselves and our place in the world. At this point, it may also be clearer why the european word "God" is inadequate to express the full complexity of what we have only begun to explore in the Osage word.

Even the architectural geography of our spirituality functioned politically to give the village group cohesion; it functions at a deep spiritual level that still pertains for a great many Indian people today. While an Osage person may be either *tzisho* or *hu"ka*, she or he is a child of parents who come from each of the divisions. Thus, each individual recognizes herself or himself as a combination of qualities that reflect both sky and earth, spirit and matter, peace and war, male and female, and we struggle individually and communally to hold those qualities in balance with each other. These value structures begin with spatial designs of existence and are rooted in those spatial metaphors as fundamental mores of communal behavior and social organization.

This is not the only spatial symbolic paradigm of existence that determines Native American individuality and community. As we have already argued, the fundamental symbol of plains Indian existence is the circle, a polyvalent symbol signifying the family, the clan, the tribe, and eventually all of creation. As a creation symbol, the importance of the circle is its genuine egalitarianness. There is no way to make the circle hierarchical. Because it has no beginning and no end, all in the circle are equal. No relative is valued more than any other. A chief is not valued above the people; nor are two-leggeds valued above the animal nations, the birds, or even trees and rocks. In its form as a medicine wheel, with two lines forming a cross inscribed vertically and horizontally across its whole, the circle can symbolize the four directions of the earth and, more importantly, the four manifestations of *wako"da* that come to us from those directions. At the same time, those four directions symbolize the four cardinal virtues of a tribe, the four sacred colors of ceremonial life, the sacred powers of four animal nations, and the four nations of two-leggeds that walk the earth (Black, Red, Yellow, and White). That is, in our conception of the universe, all human beings walk ideally in egalitarian balance. Moreover, Native American egalitarian proclivities are worked out in this spatial symbol in ways that go far beyond the classless egalitarianness of socialism. In one of the polyvalent layers of meaning, those four directions hold together in the same egalitarian balance the four nations of two-leggeds, four-leggeds, wingeds, and living-moving things. In this rendition human beings lose their status of primacy and "dominion." Implicitly and explicitly, American Indians are driven by their culture and spirituality to recognize the personhood of all "things" in creation. If temporality and historicity lend themselves implicitly to hierarchical structures because someone with a greater investment of time may know more of the body of temporally codified knowledge, spatiality lends itself to the egalitarian. All have relatively similar access to the immediacy of the spatially present.

ECOJUSTICE, SOVEREIGNTY, AND A THEOLOGY OF LIBERATION

Given the fundamental differences between American Indian cultural values and those of amer-european peoples, it should be no mystery that the relationship between the two has been consistently one of conquest, colonization, and finally the ecodevastation of American Indian territories. Our theological reflection must now move toward a sharper assessment of the systemic causes of this ethno-ecodevastation from an Indian perspective and toward the development of possible solutions. We have already begun to argue that we must understand the connection between ecological and social injustice in the world if there is to be significant transformation from the current global crisis to a healthy and sustainable future. Hence, it becomes empty quixotism to think of treating ecological devastation apart from treating issues of racism and ongoing colonialism, including especially those new forms of colonialism, which some have called neocolonialism.

In particular, I am arguing that the twofold problem of eco- and social justice is systemic in nature, and that the concerns of ethno-ecojustice must move beyond the mere naming of ecological devastations that are affecting Indian peoples and other indigenous and poor peoples today. This is a point I can illustrate with a simple example. Over the past ten to twenty years, many of us have been converted to the ecojustice vocation of *recycling*, a calling that has piqued our consciences as individual consumers to the extent that our kitchens and garages have become dangerous repositories of plastic, aluminum, and glass as we have committed ourselves to a new life-way behavior pattern. Yet our national situation with respect to garbage disposal and landfill capacity has gotten consistently worse. In spite of our committed new behavior as socially conscious individuals, the United States generated more landfill garbage during the decade of the 1980s (the decade we began actively and broadly recycling) than all the garbage generated during the first two hundred years of the existence of the United States. During the forty-three years from 1960 to 2003, the United States increased its annual municipal solid waste from 88 million tons to 236 million tons.[20] Changing individual patterns of behavior

---

20. "Municipal Solid Waste," U.S. Environmental Protection Agency, http://www.epa. gov/epaoswer/non-hw/muncpl/facts.htm. While our personal daily garbage disposal rate seems to have leveled off at four and a half pounds of trash per day, the total landfill amount continues to grow unabated.

has failed us as a strategy. We will need more holistic and systemic solutions, and systemic solutions call for theological and philosophical foundations. The crisis of solid waste management calls for societal solutions and not facile government attempts to put responsibility on the back of the individual.

It needs to be said here that by a theological response to the systemic I do not have in mind just another individualistic intellectual exercise of the sort that has plagued our universities and seminaries too much, but rather a theological reflection that is far more communal. Theology must become an exercise in expressing the self-identity of whole communities. For this sort of theology, we need stories rather than treatises, rather than essentialist discourse, problem resolution, or structuralist puzzle solving. Not even some poststructuralist deconstruction that never seems to emerge from the text will finally be able to touch the hearts and minds of whole communities. For theology of this magnitude, we must have stories.

The Amer-europeans have stories, of course, but they tend to be stories of conquest. For instance, Columbus is the quintessential all-american culture hero, the perfect exemplar for the righteous empire, the "discoverer" and conqueror who knew no sin. Even Jesus, the most important culture hero of America, has become a conqueror in western storytelling. The sacrificial cross of Jesus has become a symbol of conquest that seems to encourage more conquest.[21] Thus, the myth of Columbus and the stories of conquest continue to play themselves out with disastrous consequences in the lives of modern Indian peoples, as the case studies in this volume all too well attest.

What Amer-europeans do not yet have is a story that accounts for their history of systemic violence in the world and their easy proclivity for rationalizing any act of military or economic colonization and conquest as somehow good— whether it is the resort to violence by the foreign policy of the United States in contemporary contexts such as Iraq or Afghanistan or its older histories of violence and preemptive warfare against one Indian nation after another. Instead, Amer-europeans and their politicians seem to engage in a behavior pattern well known in alcohol and drug addiction therapy, called denial. Too many churches and too many politicians have lived out such a denial, like ostriches with their heads in the sand as if such ecodevastation and national injustice and immorality cannot possibly affect them, living in the protected comfort zones of american society. Easy answers are too often given that reflect some level of denial. It is too late, we are assured, to rectify injustices perpetrated against Indian nations; too much water has gone under the bridge. Or it is sometimes insisted that Indians are too small a percentage of the population to merit attention. We are forced,

---

21. See George E. Tinker, "Columbus and Coyote: A Comparison of Culture Heroes in Paradox," *Apuntes* 12, no. 2 (Summer 1992): 78-88.

they claim, to concentrate on the vast majority of Americans to maximize the good (and wealth) for the most people. Here the old amer-european tradition of utilitarianism (not to be confused with Jeremy Bentham or John Stuart Mill) and popular pragmatism continues to exert its powerful influence on the expediency of political practice to such an extent that abject racism can thrive with full rationalization "in the best interests of the state," and thus it becomes all too easy to think of distant and isolated Indian reservations as "national sacrifice areas."[22] Stories of conquest give way to stories of utilitarian rationalization and self-justification.

Even in those cases where we have begun to address specific cases of community well-being and ecojustice, we seem to do so with isolated strategies and a much-too-narrow focus. Especially at the level of theological reflection, the churches have not yet begun to deal with ecojustice, let alone ethno-ecojustice and racism, as a systemic whole, as a system of oppression rooted in structures of power that touch every part of our lives. At the level of liberal political action and theoretical reflection in the United States, solutions have still dealt typically with "them" and "their" problems rather than with the "us" of the United States and "our" participation in the ongoing story of world injustices. As long as the liberal amer-european story includes only Amer-europeans in the role of moral conquerors and technological geniuses providing solutions to others' problems, the real root causes of the problem will never go away. That is to say, even our proposed solutions have not been systemic enough to genuinely address the problem.[23]

In this analysis, I want to argue two correlative points, addressing what I see as a key systemic aspect of the problematic and focusing on the rise of western individualism and the systematic destruction of indigenous communities worldwide. Further, I will insist that the dismantling of indigenous communities has happened at a philosophical as well as political level. To put it another way, I am arguing that modern ecological devastation is in no small part generated by the western, european shift devaluing corporate interests in favor of the increasing prominence of the individual. This shift can be measured in the lack of political and economic respect and the lack of theoretical recognition given to the legitimacy of self-governing, autonomous, long-lived indigenous communities. Let me state the argument as provocatively as possible.

---

22. See n. 5, above.

23. A key example is the proclivity with which many northern liberals' analysis of global environmental concerns falls into blaming the south, that is the Two-Thirds World, for creating ecodevastation through overpopulation. See Andrea Smith's fine critique of this phenomenon in "Malthusian Orthodoxy and the Myth of ZPG," in *Defending Mother Earth: Native American Perspectives on Environmental Justice*, ed. Jace Weaver (Maryknoll, N.Y.: Orbis Books), 122-43.

INDIVIDUALISM AND WESTERN DEVELOPMENT

First, the western commitment to individualism colors all of the west's intellectual and theoretical posturing, whether theology, philosophy, political theory, politics, or law. For Amer-europeans, in particular, the corporate level of denial is rooted in a cultural flaw that emerges from a trajectory that has its beginning in the later greek philosophies of the hellenistic period and continues through the european reformations to modern notions of american hegemony in the new world order. From the Stoics of the third century B.C.E. in particular, but no less so the Epicureans and Skeptics, the shift to the philosophical prominence of the individual can be traced through philosophy and religious movements. While the Stoics shifted their discourse from a search for the good in a communal sense to a search for the wise individual, religious movements of the first century B.C.E. began a similar shift toward a concern for the individual. As the interest of the old mediterranean cults shifted away from communual well-being, the so-called mystery religions introduced a newly developing concern for individual salvation. It is this theological shift that eventually won the heart of greco-roman Christianity.

The resulting modern theologies of all of our churches continue this overweening concern for the individual and the individual's need for, and impediments to, salvation and well-being. Thus, our systemic interpretations tend likewise to emphasize individualist analyses: The problem is identified as original sin or, in its secularized version, the individual failings of human beings. Even our interpretations of sacred texts—themselves far less invested in the west's individualism—are regularly done from the individualist perspective. For instance, the synoptic gospels' metaphoric paradigm for the good, the goal of all life, the *basileia tou theou* (the so-translated kingdom of God) is consistently interpreted in individualistic terms. The *basileia*, we are told, has to do with the individual's relationship with God or with the individual's call to decision. Any communitarian notion of it being many people together, or all peoples, or all of creation, is little mentioned.[24]

Moreover, this problematic is not exclusive to theological education but extends to all academic disciplines in the humanities and social sciences such as political theory, international law, and economics. The culture of the west (european and amer-european) is a culture of the individual, and, through modern colonial institutions (neocolonial, some would say) such as the World Bank and the International Monetary Fund, the imposition of this culture of individualism is quickly being extended throughout the colonized

---

24. See my analysis in chap. 2, above. Also my "Indian Culture and Interpreting the Christian Bible," in *Spirit and Resistance*, 88-99.

(Two-Thirds) world in terms of economic and political development. In the ongoing disciplinary discourse about human rights, for instance, most proponents would argue for understanding human rights in terms of individual rights while vehemently denying extension of that category to groups. Human rights are rights held inherently by individuals, by definition, and not rights of culturally discrete, indigenous national communities. Hence, the cultures of these communities can be destroyed with impunity.[25]

STATISM AND INDIGENOUS SOVEREIGNTY

Second, I want to argue that the very emergence and eventual dominance of the modern state and the concomitant degradation of indigenous national entities contribute significantly to our situation of ecojustice and ethno-ecojustice devastation.[26] It should not be surprising that indigenous cultural groups, being fundamentally defined by their communitarian values and communal coherence, have been consistently attacked and destroyed by colonial intruders and usurpers of their lands and resources. Yet it needs to be said that the conquest of indigenous peoples has not been merely a military, political, or economic colonization but that the conquest has been equally engaged at an academic, intellectual level. In my own analysis, I would argue that quintessentially natural national entities of self-governance have given way to new larger and more centralized but artificial government structures identified in common parlance as the modern state.

It is symptomatic that modern political theory has little interest in defining the appropriate place of indigenous nations in relationship to states. To the contrary, it is assumed that the states have some natural sovereignty over their defined territories even if their territorial claims wholly include ancient indigenous nations that have never relinquished their own sovereignty to that state.

---

25. See Richard Falk, "The Rights of Peoples (In Particular Indigenous Peoples): A Non-Statist Perspective," 17-37; and Ted Robert Gurr and James R. Scarritt, "Minority Rights at Risk: A Global Survey," *Human Rights Quarterly* 11 (1989): 375-405.

26. Many identify the eighteenth century with the emergence of the modern state. See Cornelia Narari, "The Origins of the Nation-State," in *The Nation State: The Formation of Modern Politics*, ed. Leonard Tivey (New York: St. Martin's, 1981), 13-38. It seems more useful and accurate to date the emergence to the sixteenth century with the strong move toward centralization and bureaucratization during the reign of Henry VIII in England; or even the late fifteenth century with the formation of a "modern" spanish state in the merging of Castile and Aragon with the marriage of Ferdinand and Isabela. See Robert Williams, *American Indians and Western Legal Thought* (New York: Oxford University Press, 1990); and Stephen L. Collins, *From Divine Cosmos to Sovereign State: An Intellectual History of Consciousness and the Idea of Order in Renaissance England* (Oxford: Oxford University Press, 1989).

In general, in our critical analyses and in our imagination of solutions, we tend to concede too much to modern state systems and institutions. We assume too readily the authenticity and validity of the state and the broad bureaucratic institutions formally and informally associated with it—including our modern denominational structures.

The systemic nature of the problem as it relates to American Indians becomes apparent in the systematic erosion of Indian national sovereignty and self-determination over the past five hundred years. The erosion began the moment that Columbus first claimed Indian land as property of his spanish monarchs. It was unabated as the liberal Bartolomé de Las Casas insisted on the peaceful conquest of Indian peoples as the rightful subjects of those same monarchs. And it continued in nineteenth century U.S. jurisprudence and legislation with the legal canonization of the "domestic" and "dependent" nature of Indian sovereignty, wholly dependent on and accountable to the plenary power of the U.S. Congress.[27] Today, Indian sovereignty has become a shadow of its former self that invariably fades dimmer with each new incursion of the U.S. government and multinational corporate power brokers interested in wresting natural resources away from one Indian nation or another at unreasonably cheap prices to themselves and equally unreasonably high long-term costs to the environmental well-being of those nations.[28]

To carry the systemic nature of the problem a step further, the poverty that has consistently plagued Indian peoples since the onslaught of colonization and conquest is a natural result experienced by the colonized through-

---

27. See Chief Justice John Marshall's majority opinions in *Johnson v. McIntosh* (1823) and *Cherokee v. Georgia* (1831), which give early delineation to notions of a diminished sovereignty of Indian nations in north America—most recently explicitly affirmed by William Rehnquist's majority opinion in *Oliphant v. Suquamish Tribe* (1979). Legal scholar Lindsay G. Roberts, *Conquest by Law: How the Discovery of America Dispossessed Indigenous Peoples of Their Lands* (New York: Oxford University Press, 2005), thoroughly details Marshall's shoddy legal argumentation and the consequences of this case in terms of ensconcing the "discovery doctrine" into empiric legal discourse not only in the United States but throughout the former British Empire. See also Ward Churchill, *Struggle for the Land*, 42-45; Howard R. Berman, "The Concept of Aboriginal Rights in the Early Legal History of the United States," *Buffalo Law Review* 28 (1978): 637-67; and Felix S. Cohen, "Original Indian Title," *Minnesota Law Review* 32 (1947): 28-59. On the "plenary power" of the U.S. Congress over Indian "sovereignty" and the Congress' resulting fiduciary or trust responsibilities, see C. Harvey, "Constitutional Law: Congressional Plenary Power over Indian Affairs—A Doctrine Rooted in Prejudice," *American Indian Law Review* 5 (1977): 117-50.

28. Obviously, I have distinguished between nation and state in this essay. For the scholarly critique of statist doctrines, see Bernard Nietchmann "Militarization and Indigenous Peoples: The Third World War," *Cultural Survival Quarterly* 11 (1987): 1-16; Russell L. Barsh, "The Ethnocidal Character of the State and International Law," *Journal of Ethnic Studies* 16 (1989): 1-30; Scarritt and Gurr, "Minority Rights at Risk"; and Falk, "The Rights of Peoples."

out the modern world. And postmodernist deconstruction seems to have little creative effect on the colonizer or on the colonized—except that we, the colonized, continue to experience the deconstruction of our cultures, our ecospheres, whatever is left of our Native economies and our internal sustainability.

With a poverty level that puts American Indians chronically at the bottom of nearly every social indicator, we suffer a resulting level of community dysfunctionality that increases our lack of sustainability and makes us all the more susceptible to forces of external political and economic power. Indian unemployment is stuck chronically at more than 50 percent across the continent.[29] Per capita income is the lowest of any ethnic community in the United States. Longevity figures for Indians are more than twenty years less than the american average. The infant mortality rate is the highest of any group in the United States. And diseases such as tuberculosis (nearly eradicated for most of the U.S. population) and diabetes occur at seven and six times the average U.S. rates.[30] In some states (e.g., Montana and South Dakota) Indian inmates number more than half of the state's prison population, even though the general Indian population in the state is under 10 percent.

Given poverty statistics such as these, we have precious few political, legal, or even intellectual resources for capitalizing on or controlling our immense natural resources.[31] Of course, the cultural-economic question for Indian nations may be not how we develop natural resources but whether we feel that they can be "respectfully" developed and exploited at all. The continuing reality of our oppression, however, would leave this as a moot point, because our poverty leaves us with few defenses against the pressures brought to bear on

---

29. George E. Tinker and Loring Bush, "Native American Unemployment: Statistical Games and Cover-ups," in *Racism and the Underclass in America*, ed. George W. Shepherd, Jr., and David Penna (Westport, Conn.: Greenwood Press, 1991).

30. U.S. Bureau of the Census, Population Division, Racial Statistics Branch, *A Statistical Portrait of the American Indian Population* (Washington, D.C.: U.S. Government Printing Office, 1984); U.S. Department of Health and Human Services, *Chart Series Book* (Washington, D.C.: Public Health Service HE20.9409.988, 1988). The 2000 census has not testified to an abatement of these statistical horrors in any category for Native Americans. See also Ward Churchill, *Struggle for the Land*, 54ff., 79.

31. For an official U.S. government indication of the vast mineral resources of American Indian tribes, see U.S. Department of the Interior, *Indian Lands Map: Oil, Gas and Minerals on Indian Reservations* (Washington, D.C.: U.S. Government Printing Office, 1978). Churchill comments as follows with a bitter irony: "With such holdings, it would seem logical that the two million indigenous people of North America . . . would be among the continent's wealthiest residents. As even the government's own figures reveal, however, they receive the lowest per capita income of any population group and evidence every standard indicator of dire poverty: highest rates of malnutrition, plague disease, death by exposure, infant mortality, teen suicide, and so on" (*Struggle for the Land*, 262).

our national indigenous communities from the outside. Hence, the prior question is one of Indian sovereignty, for the sake of reclaiming Indian community sustainability, but, so I shall argue, also for the sake of the healthy sustainability of the world community as well.

First, Indians want life. But the truth is, we do not just want existence, that is, life in the sense of mere biological survivability. What we want is life in the sense of self-sufficient, cultural, spiritual, political, and economic sustainability—on our own terms. At this late date, the question is not whether Indian peoples should have the right to self-determining autonomy, but how our communities can regain this rightful heritage without the continuing colonial imposition and pressure to feed and participate in the consumptive habits of White America. We believe that the systemic justice issue involved is one of both political hegemony and ecological survivability. Moreover, the answer to this systemic question may contain something of the answer of sustainability for all people on this earth.

My suggestion that we take the recognition of indigenous sovereignty as a strategic priority is a systemic one that involves more than justice for indigenous communities around the world. Indeed, such a political move will necessitate a rethinking of consumption patterns in the north, and a shift in the economics of the north will cause a concomitant shift also in the Two-Thirds World of the south. The relatively simple act of recognizing the sovereignty of the Sioux Nation and returning to them all state-held lands in the Black Hills (for example, national forest, national park, and South Dakota state park lands) would generate immediate international interest in the rights of indigenous, tribal peoples in all state territories. In the United States alone, it is estimated that Indian nations still have legitimate (moral and legal) claim to some two-thirds of the U.S. land mass.[32] Ultimately, such an act to return native lands to native control would have a significant ripple effect on other states around the world where indigenous peoples still have aboriginal land claims and suffer the ongoing results of conquest and displacement in their own territories.

Second, American Indian cultures and values have much to contribute to the systemic reimagining of euro-western peoples and the value system that has resulted in our contemporary crisis of ecojustice. There were and are cultures that take their natural world environment seriously and attempted to live in balance with the created whole around them in ways that helped them not overstep environmental limits. Unlike the west's consistent experience of alienation from the natural world, these cultures of indigenous peoples con-

---

32. See Churchill, *Struggle for the Land*; and idem, "The Earth Is Our Mother: Struggles for American Indian Land and Liberation in the Contemporary United States," in *The State of Native America,* ed. M. Annette Jaimes (Boston: South End Press, 1992), 139-88.

sistently experienced themselves as part of that created whole, in relationship with everything else in the world. They saw and see themselves as having responsibilities, just as every other creature has a particular role to play in maintaining the balance of creation as an ongoing process. This is ultimately the spiritual rational for annual ceremonies like the Sun Dance or Green Corn Dance. Lakota peoples, for example, planted cottonwoods and willows in their tipi rings and campfire sites as they broke camp to move on, thus beginning the process of reclaiming the land that humans had necessarily trampled through habitation and encampment.

We now know today that indigenous rain-forest peoples, in what is today called the state of Brazil, had a unique relationship to the forest in which they moved away from a cleared area after farming it to a point of reduced return, thus allowing the clearing to be reclaimed as jungle. The group would then move to clear a new area for a new cycle of production. The whole process was and is relatively sophisticated and functioned in harmony with the integrity of the jungle itself. So extensive was their movement that some scholars are now suggesting that there is actually very little of what might rightly be called "virgin forest" in what had been considered the "untamed" wilds of the jungle.

I have described here more than just a coincidence or, worse, some romanticized falsification of Native memory. Rather, I am insisting that there are peoples in the world who live with an acute and cultivated awareness of their intimate participation in the natural world as part of an intricate whole. For indigenous peoples, this means that when they are presented with the concept of development, it is *sense-less*. It is important to realize that this worldview is the result of self-conscious effort on the part of traditional American Indian national communities and is rooted first of all in the mythology and theology of the people. At its simplest, the worldview of American Indians can be expressed as Churchill so aptly describes it:

> Human beings are free (indeed, encouraged) to develop their innate capabilities, but only in ways that do not infringe upon other elements—called "relations," in the fullest dialectical sense of the word—of nature. Any activity going beyond this is considered as "imbalance," a transgression, and is strictly prohibited. For example, engineering was and is permissible, but only insofar as it does not permanently alter the earth itself. Similarly, agriculture was widespread, but only within norms that did not supplant natural vegetation.[33]

---

33. Churchill, *Struggle for the Land*, 17.

Like the varieties of species in the world, each culture has a contribution to make for the sustainability of the whole. Given the reality of the ecodevastation threatening all of life today, the survival of American Indian cultures and cultural values may make the difference for the survival and sustainability for all the earth as we know it. I have implicitly suggested in this essay that American Indian peoples may have something of value, something corrective to western values and the modern world system, to offer to the world. The loss of these gifts, the loss of the particularity of these peoples, today threatens the survivability of us all. What I am most passionately arguing is that we must commit to the struggle for the just and moral survival of Indian peoples as the peoples of the earth, and that this struggle is for the sake of the earth and for the sustaining of all of life. It is now imperative that we end the modern value of acquisitiveness and the political systems and economics that consumption has generated. The key to making this massive value transformation in the world system may lie in the international recognition of indigenous political sovereignty and self-determination. Returning Native lands to the sovereign control of Native peoples around the world, beginning in the United States, is not only just but the survival of all may depend on it.

Chapter 4

Christology and Colonialism
Jesus, Corn Mother, and Conquest[1]

"Who do you say that I am?" The question Jesus asks of his disciples in the synoptic gospels has become the most enduring question for Christians, in terms of the faith of individuals, the character of denominations, and christian intellectual discourse. Because of five hundred years of euro-western colonialism and the imposition of Christianity on Indians, any American Indian theology must also make some attempt to address the question. This chapter will move in two disparate directions to address this christological concern. It will first press the issue of the inappropriateness in American Indian communities of the use of the customary christian language for calling on Jesus and to propose other, more applicable metaphors, both scriptural and indigenous, for referencing Jesus and the Christ in a christian Indian context. Next, however, it will move to reevaluate the suitability or appropriateness of even this project in the healing process of a colonized community damaged socially, emotionally, and spiritually by the past five hundred years of conquest and destruction. Many Indian people have been missionized and continue to find personal solace in their connection with the church, and the initial project may help them to rediscover a more culturally appropriate christology for an Indian church. A great many others, however, have found any affirmation of the Christ of Christianity to be merely another imposition of colonial control.

In any event, this essay is a small exercise in neocolonial resistance in search of genuine American Indian liberation, part of a much broader quest engaging Indian peoples today. This chapter intends to speak somehow to both colonizer and colonized, to Amer-european and American Indian, about the nature of this thing called christology and the place of Jesus in the thinking of the respective peoples.

---

1. This essay brings together material that was published earlier in two separate essays by Tink Tinker: "Jesus, Corn Mother, and Conquest: Christology and Colonialism," in *Native American Religious Identity: Unforgotten Gods*, ed. Jace Weaver (Maryknoll, N.Y.: Orbis Books, 1998); and "American Indians and Jesus: Towards an EATWOT Christology," *Voices from the Third World* 18, no. 2 (Fall 1995): 115-34 (a special issue edited by James Cone).

THAT THE PEOPLE MIGHT LIVE!

"What can the death of a man two thousand years ago possibly have to do with people who live today?" Covered in black grease, my brother looked up from the engine of an old truck long enough to ask a serious theological question. He had been raised a christian Indian but had begun incorporating traditional spiritual practices, including the Sun Dance, back into his life for several years. An insightful genius, he was always the visionary at Four Winds American Indian Council, an urban project in Denver, always pushing the community further than they imagined they would go, at times even further or faster than they wanted. On this occasion, he was initiating a process that would call on urban Indians to reconsider once again the nature of the relationship between Four Winds's vision of Indian community healing and a public christian commitment. For the moment, however, there was an answer for him that slowed him down, even if only temporarily. "Why do you dance?" was the question I asked in return. Sometimes the deepest theological discussions are very short and to the point. His only reply as he dove back into the engine compartment was, "Oh!... Yeah." No more words were needed, since both of us, as Indians, knew full well the vicarious suffering aspect of Indian spiritual commitments at Sun Dance, the Rite of Vigil, and the Purification Ceremony (called sweat lodge in english, by some).

Virtually every tribal nation in north America has had a variety of ceremonies whereby the individual might take on a discipline of ceremonial vicarious suffering for the sake of the people as a whole. In every case, the first european and amer-european invaders of their lands, including especially the missionaries, mistook these ceremonies for something they never were intended to be. Because they misunderstood, sometimes very intentionally, these ceremonies, the missionaries and the amer-european government proceeded to condemn our ancient rites as devil worship or idolatry. Yet, these ceremonies have much in common with the suffering of Jesus in the christian gospels because the individual undertaking the ceremony willingly undergoes a discipline of suffering on behalf of the people. This is true even in the case of the Rite of Vigil, often called the vision quest in the literature. While there are particularly individual benefits that can accrue from engaging this ceremony of fasting and prayer, even the eventual benefits are enjoyed by the individual for the sake of the community as a whole.[2]

---

2. This ceremony is persistently and wrongly signified in anthropological and history-of-religions literature as quintessential evidence for the radical individualism of plains Indian societies.

Our understanding of vicarious suffering in such ceremonial contexts gives Indian people an inherent understanding of the christian concept of grace, an understanding that precedes the arrival of the missionaries. We could even go so far as to insist that we already knew the gospel! We were taught differently by the missionaries, of course. They had a vested interest in separating Indian people from their ancient ceremonial structures and consistently taught that those ceremonies fell far short of the christian ideal. They were, the missionaries insisted, merely vain human attempts to placate an angry god—an impossibility in the first place, went the message, and unnecessary in the light of God's grace revealed in the gospel of Jesus Christ. More and more, contemporary Indians are realizing that the missionary interpretation was a self-serving lie, a colonial act of domination.

There is nothing in any of our traditions that suggests any attempt to make "God," a god, or the spirits happy with us or to placate the judgment of God against a sinful humanity. There is no sense of God's anger. In fact, the whole notion of *wako^{n}da* becoming angry is far too anthropomorphic a notion of deity for Indian people. Rather, our traditions are more complex than that. Our notion of *wako^{n}da* cannot conceive of ascribing human emotions to *wako^{n}da*. Yet, we do conceive of *wako^{n}da* as functioning in the best interests of the created world. We know *wako^{n}da*, however, much more as a sacred but impersonal force that only becomes personified in order to facilitate human understanding. We were given ceremonies in order that we might do our share as two-leggeds in maintaining the world, just as all other species contribute their part. Thus we participate with *wako^{n}da*, the Sacred Energy or Mystery or Power. And we likewise participate with the more personified spirits that are part of *wako^{n}da*'s self-manifestation.

Yes, there were and are ceremonies to make right an imbalance that we ourselves as two-leggeds in moments of foolishness may have instigated through our laziness, inattention, oversight, anger, or some unknown mistake. But even here, the anger of the spirits is never at stake in most of our traditions when those traditions are understood at their most complex level. The spirits are, rather, neutral and follow a natural, predeterminable course. We are mere players in this drama and have been given ceremonies and ways of being that can help to determine the outcome. Thus, our ceremonies are gifts to us, signs of what euro-christian theology would call God's grace, or the intrinsic goodness of *wako^{n}da* and all of its various manifestations and personifications as Grandmothers and Grandfathers.

If our native ways already had some notion of what Christians call God's "good news," then it becomes important for us to hang on to the good news *wako^{n}da* originally gave us rather than blindly consume the good news that the missionaries would impose on us at the cost of losing our own set of cultural values and losing our inculturated sense of community and individual self-esteem.

POLITICAL AND CULTURAL ANALYSES

Given the particularity of our history of oppression and particularly the role of missionization in the conquest of our territories and our indigenous nations, it is important to begin the process of sorting out what the function of Christianity and christology is and might be for us as we continue our struggle and resistance against ongoing colonization. The conquest is not yet complete.[3] Our resistance against the continuing conquest and our healing process of decolonization demand both a political and a cultural analysis of christology. Two-Thirds World theologians are well aware of the historical tension between political and cultural analysis.[4] Although political and cultural analysis arose in separate contexts, they are closely related and symbiotic exercises. As colonized Indian peoples whose cultures have been systematically destroyed and denied, we suffered the loss of culture as a significant part of our experience of political oppression.[5]

Political Analysis

It was first of all from latin America that the christian world finally discovered the critical truth that all theology is inherently and at least implicitly political.[6] Euro-western theologians now know that there can be no existentially useful

---

3. This is an allusion to a very useful book by an American Indian legal scholar, Robert Williams, *The American Indian in Western Legal Thought: The Discourses of Conquest* (New York: Oxford University Press, 1990). Williams demonstrates historically from legal texts of the time that systemic forces running through european and amer-european colonization history could not be satisfied until the "conquest" was decisive to the extent that all normative divergence was disallowed.

4. Tissa Balasuriya, "Christologies in Dialogue in EATWOT: An Asian Historical Perspective," *Voices from the Third World* 18, no. 2 (Fall 1995): 46-70.

5. George E. "Tink" Tinker, "Asian Christologies: An American Indian Response," *Voices from the Third World* 18, no. 2 (Fall 1995): 70-73.

6. We have in mind, for example, Gustavo Gutiérrez, *A Theology of Liberation: History, Politics, and Salvation,* trans. and ed. Caridad Inda and John Eagleson (Maryknoll, N.Y.: Orbis Books, 1973); José Miguez Bonino, *Doing Theology in a Revolutionary Situation* (Philadelphia: Fortress Press, 1975); idem, ed., *Faces of Jesus: Latin American Christologies* (Maryknoll, N.Y.: Orbis Books, 1984); see also the writings of Leonardo Boff and many others who taught us so much in the 1970s.

theological or christological reflection that does not engage in critical political analysis. How one identifies the Christ and understands the functions of christology determines much of one's political reality and how one deals with it. A comfortable christology, which ignores the reality of systemic injustice in the world, can do much to ease the consciences of those who function as oppressors and to rationalize the oppression they perpetrate as just or at least necessary. As R. S. Sugirtharajah describes the practical christology of the colonizer's mission efforts, Jesus was made to be the ally of the colonizer:

> [Jesus] was manipulated to validate the ideological and class interests of the exploiters, the privileged and the powerful. He was projected as a preacher of timeless truths who conquers and vanquishes the cultures and religious traditions of other people, a proclaimer of cosmic catastrophe who was indifferent to current social issues and a pacifist who was remote from human tensions and turmoils.[7]

This too continues to be the American Indian experience of amer-european missionary colonialism and their preaching about Jesus in our communities.

In contrast to such theological rationalizing of power and privilege, liberation theologies decidedly established that a genuine understanding of the gospel of Jesus Christ results in a commitment to the liberation of the oppressed and poor of the world. Thus, christological interpretation in the Two-Thirds World has been an exercise in articulating Christ as a spiritual force for liberation from political contexts of oppression.[8]

---

7. R. S. Sugirtharajah, "Jesus Research and Third World Christologies," *Theology* 93 (1990): 387.

8. Of course, one of the consistent criticisms of liberation theology in the United States—by both government and church officials—has been that it explicitly politicizes Jesus. To the contrary, it was early latin american liberation theologians who first exposed and described the political currents inherent in the theologies dominant in the european immigrant churches. It was the colonizers who first politicized Jesus in the Americas. It seems evident from the colonizers' own strategy and view that Jesus exists in the world and is not divorced from political realities in the world. Latin american liberation theologians in particular met this oppressors' idea head-on with their own rendering of how Jesus exists in the world—including the political/economic world—but articulated this from the underside of history. This is what gives liberation theology its power and authenticity. I do not yet understand how to press this discussion with American Indian thinkers who have already decided on the outright rejection of Jesus as the culture hero or spiritual center of the oppressor. It could be powerful for Indian thinkers to challenge the persistent rendering of Jesus by the privileged as a means for ensuring the continuation of their privilege at the cost of American Indian well-being. While I am very sympathetic to Indian reluctance to invest themselves in any type of Christianity, an argument could be made for an Indian christology that would respond effectively to the resurgence of right-wing, racist, oppressive theologies in the United States that pose a new

In the United States, it is crucial that American Indian intellectuals pay close attention to the past five hundred years of colonialism and conquest if we are to plan a future that includes genuine healing and empowerment of our indigenous communities. Since our history of colonialism includes a correlative history of colonial missionization, our political analysis must focus in no small measure on the ways that Jesus and the doctrine of the Christ have been used as a tool of the conquest of our nations and our eventual subjugation as small, poverty-ridden internal minorities in what has become the wealthiest and most politically powerful state in the world community of states. As an example of missionizing colonialism, let me point to the relationship between Jesus and the amer-european cultural affectation of individualism. Much of the missionizing process among Indian peoples has been a studied attempt to encourage Indian converts to develop an individual relationship with Jesus at the cost of the inherent Indian cultural commitment to the community as a whole and to a communitarian value system. Thus, the missionary victory involved cultural conversion as well as spiritual conversion, the destruction of one set of cultural values and the imposition of a new set. It is much clearer today in retrospect that this sort of amer-european cultural proclamation of the gospel did as much as the U.S. Army to change the political landscape of each Indian nation.[9] It needs to be said here that the oppression of Indian peoples in the United States continues today. We remain colonized peoples, more or less rigidly controlled by the government that surrounds us, too often appealing targets for the extraction of natural resources, and the ongoing subjects of poverty, joblessness, disease, and other symptoms of colonization.

Cultural Analysis

It was theologians from Asia and Africa who pressed euro-christian thinkers toward the step beyond political analysis. Today, it would be unthinkable to do political analysis in theological and christological reflection without paying close attention to cultural analysis as well.[10] In the American Indian world,

---

(renewed) threat to Indian peoples today. A serious Indian reflection on christology could provide new energy and creativity to confront this new round of colonialism (which we call "internal colonialism").

9. George E. Tinker, *Missionary Conquest: The Gospel and Native American Cultural Genocide* (Minneapolis: Fortress Press, 1993).

10. For Asia, see, for example, the writings of David Kwang-Sun Suh, Chung Hyun Kyung, Kwok Pui-Lan, Virginia Fabella, and Samuel Rayan. For Africa, see Jesse N. K. Mugambi and Laurenti Magesa, *Jesus in African Christianity: Experimentation and Diversity in African Christology* (Nairobi: Initiatives Publishers, 1989). In his "Response to the Presentation by Diego Irarrázaval," *Voices from the Third World* 18, no. 2 (Fall 1995), David Kwang-Sun Suh acknowledges a similar shift in latin american thinking: "It is good news to us Asian

we have found that it is important to affirm who we are, not just socially and politically but in terms of our traditional cultures and value systems. Having begun the unending process of analyzing the ongoing political aspects of our colonial reality, it is apparent to many of us that we must move intentionally and assertively to affirm in great detail the ongoing importance of our own traditions. This means that some of us will struggle to understand the Christ in terms that are more culturally compatible with those traditions. Others in the Indian world will continue to press the more radical question as to whether Jesus and Christianity can be rescued as a significant source of spiritual sustenance for Indian peoples at all.

One important example of the role of cultural analysis in articulating an American Indian christology would be the destructiveness caused by the varieties of the typical fall-and-redemption evangelism proclaimed in Indian mission contexts. In the lutheran variation of this type of theology, the "law" (*nomos*) is paired with the gospel as the gospel's natural and logically necessary antecedent. One must be convinced of the need for salvation by the preaching of the law as a preparation for hearing the good news of the gospel. Yet this intrinsic emphasis on human sin and sinfulness violates Indian people in two devastating ways. First of all, Indian cultures do not inherently share the same sense of human depravity that is so pervasive in european cultures and has there given rise to the doctrine of original sin. Thus, Indian peoples, who are inherently open to varieties of spiritual expressions and experiences, are forced to experience the foreign emotive sense of depravity and sinfulness before they can enjoy the deep spiritual insights of the power that emanates from God in the witness of Jesus. Second, and more important, given the social dysfunctionality that reigns in Indian communities as a result of our history of colonialism and oppression, this emphasis on sin and depravity impedes any hearing of the good news among a people demoralized both spiritually and emotionally by their experience of conquest. In our internalizing of our own oppression we have taken to heart too much the continual insistence of the missionaries, the government, and virtually all White amer-european peoples and social structures that everything Indian is necessarily less good than the superior cultural values and structures brought to us by the amer-european invasion. Yes, it is unfortunate, but we have learned to hate and demean ourselves and to value things that are White. Generations of abuse have caused us, like too many abused children, to internalize the abuse as wholly deserving on our part. As unhealthy and wrong as this is, it is only reinforced by fall-and-redemption notions of christology.

---

theologians that the Latin American colleagues are taking the peoples' cultures and religions seriously" (81).

Culturally, any proclamation of the gospel among Indian peoples must begin with some sort of affirmation of Indian people as Indian and as human beings. It is not even enough to focus on the affirmation of Indian individuals as such; rather, it is the whole of an abused community who must be built up by such affirmation. Thus, I have always proposed that spiritual proclamation or teaching in American Indian communities must begin with creation and the affirmation of the community and each individual as an equal part of the whole of creation. In a christian or biblical context, for instance, this would mean an initial emphasis on human beings as created "in God's image." Hence, if God has created me, and created me as an Indian, then I must be good, just as all of creation is good; and being Indian must also be a part of God's good design. Likewise, our Indian communities with our unique cultures and values must also be rooted in some sense of the goodness of all of creation.

Of course, those christologies that build first on some notion of human sin and the need for salvation that is answered by Jesus as the Christ of God also tend to emphasize the universality of both this worldview and of Jesus. As a result, amer-european missionaries have consistently tried to disallow any traditional expression of spirituality on the part of Indian people. Their notion of original sin allows for access back to an alienated God only in the way they would prescribe. Any notion that God may have provided a panoply of ways to relate to God's self would be anathema. Again, Indian people are taught that they are somehow less than White people. Again, we are excluded. Any American Indian christology must do better than that.

DECOLONIZING INDIAN CHRISTOLOGY

There are a number of considerations involved in thinking about how an American Indian christology might be constructed as part of the decolonization process. There are several aspects that are unique to the situation of indigenous peoples and are not universal to the context of all marginalized peoples. These involve aspects of both political and cultural analysis and must invariably gravitate around traditional Indian community patterns of thought and values, especially in terms of the spiritual well-being of the people. This christology must begin with and continually be in touch with the analysis of the political context, but it must today especially include the results of colonization, particularly the psychological state of the community and the psychology of the act of colonization.[11] At this point perhaps it is

---

11. I have in mind here the works of Albert Memmi, *The Colonizer and the Colonized* (Boston: Beacon Press, 1967); and Ashis Nandy, *The Intimate Enemy: Loss and Recovery of Self under Colonialism* (Delhi: Oxford University Press, 1983). But note also Franz Fanon's

enough to simply list a few of these considerations and then to reflect further on the basis of these.

1. Jesus, that is, the Jesus manufactured by the colonizers, has been systematically imposed on Indian peoples as a replacement for internal, cultural forms of spiritual involvement. The mission program dictated by this artificial Jesus construct had more to do with altering the traditional social, economic, and political foundations of self-sustaining communities, attempting to bring them into line with european and amer-european norms, than it had to do with supporting social structures that nurtured the well-being of Indian communities. In the course of this imposition (missionization), traditional forms of spirituality have been defamed, belittled, disallowed, and even outlawed by the missionaries or by the government under explicit pressure from the missionaries.

2. The U.S. government has been historically involved in encouraging missionary activity as a means pacifying of Indian peoples. In spite of its constitutional claim to insure freedom of religion, the government has consistently supported and even funded missionary projects among Indian peoples. Christianization was assumed to be an important foundation for the civilization of "savage races."

3. The christology that has been imposed on Indian peoples in the course of missionization has been, in every context, one of control and manipulation of Indian peoples by the denominations that did the missionization. The churches have provided little or no opportunity for Indian communities to determine the parameters of the gospel for themselves, let alone for them to determine their own christology.

4. Christianity has been from the beginning and continues to be divisive of Indian communities. In every case, the first missionary to win a convert in an Indian community effectively split the community into two camps that have not been reconciled to this day. The tragedy in this process is that, ideally, Indian cultures function as communist value structures, as integral wholes with each person and each part of the community's life related to everyone and everything else. In traditional life, one was never forced to make a choice between competing spiritual forms. If the community had a ceremony on a given occasion, everyone was included and had a part to play in fulfilling the ceremony. Suddenly, with the arrival of the amer-european missionary, the church imposed on Indian peoples, and ultimately on each individual, a

---

The Wretched of the Earth (New York: Grove Press, 1963); and the writings of Aimé Césaire. I mention these "classics" out of concern that they are too often overlooked in our concern for liberating theologies, yet their analyses of colonialism and the ongoing symptoms of colonial oppression are crucial to our own agenda.

choice between the community's ceremony and the new form of spirituality proclaimed by the missionary. Our communities would never again be whole and would never again pray together as a whole and united people.

5. Any attempt at this late date to develop an Indian christology as part of the decolonization process must begin by claiming its own freedom in Christ Jesus: "For freedom Christ has set you free. Do not submit again to the yoke of slavery" (Gal 5:1). Our question about this "freedom" eventually must extend to asking if it includes the freedom to choose a return to traditional native religious structures. Pressing toward an Indian articulation of this gospel, freedom begins with (1) defining christology and the gospel for ourselves in ways that might be more compelling and more culturally appropriate for us. It moves then toward (2) claiming the freedom to embrace and participate as Christians in the traditional ceremonies and belief structures of our own peoples. But at its most radical, the question must (3) ask whether a colonized, conquered, and subjected people might now choose to return entirely to its own traditional forms of prayer, even if Jesus does not bless us in our prayers apart from reciting his name. The contemporary Indian experience in north America is that many people are finding greater health and liberation in abandoning the colonizing religion in favor of such a return to the ancient ways of the people.

6. Great care must be taken to insure that, whatever sort of christological statement we decide to make, it not result in another exercise of participating in our ongoing colonization and oppression.[12]

AMERICAN INDIANS AND JESUS

The question that emerged from under the hood of that old truck was much more persistent than the quick response had initially allowed for. Indeed, the question will not go away. Given the implicit and explicit participation of the churches' missionaries in the oppression and cultural genocide of American Indians, what relevance can Jesus have for Indian peoples? That, ultimately, was the question my brother was asking, and this question became a constantly recurring problem for Indian people at ministry centers like Living Waters Indian Lutheran Ministry, a project that has transformed itself as Four Winds American Indian Council. How could we proclaim Jesus to a community that

---

12. To wit, note the critique of intra-asian missionary endeavors today voiced by Aruna Gnanadasan, "Asian Theological Methodology: An Overview," *Voices from the Third World* (June 1995): "An added phenomenon is the growth of missionary movements within Asia— notably from South Korea. These groups replicate the same mistakes the Western mission movements had made in the last century. They impose a religious mindset which is alien and which exploits the vulnerability of the poor in some countries in Asia, including China, but also in Eastern Europe" (85).

has been constantly hurt by the proclamation of the gospel and those who have proclaimed it? There are three points to be made here. First, the initial problem is not with Jesus but with Christianity and the church. Second, if Jesus is not necessarily a problem, language about Jesus can be quite problematic, and the churches might reasonably make some linguistic/theological shift that might be more inclusive of Indian peoples and their cultures and values. And, third, in the final analysis, the historical experience of colonization and conquest may continue to make any use of Jesus problematic for American Indian people. It is difficult for many Indian people to concede efficacy to a system of religious belief that they have consistently over several generations experienced as an intimate and symbiotic part of conquest and the ongoing colonial presence.

Jesus and the Church

Traditional spiritual elders and medicine women and men rather consistently express their respect for Jesus as a spiritual person and even as a manifestation of the Creator (namely, God, or something like what Amer-europeans mean by God). While these spiritual elders and medicine people may have significant resistance to church and to Christianity, they found that they were quite able to participate at Living Waters, since Living Waters represented in its day an Indian community more than it represented church. Moreover, these elders were more likely than many other traditional people to participate fully in the liturgy at Living Waters, even participating in the sacred meal of communion. Jesus, it seems, poses little problem for these elders. They can respect him as having been a spiritual presence and even as a continuing spiritual presence in the world. As these people have expressed themselves, Jesus is much more acceptable than the church.

When traditional Indian people came to Living Waters' Sunday service—and many of our regular participants were traditional—they were faced with a choice when it came to the eucharist, whether to participate or not. Many found Living Waters a comfortable place to pray with Indian people, yet they were not always ready to concede the efficacy of this important christian ceremony. The political compromise and resulting disempowerment that come from participating in the conqueror's ceremony were and are simply too great. Abstaining from bread and cup became a final act of resistance and a clear political choice, even in a church that was clearly and more radically Indian.

On the other hand, many chose to go ahead and participate.[13] There were

---

13. For White, amer-european Christians there is a curious aspect in nearly every case. Whether an Indian participant in eucharist is Christian or not, they came to Living Waters' communion with a belief (even faith) in the presence of Jesus in the sacrament. I would even

various reasons for their acquiescence. (1) Traditional values often dictate that spiritual respect for another's ceremony supersedes one's political conviction. (2) For many there is a recognition of spiritual power in Jesus that goes beyond ethnicity or culture and is similar to the spiritual power already experienced in traditional Indian ceremonial life. (3) There is a traditional valuing of shared hospitality: when in someone else's camp, one does what they do. (4) Most important, many were simply expressing a sense of solidarity with those Indian people who have been converted to Christianity by participating occasionally with them. Among these elders there is a sense that those who have remained with the traditional ways or returned to them cannot abandon converted Indians as if they no longer belonged to the community. Decolonization is a process that requires some patience, especially as those who have worked more consistently at the process extend their solidarity to those who are not yet at the same place in that process. The Indian concern for community will not permit the individual to exclude others from the group.

In any case, the distinction between these traditional people's response to Jesus and the church or Christianity as an institution is critical. They have largely screened out christian language about Jesus and focused only on the mythic person. Language about Jesus, however, takes on importance because so many Indian people have been missionized and continue as members of mainline denominations. One response to the problem of language, then, is to search for more culturally appropriate translations of metaphors. Thus, it has become axiomatic in Third World theological contexts to talk of contextualizing and inculturating theology.[14] Likewise, culturally discrete interpretations of Jesus have become commonplace in world Christianity. In the interests of American Indian Christians, one might propose the development of an American Indian christology that would make Jesus more authentically accessible to Indian people. This process might begin by identifying existing euro-christian language that is unhelpful or even destructive. One example of this latter is the common christian reference to Jesus as lord.

Language and Lordship: Jesus as Conqueror

The scene was the 1990 World Council of Churches Consultation on Justice, Peace and the Integrity of Creation in Seoul, South Korea. "Jesus Christ is

---

go so far as to say that there was a stronger or more lively sense of the "real presence" of Jesus in the sacrament than there is in most suburban lutheran congregations.

14. See Edward P. Antonio, *Inculturation and Postcolonial Discourse in African Theology* (New York: Peter Lang, 2006), especially the first chapter, entitled "Introduction: Inculturation and Postcolonial Discourse," 1-28.

Lord!" So read the huge banner above the dais, the last gasp of triumphalism at an antitriumphalist event. The banner represents the bare-bones common confession of the great variety of communions who make up the World Council of Churches, the doctrinal glue that holds us all together. Yet the colonial oppressiveness of the proclamation began to weigh heavily on at least one Indian person present at the consultation in ways never before considered. The cultural otherness of the language used in this common confession once again meant that American Indian peoples were being co-opted into a cultural frame of reference that necessitated self-denial and assimilation to the language and social structures of the conqueror. The reflection at that moment began a much deeper and longer-termed reflection on issues of christology and conquest that resulted in a radical shift in that Indian person's theological thinking and in the self-identity of the ministry project with which he had been affiliated for the past dozen years.

As foundational as the confession "Jesus Christ is Lord" is for the World Council of Churches, it is the one scriptural metaphor used for the Christ event that is ultimately unacceptable and even hurtful to American Indian peoples. There was no analogue in north american indigenous societies for the relationship of power and disparity that is usually signified by the word "lord." To the contrary, north american cultures and social structures were fundamentally marked by their egalitarian nature. Even a so-called chief had typically very limited authority, which even then depended much on the person's charismatic stature within the community and skill at achieving consensus. The American Indian experiential knowledge of lordship only begins with the conquest and colonization of our nations at the onslaught of the european invasion. What we know about lords and lordship, even today, has more to do with Washington, D.C., the Bureau of Indian Affairs, and the modern tribal governments created by an act of Congress. Unfortunately, by extension, even the church becomes a part of these new colonial relationships, with lords in the form of bishops and missionaries (both male and female) to whom we have learned as conquered peoples to pay lordly deference.

To this extent, then, to call upon Jesus as lord suddenly began to strike me as a classic example of the colonized participating in our own oppression. To call upon Jesus as lord is to concede the colonial reality of new hierarchical social structures; it is to concede the conquest as final and become complicit in our own death, that is, the ongoing genocidal death of our peoples.[15] It is an act of the colonized mind blindly reciting words that the colonizer has taught

---

15. For a description of missionary participation in injustices committed against Indian peoples, see Tinker, *Missionary Conquest*.

us that violate our own cultures but bring great comfort to the lordly colonizer and his missionaries.

Lordship and the Shaping of the Amer-european Experience

It can be objected that the lordship metaphor for Christ is actually helpful for White, amer-european Christians because it puts many people into a posture of humble surrender to another, a posture to which most are quite unaccustomed. Yet, I would argue that the metaphor does exactly the opposite and that it is ultimately not helpful for amer-european Christians any more than it is for American Indians. Rather, the metaphor excuses White amer-european folk from any earthly humility or surrender, and facilitates a lack of consciousness with regard to the impropriety of relationships of exploitation. Since one has surrendered to an overwhelmingly powerful numinous Other, no other surrender or act of humility is called for within the human community. Indeed, many amer-european Christians seem to feed on a hierarchical view of the world that has historically privileged and continues to privilege White people on this continent and in other Two-Thirds World colonial contexts. Thus, rather than being humbled in submission, they are empowered and emboldened—sometimes even explicitly empowered for imposing their own brand of submission on others. Having submitted to the lordship of Jesus, one must submit or pay homage no longer to any earthly authority. Indeed, humbled as a vassal before Jesus, one becomes empowered as Jesus' champion in the world, a soldier for Christ. Unfortunately, this notion of White superiority and White privilege regularly serves White political and economic interests as well, defining those interests as somehow naturally concurrent with the interests of God.

Moreover, "lord" is one of those biblical metaphors that seems to have lost all symbolic cognitive moorings in modern american society. The problem is that there are no "lords" in our society and no use of "lord" as a form of address that might conceivably give the metaphor content. Indeed, any use of the word in the United States today is an anachronistic metaphor requiring the hearer to summon up memories of historical uses of the word in english history and literature that predate the american Revolution, or it requires a crosscultural understanding of the living anachronism in contemporary english society. Like the language of the "kingdom of God," these persistent metaphors from the first-century mediterranean world require that modern north Americans engage in enough of a linguistic-cultural history lesson to have any idea what the word might have meant in the past before they can appropriate any spiritual content from the proclamation of Jesus as lord for the present.

Modern biblical exegesis is an ongoing attempt to recover meanings in the biblical texts from research in ancient biblical societies and languages. Thus, exegesis would attempt to explicate the lordship metaphor in terms of the social and political arrangements that dictated the use of language in Palestine and the greco-roman world of the christian gospels. This, however, does not solve the problem that the most accessible use of the word for amer-european people (and undoubtedly for many of the rest of us because of our experience of colonialism in America) is not its use in the eastern mediterranean world of Jesus' day but rather its use in european cultures, which continues to some extent even today in places such as England, for instance, which still maintains in its Parliament a House of Lords. Yet the european use of the word, rooted as it is in the social structures of medieval feudalism, is in actuality a far cry from the palestinian (aramaic) use that would have been familiar to the author of the greek testament called Mark or even the hellenistic (greco-roman) use that would have been the experience of the author of the gospel called Luke.

What we are close to saying here is that to continue to use the metaphor in literal translation may be leading the faithful astray even in White, amer-european churches, quite apart from the more complex issue of translating what is culturally foreign for American Indian hearers. Of course, it can be argued that it is the preacher's responsibility to interpret, to teach the correct meaning, to unpack the metaphor for the ecclesial community. Yet, it seems ludicrous to think that the only path to salvation is in a transcultural, ancient history lesson. Especially when one considers the needs of children in amer-european churches, one must ask if it is fair to them to insist that they must come to understand something quite outside of their lived experience in order to engage the spiritual traditions of their families.

More to the point, we are experiencing a shift away from the useful, mean-ingful, experiential use of language to what can only be categorized as "reli-gious language." And it can be further argued that religious language is by definition and de facto language that has lost its meaning; that is, religious language has no currency of meaning in the day-to-day, real world use of lan-guage. Religious language is made up of old-language usages that now con-tinue to have meanings only insofar as they continue to function in that small slice of modern life reserved for religion.

No Other Name: Colonizer's Claim to Universal Truth

Many would, of course, insist that the American Indian case for spiritual self-determination can and must be made on its own merits without recourse to amer-european discourse. While Indian peoples have a spiritual understand-ing of the world that is inherently amenable to some central christian concepts, such as grace, we must understand Indian spiritual traditions in their own right and in their own uniqueness. They are not spiritual "puzzle pieces" that can be locked into a universal christian truth but have their own meaning and vibrancy within each discrete Indian culture. Yet, for the sake of those Indian people who have made a lasting commitment to the colonizer's religious traditions and have converted to Christianity, it can be important to demonstrate the plausibility of Indian religious traditions on the basis of an interpretation of the colonizer's own texts. In the following section, I propose to interpret two of those texts with a different eye than most amer-european or european biblical scholars would bring to the task. The first text is from the fourth chapter of the Acts of the Apostles:

> [9] ... by what means has this man been *healed*? [10] Be it known to you all, and to all the people of Israel, that by the name of Jesus Christ of Nazareth, whom you crucified, whom God raised from the dead, by him this man is standing before you well. [11] This is the stone which was rejected by you builders, but which has become the head of the corner. [12] And there is salvation in no one else, for there is no other name under heaven given among human beings by which we must be *saved*. (Acts 4:9-12)

"There is *no other name* under heaven given among human beings by which we must be *saved*" (Acts 4:12): the Rev. Harry Long, a legendary Muskogee methodist pastor, a radical and troublemaker in his own right, asked me some years ago if I would not give some attention to this particular text. I think Long had decided many years prior to our conversation to pay less attention to this text and lend his own affirmation to the revival of traditional native spirituality both in our national (meaning reservation or "tribal") communities and in the context of urban Indian communities. Yet, I think, the text continued to trouble him as an ordained methodist minister, and he hoped that an Indian with some training in biblical studies might be able to clarify the text for Indian people in a new way.

For us the question is indeed whether there is salvation in our traditional religious beliefs and ceremonies or whether the missionaries were right, that our old ways were mere devil worship that badly needed to be replaced by this new "good news" brought to us by the White amer-european missionaries, who all too often came with the colonizer army and paved the way for government treaty swindlers.

This is serious business. If the missionaries are right, then we Indian peoples have at least three problems. First of all, I can be saved now, because God sent us White people, but what about my Indian ancestors? They were directly accused of engaging in devil worship by the earliest european invaders of Indian lands, and, unfortunately, classical christian doctrine holds out little hope for their rejoining any of us who have heard the "good news" and have been converted to Jesus since then. According to the missionary gospel we have been taught, in heaven we will be separated from our ancestors and will live for eternity in a world ("new heaven and new earth") populated primarily by our conquerors and colonizers and separated from our own ancestors.[16]

Second, and more immediately pressing, we will also be separated from many in our national communities (tribes) and many of our relatives because they have chosen not to convert or even to revert to their old traditional belief systems. Discouraged by the dominance of White missionaries and the collusion of those missionaries with oppressive government and military subversions of our communities and our native economies, many of our relatives have decided that there is no good news in the good news and have helped to fuel the revival of our traditional ceremonial life. Thus, there is a distance placed between those who have become christian and those who have as a matter of conscience decided that they cannot be christian because Christianity represents the worst of the history of colonialism among Indian peoples in north America. The third problem has to do with many contemporary Indian clergy. While they genuinely want the healing of Indian peoples, they find themselves caught in a quandary between the claim of christian exclusivity and the revival of traditional ceremonial life among our peoples.

Yet the biblical text at hand does not necessarily read as the missionaries have insisted. Is there salvation only in Jesus? This is the way we have been conditioned to read the story in Acts, but a closer reading makes interpretation much more complex. To begin with, the use of the noun *salvation* and the verb *saved* must be read in the context of the story itself and not merely read as if the author had the usual english language meanings in mind in verse 12. The story actually begins earlier, in chapter 3, when Peter and John heal a lame man at the entrance of the Jerusalem temple. They are taken to court because they have healed him on the Sabbath, the traditional day of rest for Jewish peoples, on which no work was to be performed by divine law. Proceeding carefully, the lawyers wished to know, "By what means has this man been healed?" (Acts 4:9).

---

16. Las Casas relates a famous illustrative incident from early in the sixteenth century during the conquest of Cuba, one that is still remembered in Cuban oral tradition. In 1512 a franciscan friar attempted to offer baptism and the chance to go to heaven after his immanent execution to a captive cacique named Hatuey. Hatuey, who was bound to the stake with firewood already piled up for the brutal execution, asked whether the spanish soldiers would also be in heaven. Told that their baptism assured their going to heaven, Hatuey refused the offer, resolutely announcing that he would rather go to the other place. Bartolomé de Las Casas, *Historia de las Indias,* book II, chap. 25. Gustavo Gutiérrez (*Las Casas: In Search of the Poor of Jesus Christ* [Maryknoll, N.Y.: Orbis Books, 1993], 546 n.47) also mentions the story in passing.

The use of the verb for healing is important. Indeed, it is the same verb that is translated as *saved* in verse 12. This verb (*sōzō*) carries a range of meanings, including medical healing and spiritual salvation. The question is, how have english translators moved from one meaning of the word to another in four verses with no explanation? The related nouns (*sōtēr* and *sōtēria*) likewise carry a range of meanings, including savior and healer, salvation and healing. Before we offer another translation of the text, it is important to ask how the word was first used in the story. It would seem reasonable to think that the author would have used the words in the immediate context in not terribly disparate ways.

To understand these related words in their greek cultural context requires a reading of several hundred years of greek literature. Already, some six hundred years before Acts was written, the greek poet Pindar called Asclepios, the greek god of healing, "the savior of his people." He was clearly a savior because he visited patients in his temples at night and brought to them miraculous, overnight healings of a great variety of physical maladies. As yet in greek consciousness, there was little attention to any notion that might be similar to the modern christian notion of salvation. So *savior* clearly meant *healer*. Likewise, it is well known that the word *salvation* originally referred to physical healing of an illness, and that the verb *save* referred to the action of *healing*. Luke clearly uses this meaning of the verb in the early part of this story. After Peter says to the man, "In the name of Jesus Christ of Nazareth, rise up and walk" (3:6), five verses later Luke describes the man as "the lame man who was healed" (3:11). That is to say, the lame man was saved not for eternal life but from his lame leg. Surely, we cannot discount the possibility that there was also a spiritual saving that happened, but that is not a part of this story. In this context *sōzō* means physical healing.

When the priests and lawyers ask Peter and John, "By what power or by what name have you done this?" (4:7), they are asking about the physical healing. Peter's response is equally clear. The physical healing (saving) of the lame man was done by "the name of Jesus Christ of Nazareth" (4:10): "By him is this man standing before you well." This seems clearly to imply a spiritual power for physical healing (saving) that can be summoned by using the name of Jesus. And here I say the name of Jesus because the rest of the identifying label is not name but title ("Christ") and geographical locator ("of Nazareth").

Hence, when we finally get to the key verse (4:12), there is little reason to shift the meaning of the words in a wholesale fashion. Peter must be saying, "There is *healing* (not salvation) in no one else, for there is no other name under heaven given among human beings by which we must be *healed* (not saved)." While this use of language can certainly carry a double meaning, it is important to understand that this whole story is about a healing—the miraculous, physical healing of a lame man. To change the story to meet our own needs for salvation language does an injustice to the author and to the meaning of the story.

We are still left with Rev. Long's original question, however. What can the text mean when it says there is no other name by which healing can take place? At the surface level, this claim seems ludicrous if not patently false. Even in Peter's day there were trained (however poorly by modern standards) physicians who effected healing and gave healing care to the sick. There are numerous stories from the time of Jesus that attest to the miraculous healing work of other charismatic healers in Palestine. In our American Indian communities, we have considerable experience with healing styles that use spiritual medicine and ceremony. What are we to believe then of Jesus' world? That these healings did not occur?

I want to suggest that this verse, typically used by amer-european missionaries to coerce our conversion to Christianity, has been consistently misread and misinterpreted in the missionary claim of christian exclusivity and superiority. Commentators consistently miss the most obvious point of the story, namely, that the reader is supposed to know a bit more about the name of Jesus and to draw out the meaning of the story from the meaning of the name. Like many of the particularities of ancient palestinian culture, this is not foreign to Indian hearers of the story, because we come from cultures where names still have meaning. In the amer-european world, however, names have largely ceased to carry any real meaning beyond euphony or family sentimentality. What do the names George, Betty, Bob, Kathy, Bill, or Ted actually mean? Eagle Elk, Red Eagle, Bacon Rind, Earth Walker, Crazy Horse, Tall Buffalo: those names can be explained. They have meaning and are carefully given to the bearers because of their meanings.

I want to ask, then, can the meaning of the name Jesus help us to understand why Peter would insist that healing can happen only by means of this name? Few modern Christians remember that Jesus was a very common name in Palestine two millennia ago. Some will remember that it was actually a shortened form of the hebrew Bible name of Moses' successor, Joshua. This hebrew name was a combination of two elements, a noun and a verb, *ja* and *shua*. The first part of the name occurs also in the name Jonathan (*ja - nathan*), which is actually a similar name to Nathaniel (*nathan-el*). These last two names have a counterpart in two greek names, one male and one female: Theodore and Dorothy; both are combinations of the greek words for God (*theos*) and gift (*dorea*). In hebrew, *nathan* means gift, while *ja* and *el* are shortened forms of *jahweh* and *elohim*, variant names for God. All mean "gift of god." The name Jesus or Joshua includes this shortened form of *jahweh*. The verb, or action part of the name (*shua*), is translated as "saves" or "heals." Thus, the name Jesus means "God heals (or saves)."

Here finally we have the meaning of the text clearly stated. The focus, suddenly, is not on Jesus at all but on God! Jesus is not identified here as the only source of salvation or as the only savior. Rather, God is identified as the only ultimate source of healing, a meaning embedded in the name Jesus itself. God is the healer. This much every Indian person can readily acknowledge. So it has always been in our ceremonies and among our healing specialists since time immemorial. The power to heal always comes from the spiritual energy of *wako^{n}da*, even when particular individuals have been identified as the vehicles through whom certain kinds of healing or help can be facilitated.

Yet the missionaries have used this story to proclaim to us a self-serving untruth, that God has spoken only to them and only communicated through Jesus. And under the immense pressure of colonization and conquest, many of our ancestors felt they were left with little choice but to accede to the self-proclaimed superiority of the White invaders of our land, to convert to their religious belief, and to acknowledge the superiority of their God. The nature of colonization is such that it entices the strong to take advantage of the weak in all aspects of life: social, political, economic, and religious. Such domination in the sphere of religion serves as an essential reinforcement for these other modes of domination. And so the missionaries, whose minds were every bit as much colonized as ours, saw Indian vulnerability and used that vulnerability to advance their own cause quickly and decisively.

Perhaps now that the land is in their possession or at least under their political control the churches will leave Indian people alone to find our own way spiritually. Indeed there are signs that the mainline denominations intend to abandon Indian peoples and the churches they have created in our communities. Funds have been regularly cut back from reservation churches, and the growing urban Indian population, fostered by ill-intended government policies of trying to force assimilation, have been regularly ignored by the same churches that rushed into the missionary enterprise on the ever-expanding frontiers of Manifest Destiny a century ago. Unfortunately, the signs are not entirely positive. As the mainline denominations pull back from us, the even more doctrinally rigid pentecostal and right-wing evangelical groups have moved in like vultures to clean up the remaining scraps on the garbage heap of Indian colonized vulnerability.

We are not yet done, however, with the colonizer's texts. We must look at one other passage before we conclude. The beginning of the Gospel of John (1:1-4) is a wonderful, poetic statement that identifies the spiritual power that John associates with Jesus. That power, he calls *Logos*.

CHRIST, *LOGOS*, PREEXISTENCE, AND CORN MOTHER

> In the beginning was the *Logos*; and the *Logos* was with God; and the *Logos* was [a] god [or "divine"]. This one [*It*] was in the beginning with God. All things came into being through *It*, and nothing happened without *It*. What came into being through *It* was life; and life was the light of humanity [human beings]. And the light shines in the darkness, and the darkness cannot overcome it. (John 1:1-4)

As american Indian readers of this important colonizer sacred text, we must first come to terms with the gender of this *Logos* concept in John 1. It is clear from John's telling of the story that he intends us to understand the *Logos* as personified, but it is certainly not clear at all that he intends us to understand it as a male personification that should thereafter be referred to as "he," which is how english translations regularly translate the pronouns of verses 2 to 4. The initial problem for english-speaking interpreters is that the greek noun *logos* does carry an assigned masculine grammatical gender. English-speaking interpreters have regularly made the mistake of assuming that grammatical gender is necessarily a real indication of the gender of the object or person to which the noun refers. This is not, however, how human languages usually function, as any speaker of an american indigenous language knows already. In german, for instance, young men and young women are often referred to with a noun whose grammatical gender is neuter (*das Mädchen*; *das Herrlein*), yet no one would suggest that these people actually are neuter gender. Likewise, french can shift in its reference to God from *le dieu* (masculine) to *la divinité* (feminine) without substantially affecting the actual gender of God. Yet even the french pronouns will automatically shift to match the grammatical gender of the noun, so that after *le dieu*, God will be referred to as *il* (literally, he), and after *la divinité*, the reference to God will change to *elle* (literally, she). We must carefully guard against ascribing gender to a person or object on the basis of the grammatical gender of the noun (or even pronoun) used to refer to that person or object.

Thus, I have chosen to play it safe and refer to the *Logos* as It with a capital initial letter to indicate Its divine status in John's mythic construct. This does not mean that I believe God to be neuter gender any more than I believe God to be exclusively masculine. Rather, I know God to be both male and female, because my ancestors have always called on God as grandfather and grandmother together, as *wako"da mo"shita* and *wako"da udseta*, the Sacred Above and the Sacred Below. Philip Deere was fond of making the point that God, or the Sacred Other, is ultimately the Unknowable and, as such, has no gender until It makes Itself known. And in most of our American Indian cultural traditions, God, the Unknowable, makes Itself known in a reciprocal duality that is both male and female. Hence, I argue that to follow the missionaries by simply always ascribing maleness to God would be wrong and that to ascribe maleness to the *Logos* would be to fall into that same trap. There is no compelling reason to interpret the *Logos* as male. Some amer-european biblical interpreters have even entertained the possibility that the *Logos* is a metaphor for the old testament personification of *sophia,* or Wisdom, as a female aspect of divinity.

Of course, the *Logos* does eventually become manifest in the text as a male entity a few verses later when, implicitly, the *Logos* becomes incarnate and is identified as Jesus. This introduces a second and most interesting problematic in our interpretation. Namely, how are we, precisely and accurately, to make the identification between Jesus and the *Logos* or between Jesus and the Christ, ultimately, since John seems to clearly infer a philosophical or theological identification between Christ and *Logos*? While this topic has been explored with considerable finesse by biblical scholars over the past century, it has a particularly promising potential for American Indian Christians in their discrete interpretation of the gospel. This potential begins with an understanding not of the identity between Jesus and the *Logos* in John's introductory paragraph but rather with a clear distinction between the two that must help to define the ensuing connection.

While most american Christians, especially those who are more conservative, live with a simple notion of a one-to-one equivalency of the names Jesus and Christ, a majority of theologians and biblical scholars have, especially since Rudolf Bultmann, distinguished the two both as names and as concepts. Bultmann, for example, introduced the distinction between the "historical Jesus" and the "historic Christ." He found the historical Jesus to be very elusive and unrecoverable, arguing that the documents (primarily the gospels) were not written as or intended to be read as history. Rather, they were always intended to be generative of faith in Jesus as the Christ. Hence, they were written not to convey historically accurate information; rather, the story, and each part of it, was told in ways to enhance the faith of the believer and to teach the continuing importance of Jesus as the Christ of God. Thus, Jesus becomes the human vehicle for experiencing and for communicating the more mythic, spiritual, theological, and enduring function of the Christ of God.

To apply this understanding to the *Logos* hymn at the beginning of the Gospel of John means that we must begin to distinguish Jesus and the Christ of God in one very decisive way. Namely, it is clear from John 1:1-4 that the *Logos,* that is, the Christ of God, is a preexistent part of God. Jesus is not preexistent in this same way. Rather, Jesus is a human being who has a birth, a beginning in time, and whose birth is identified by early Christians as a particular incarnation or manifestation of the Christ or the *Logos*. While Christians can claim that Jesus became the incarnation of the Christ, it would violate nearly two thousand years of european christian history to claim that Jesus was pre-existent in the same way that the *Logos* is presented here as preexisting all things and participating with God even in the creation of all things. What we have said here should already signal that the two terms, Jesus and Christ, have different meanings and functions in the biblical texts; they are not just two names for Jesus like modern american first and last names.

Up to this point, the text at hand has described the *Logos* as having had two functions only. It was a part of creation; and some millennia later It returned to action in Its incarnation in Jesus. Yet this seems terribly limiting of God on the part of human interpreters. Why would this *Logos*, which was so instrumental in the creation act, have lain dormant for so much of human history? Surely there must be another way of interpreting this text.

The first question we must raise, of course, is the functional question. What is it this *Logos* does? How does it function as a part of God? From the little bit that we have in the Gospel of John, it seems that the *Logos* is some aspect of God, perhaps the creative aspect of God's self, perhaps the creative, communicative aspect of God's self as God communicates with human beings. If this is plausible, then it is unlikely that we could defend any period of inactivity or dormancy, as this would claim dormancy on the part of God. Rather, it would seem that John merely does not mention other occurrences where the *Logos* or Christ was functioning in the world. Indeed, nowhere does John claim that this is the only action of the *Logos* since creation. Jesus, it seems, is merely one, albeit very powerful, occurrence of the *Logos* in human history.

This, suddenly, is a notion of Christ that Indian people can begin to understand naturally within their own cultural experiences and knowledge, without attempting to impose upon us or inculcate in us new cultural categories of knowledge that come from the colonizer's culture and history. If the *Logos* or the Christ is merely that aspect of God that communicates creativity and healing or salvation to human beings, then we can even add to Christianity's knowledge of salvation from our own experiences and memories of God's functioning among Indian communities throughout our history. In this sense, we can claim to have a history of many such experiences of the Christ and can even begin to name some of them and tell the stories that go with the naming. But this also means that we can never be trapped into saying that God has only spoken this good news through Jesus, or that the only way to salvation is through a euro or amer-european message brought by the colonizer to the conquered.

In the final section of this essay, I want to suggest the comparison between the mythic truths inherent in the gospel stories of Jesus and one of our American Indian traditional foundation stories.

CORN MOTHER AS CHRIST

Because our experience of *wako^nda* is always a bi-gender duality, any Indian equivalent for the euro-christian notion of the Christ would include examples that are explicitly female. Thus, the revered mythic and historic figures of Corn Mother and White Buffalo Calf Woman, examples from two different Indian cultural traditions, would perhaps come close to functioning in ways that could be conceived of as christological. As narrative oral texts, they certainly approximate the earliest asian mediterranean narratives about Jesus; and, as in Christianity, each of these figures continues to be significantly involved in the day-to-day well-being of the communities that tell these stories. Both recount a salvific moment in the community's past, yet both function to bring some element of "salvation" and wholeness to the peoples who honor the stories today. This essay will focus on the Corn Mother narratives.

The story of Corn Mother is told in a multitude of versions among Indian communities of different language families, from the east coast of Canada, throughout eastern north America to Florida, and across the southern United States as far west as the Keresan Pueblos in New Mexico. The story is a part of the foundational mythic life of these different peoples, not only as an etiology for corn but for the sacredness of life and the sacredness of food. The story involves the willing self-sacrifice (vicarious suffering) of the First Mother (Corn Mother) on behalf of her children. While initially First Man was the hunter and alone provided for the sustenance of his family, as the family grows ever larger, it became important to introduce new sources of vegetable foods. The details of the story work themselves out quite differently in different communities, with some variety in teaching emphases, but the central mythic themes are intact in all the tellings of the story.

In the Penobscot telling, the death of First Mother is actually requested by the woman herself, against the wishes of her husband, and only completed after he makes a long journey and consults with the Creator himself. In a great variety of other tellings, the woman is murdered by her own children, although in each of these tellings she nevertheless willingly agrees to the killing and even invites it. In some of these stories, Corn Mother provides food in the absence of game by privately scraping or shaking the corn (and sometimes beans) off of her own body. When two of her children sneakily discover where the food is coming from, they accuse her of tricking them into cannibalism, and this becomes the excuse for the murder. In a Natchez version, two daughters accuse their mother of feeding them defecation and proceed to kill her. In another set of tellings, the murder of the woman happens as a result of the foolishness of a powerful, mythic boy child, called Blood Clot Boy, who entices the participation of his sibling. But in all these tellings the self-sacrifice of the woman is emphatically consistent and results in the enduring fecundity of the earth and the production of vegetable foods.

In these stories, First Mother's death is also the first human experience of death. Her burial is accompanied by ceremony and sometimes pronounced weeping. In a fairly typical telling, the surviving family discovers that the clearing where she had been buried is miraculously filled with fully mature food plants, most prominently corn. That is, First Mother, who is buried in the earth, becomes productive in ways that were unexpected and continues to nourish her children long after her death.

Common Theological Themes

There are a number of common theological themes in these stories. The first and perhaps most important is that food must henceforth be considered sacred. Eating becomes what euro-christian theology would signify as sacrament, because eating always involved the eating of the flesh of First Mother. She, in her dying, becomes identified with the earth, with Grandmother, with what the Osages call *wako^{n}da udseta*. In one telling of the story, tobacco is provided by Corn Mother in the middle of the vegetative cornucopia that grew in what had been a clearing in the forest the day before. Her voice is heard as her children approach the clearing, announcing the import of their discovery of this surfeit of food and adding that the tobacco is to be used as a part of their prayers. It is the breath of the Mother and is to add power to their prayers as the smoke is carried up to the sky.

There is more to this story than is conveyed in the simple telling of it. Out of this story emerges a considerable theology that includes the important teaching that all life—including that life considered un-alive by euro-science, rocks, rivers, lakes, mountains, and the like—is interrelated. When one fully understands this teaching—a simple sounding notion that requires years (if not generations) of learning—one finally understands the sacramental nature of eating. Corn and all food stuffs are our relatives, just as much as those who live in adjacent lodges within our clan cluster. Thus, eating is sacramental, to use a euro-theological word, because we are eating our relatives. Not only are we related to corn, beans, and squash, since these things emerge immediately out of the death of Corn Mother, but even those other relatives such as Buffalo,

Deer, Squirrel, and Fish ultimately gain their strength and growth because they too eat of the plenty provided by the Mother—eating grasses, leaves, nuts, and algae that also grow out of the Mother's bosom. More than that, when we eat, we understand that we are benefiting from the lives that have gone before us, that all our human ancestors have also returned to the earth and have become part of what nourishes us today. Thus, one can never eat without remembering the gift of the Mother, of all our relatives in this world, and of all those who have gone before us. Indian people are not cannibals.[17] Indeed, the idea is so abhorrent, even at the mythic level, that a Seminole version of the story has the two boys deeply offended to the point of murdering their mother because they fear that she has forced cannibalistic practice on them in the eating of foodstuffs from her own body.

Another key theological theme and a continuing cultural value among Indian peoples of different cultural affiliations is the concept of Corn Mother's vicarious, self-sacrifice. In all these stories, Corn Mother sacrifices herself willingly for the sake of her children. And so it is that individuals in our communities have lived with the notion of both ceremonial and very real physical sacrifice for the people—"that the people might live!" Ceremonially, this is lived out in our communities in rites like the vision quest, the Sun Dance, and even the purification rite called sweat lodge by many.

The first experience of death by the people in the death of Corn Mother teaches also the truth of the old saying attributed to Seattle (or Sealth): "There is no death; only a change of worlds."[18] What is more important, in terms of our day-to-day existence in Indian communities throughout north America, we understand that our ancestors continue to live in very real ways. This happens in two important ways. First of all, they continue to live in a spirit world where we hope to join them at the ends of our lives here. Second, and just as important, these ancestors continue to live in us, both in our memories and in our physical lives as we continue to eat the produce of the earth where they have returned in one way or another.

Finally, these stories contain some ethical/theological content as well, focused especially toward our young men. In those variants of the story in

---

17. Of course, even the existence of cannibals in the world is a european, amer-european mythic construction. There is no evidence of any indigenous peoples who were cultural practitioners of cannibalism. Yet, it should be remembered that the earliest christian converts in the world of the old roman empire were also accused of cannibalism in their teaching of the sacrament of communion by those who found Christianity to be a threat to society in the first three christian centuries.

18. The speech, commonly attributed to Seattle, is actually not his in any real sense but begins as a recreation in translation of a White onlooker who wrote down, in english, what he remembered of Seattle's speech.

which Corn Mother is killed by male off-spring, there is an implicit warning to men about the potential for male violence in society. Men are to pay attention to the results of immature male decision making, especially when it leaves women out of the decision-making process. We are to be particularly attentive to the potential for inherent male strength to explode in foolish, unpredictable, and irreparable ways against the females in our midst. Moreover, we are to pay attention to the inherent valuing of female gifts and wisdom in our communities. We are to forever remember that healing in the form of both food and spiritual sustenance have come to us traditionally not through men but through a woman, whether it is White Buffalo Woman or Corn Mother. This wisdom is a constant tempering of male dominance, aggression, and assertiveness in our communities.

CONCLUSION

The story of Corn Mother is one example of the power and cosmic balancing of American Indian mythic traditions. Eventually, the healing power of such stories and the ceremonial ways that they undergirded caused a more interesting and persistent rephrasing of my brother's initial question. Why should Indian people be coerced to give up God's unique self-disclosure to us? Why ought Indian people learn to identify after the fact with God's self-disclosure to some other people in a different place and time in a mythic tradition that is culturally strange and alienating? To many in our contemporary American Indian community the answer to this question is obvious. Our traditions, they will argue, are ancient and precious and are to be revered and lived. To the modern Indian traditionalist, there is little need to pay any heed to the colonizer's churches or doctrines.

Nevertheless, many who have been converted to those churches may also find these ancient traditions to be precious. Indian Christians will want to struggle in the coming generation to understand their christian commitments increasingly in their own terms, in ways that incorporate their own cultural traditions of the sacred. The christian Indian interpretation of Jesus as the Christ will eventually differ considerably from the interpretation offered in the colonizer churches and hierarchies. This process of nativizing Indian Christianity already began with the first Indian ministers in the seventeenth century and continues in the bold and energetic work of modern Indian ministers such as Harry Long.

In terms of an emergent communal vision of healing for a people that have been long abused and marginalized by the colonial relationships in north America, it seems that more and more Indian people are making the former choice. They are insisting that the relationship between Indian peoples and the churches is so fractured as to be irreconcilable from the vantage point of American Indian liberation. The spiritual hope today for Indian nations, they argue, is to recover their historical and traditional ceremonial forms. A great many Indian families have been evangelized into the churches, of course, and the churches will continue to be a force in every Indian community. Yet, those congregations and missions have long ceased to grow and are rather in decline these days. The younger members of churched families have tended to be among those who have made the transition back to traditional ceremonies and religious traditions.

In any case, it would seem that the colonizer churches themselves will necessarily have to rethink their notion of christian exclusivity and make room for American Indian religious traditions as being potentially as powerful and salvific as the best vision well-intentioned peoples have for Christianity. I hope that my interpretation of two important texts will make it possible to understand the notion of Christ with much greater inclusivity and parity of power between colonizer and colonized. Likewise, it should be possible today for a mutual respect to emerge that will allow Christians to acknowledge the inherent spiritual power and goodness of American Indian religious traditions. My brother came to the end of his life having forsaken his early christian connection in favor of a more traditional religious life. Yet he maintained a respect for the churches and never hesitated to dialogue with the colonizer in the hope of healing, not only for Indian people but for the colonizer people of north America as well.

Chapter 5

Abjection, Violence, Missions, and American Indians

Missionary Conquest in an Age of Pluralism[1]

Is there a universal religion that applies or should apply to everyone? Is Christianity that religion? Or should there indeed be a dialogue between and among religious thinkers today in which all (including especially christian thinkers) ought to listen carefully and closely to the other? As an American Indian scholar teaching cultural and religious traditions in a christian[2] seminary, I want to affirm strongly Joseph Hough's clearly articulated theology of religious pluralism. Indeed, all amer-european Christians owe him a round of applause for a message that helps them come to a different and more life-affirming understanding of their own past.[3] His essay represents a major step

---

1. This chapter was published originally as my response to an invitation to join a discussion initiated by Joseph C. Hough, Jr., then president of Union Theological Seminary, through his essay titled "Christian Revelation and Religious Pluralism." Both essays appeared in the same issue of *Union Seminary Quarterly Review*; this issue also included Hough's "Continuing the Discussion," in which he addressed all seven of the scholars who had responded to his essay (*Union Seminary Quarterly Review* 56, nos. 3-4 [2002], 65-80, 106-21, 179-93).

2. As noted in the introduction, my use of the lower case for adjectives such as "christian," "protestant," "catholic," "european," and "american" is intentional. While the noun might be capitalized out of respect for each Christian—as for each Muslim or Buddhist—using the lower case "christian" or "biblical" allows us to avoid any unnecessary normativizing or universalizing of the principal institutional religious quotient of the euro-west. The language of "christian civilization" was widely used during the conquest. It is an explicit part of Bishop Henry Benjamin Whipple's programmatic missionizing on the north-central plains in the latter half of the nineteenth century. See my analysis of Whipple in chap. 5 of *Missionary Conquest: The Gospel and Native American Genocide* (Minneapolis: Fortress Press, 1993). I have likewise avoided capitalizing adjectives such as american, amer-european, european, and so on for the same reasons. Paradoxically, I insist on capitalizing the w in White (adjective or noun) to indicate a clear cultural pattern invested in Whiteness that is all too often overlooked or even denied by american Whites.

3. "Christian Revelation and Religious Pluralism." I also need to express my gratitude to Loring Abeyta, a Chicana scholar in international relations, for her critical reading of the first draft of this essay and for her helpful suggestions for improving it substantially.

in the direction toward transformation both of personal attitudes and social structures in the United States and, perforce, in the world. His emphasis on moving beyond euro-western christian triumphalism, with its emphasis on salvific exclusivity, is important to ensuring Christians some sense of genuine moral parity with so many other religious expressions in the world today. At the same time, he begins to offer some paradigmatic guidance to fundamentalist versions of so many religious expressions in the world today, including an increasingly large segment of amer-european Christianity. However affirming my response to Hough, I want to offer a critique of Hough's important article from an American Indian cultural perspective, a critique that may prove helpful to the continuing dialogue among Christians on the subject of pluralism.

Let me begin my critique by acknowledging that American Indian religious traditions have long suffered disavowal and outright abjection as a demonic evil by the colonial settler society.[4] Islam has experienced a similar response from some quarters in the United States regularly, and especially so since the September 11th tragedy. A recent example was reporter Bob Simon's October 2002 interview with Jerry Falwell on *60 Minutes*. Falwell referred to Muhammed as a "violent man" and a "terrorist."[5] Falwell is joined in these sentiments by other prominent religious figures in America such as Franklin Graham (Billy Graham's son), Pat Robertson, and leaders in the Southern Baptist Convention. An Associated Press report on the *60 Minutes* interview includes comments of Ibrahim Hooper, spokesman for the Council on American-Islamic Relations in Washington, D.C.: "Anybody is free to be a bigot.... What really concerns us is the lack of reaction by mainstream religious and political leaders, who say nothing when these bigots voice these attacks." Hooper noted that "Falwell and Robertson would speak at [the] Christian Coalition Convention in Washington alongside House Majority Whip Tom Delay."[6]

---

4. Anne McClintock, *Imperial Leather: Race, Gender and Sexuality in the Colonial Contest* (New York: Routledge, 1995), 71-74, gets at the texture of the word "abjection" that I intend here. See also Julia Kristeva, *The Powers of Horror: An Essay on Abjection*, trans. Leon S. Roudiez (New York: Columbia University Press, 1982). The colonized, American Indians in this case, are abject peoples. Ward Churchill discusses federal policies of "national sacrifice areas" as they relate to certain Indian reservations in *Struggle for the Land: Indigenous Resistance to Genocide, Ecocide and Expropriation in Contemporary North America* (Monroe, Me.: Common Courage Press, 1993)..

5. Associated Press, October 3, 2002, reported on the *60 Minutes* interview with Falwell. The item can be retrieved from Fox News online: "Falwell: 'Muhammad Was a Terrorist,'" http://www.foxnews.com/story/0,2933,64770,00.html. For further evidence of Falwell's views on Islam, see the Jerry Falwell Ministries Web site posting at http://www.falwell.com/historical_data.html.

6. "Falwell: 'Muhammad Was a Terrorist,'" http://www.foxnews.com/story/0,2933,64770,00.html.

One crucial difference in the experiences of north american indigenous communities and modern-day Islamic communities in the United States is that Indian traditions were denounced even more persistently in the long-term historical colonial context of dominance, having been formally disavowed as satanic by the first pilgrim and puritan colonizers to settle on Indian lands, by both their governments and their religious functionaries, then by the mainline denominations and their missionaries to Indian people throughout U.S. history, and by the U.S. government. Quite late in the process of conquest, Indian religious traditions were even disallowed by specific colonial legal interdiction in federal law, a condition that persisted even after the Indian citizenship law (1924) should supposedly have extended the protection of the Bill of Rights and the First Amendment to Indian peoples.[7] This was supposedly rectified in 1978 when the U.S. Congress passed the American Indian Religious Freedom Act. Curiously enough, Indian people have not yet been able to win a single court case predicated on this congressional resolution.[8] While differences in experience certainly don't diminish the respective suffering experienced by these "normatively divergent" communities, a closer historical examination reveals how the dominant narrative is able to manipulate the rhetoric of respecting cultural diversity, while simultaneously imposing institutional denunciations of, and structural punishments for, any kind of substantive "difference."

Long before contemporary new-age aficionados discovered American Indians as the hottest atavistic fetish commodity and turned us into the most exotic other on the periphery of euro-western "civilization," it was the announced policy of european and amer-european missionaries to wrestle Indian peoples away from their "savage" and "pagan" tribal ceremonial traditions (from Toribio de Benavente Motolinia in Mexico and John Eliot in New

---

7. As Secretary of the Interior, Henry M. Teller established the Indian Courts of Offenses in 1883 to force compliance with White codes of civilization in Indian communities. See a lengthy excerpt of his *Annual Report* in *Documents of United States Indian Policy*, ed. Francis Paul Prucha (Omaha: University of Nebraska Press, 1975), 160-62. The list of offenses included dances and ceremonies and even extended to the so-called give-away. In Teller's note prefacing an 1898 speech of Short Bull, James R. Walker reports: "The U.S. Indian agent had sent U.S. Indian police to arrest a member of Short Bull's band for giving away his property when his son, a young man, had died" (Walker, *Lakota Belief and Ritual*, ed. Raymond J DeMallie and Elaine A. Jahner [Omaha: University of Nebraska Press, 1980], 141).

8. See Vine Deloria, Jr., "Trouble in High Places: Erosion of American Indian Rights to Religious Freedom in the United States," in *The State of Native America: Genocide, Colonization and Resistance*, ed. M. Annette Jaimes (Cambridge, Mass.: South End Press, 1992), 267-90. Also, on American Indian sacred sites and religious freedom, now see Christopher McLeod, producer and director, *In the Light of Reverence: Protecting America's Sacred Lands*, a documentary film narrated by Peter Coyote and Tantoo Cardinal (San Francisco: Earth Island Institute, 2001).

England, to Pierre Jean DeSmet and Henry Benjamin Whipple) and to train them in euro-western cultural behavior patterns and the use of euro-christian religious language appropriate to their newly imposed faith.[9] Ignoring the reality that all human beings have distinct cultures and corollary modes of civilization that are equally distinct, colonizing Europeans, particularly their missionaries, invariably signified the colonized other as lacking in civilization and in dire need of conversion to a *christian* civilization. Thus, religious conversion to Christianity meant the concomitant imposition of european cultural modalities (meaning, "civilization") in terms of architectural styles, family structures, dress codes,[10] relationship to land (the disposition of real estate), interpersonal relationships (individualism), and the like.[11] Thus, the euro-colonizer conveniently dismissed Indian cultural modalities of civilization out of hand as inadequate, primitive, and savage.[12]

This abjection of Indian religious traditions and ceremonial rites is not merely a historical *factum*, a quaint part of our colonial past. Rather, this abjection becomes incorporated into the dominant discourse by subliminal mechanisms that the popular media and the average "person in the pews" fail to notice. As a result, the privileging of one particular worldview, which has actually occurred, is not resisted but rather is perpetuated by the exclusionary narrative. The process has suddenly become quite contemporary with the catholic pope's announcement in July 2002 of the beatification of two "martyrs" of its own violent history of colonial conquest in Mexico. The beatification of Juan Bautista and Jacinto de Los Angeles is as deeply sinful today on the part of the Roman Catholic Church as has been the long exclusivist history of Christianity (protestant and catholic) in general in this regard.

Both of the beatified persons were seventeenth-century Indian inform-

---

9. This is the substance of my 1993 book *Missionary Conquest*.

10. Never mind that Indian cross-dressing has today become a favorite pastime of many White new-agers and sports fans.

11. See Tinker, *Missionary Conquest*, for a general analysis of euro-western missionary confusion of gospel with culture and the imposition of the latter. For a compendium of late-nineteenth-century primary documents demonstrating the imposition of cultural change on Indian peoples, see Francis Prucha, ed., *Americanizing the American Indian: Writings by the "Friends of the Indian," 1880-1900* (Omaha: University of Nebraska Press, 1973).

12. This process continues today, of course, in the American insistence on Two-Thirds World countries falling into line politically and economically by engaging models of procedural democracy that fit our guidelines and instituting globalized economic models of privatization that further impoverish already desperate populations. And it should be noted forthwith that the globalization of capital certainly is a political and economic system with distinctly religious undertones. See Jonathan Crush's description of "development" as "redemptive power," in his "Introduction" to *Power of Development*, ed. Jonathan Crush (New York: Routledge, 1995), 10.

ers, serving the colonial spanish government as spirituality police helping the spanish to stamp out indigenous religious traditions, in this case in a Zapotec tribal community. The two were executed by their community—that is, martyred for the spanish cause—in September 1700. They had exposed their community's attempt to conduct a traditional ceremony in private by reporting the offense to their spanish lords (the Dominican priests in charge of their local parish and the local spanish military authorities). Spanish police, along with indigenous servants including the two now-beatifieds, proceeded to raid the ceremony and to shut it down, stealing (legally confiscating?) all religious paraphernalia in the process.[13] The local community became rightly angered at the betrayal and the theft of religious items, and rightly or wrongly they decided to execute the two traitors. Catholic propaganda reports that fellow villagers of the two "dragged them, hung them and finally decapitated them, cut open their sides to pull out their hearts and gave them to the dogs."[14] The propaganda does not report that these colonial catholic Christians responded with even greater violence by decapitating and quartering the principal administrators of community justice.

Thus, the beatification of these two is more precisely a beatification of a catholic history of violence and a validation of the triumphalist euro-christian history of forced conversions. It is the highest ecclesial disavowal of indigenous resistance and a self-justification of the violent imposition of missionary conquest. At the same time, it is a new kind of tool in the church's manipulation and pacification of indigenous peoples. Using the sop of beatifying two of their own, that is, two Indians, the beatification is an attempt to hold all latino indigenous people's feet to the fire with regard to their historic conversion and to combat the increasing movement back toward indigenous cultures and the ceremonial traditions that embody those cultures. It is, thus, a new denigration of the colonized other by the roman catholic colonizer and a new abjection of indigenous religious traditions.

---

13. The event, of course, must be placed into its proper colonial context of the extirpations being pursued by spanish/catholic officials throughout latin America at the time. See especially Kenneth Mills, *An Evil Lost to View? An Investigation of Post-Evangelisation Andean Religion in Mid-Colonial Peru* (Liverpool: Institute of Latin American Studies, University of Liverpool, 1994); and idem, *Idolatry and Its Enemies: Colonial Andean Religion and Extirpation, 1640-1750* (Princeton: Princeton University Press, 1997).

14. The Vatican news release came in at least two versions (not identical)—one in spanish and one in english: "Juan Bautista y Jacinto de los Ángeles (1660-1700)," http://www.vatican.va/news_services/liturgy/saints/ns_lit_doc_20020801_los-angeles_sp.html; and "Juan Bautista and Jacinto de los Ángeles (1660-1700)," http://www.vatican.va/news_services/liturgy/saints/ns_lit_doc_20020801_los-angeles_en.html. Locally in Denver, the news reports included this item: Jeannie Piper, "Pope Winds Up Three-Country Trip, Beatifying Two Indians," 9NEWS.com, August 1, 2002.

At the same time, it needs to be acknowledged that the Roman Catholic Church seems to think that it is honoring Indian people by beatifying these two traitors. What on earth can the Vatican be thinking—except that coopting people to participate in their own colonization will more firmly lodge them in their abjection as faithful (?) members of the colonial religious organization? In other words, the action seems entirely oriented toward legitimizing catholic participation in the genocidal history of conquest and colonization in the Americas. As such, it is absurdly and indulgently sinful—that is, sin in its usual, if broad, set of christian meanings.

Joseph C. Hough's Proposal

Hough, of course, is no party to such neotriumphalism. To the contrary, he traces some of the history of christian triumphal exclusivism in order to disavow those old forms of colonial conquest in our modern moment of magnanimity. Yet for very different reasons, it must be said that he still misses the heart of the matter, at least from my perspective. Social attitudes of tolerance and intercultural affirmation are not merely intellectual matters of intellectual history, or the history of euro-western theology. Nor are they merely religious affectations that can be dealt with by clarifying subtleties in contemporary theological positions—even while making some room for positions posited by other religious traditions. Rather, the concerns before us are so deeply complex that the complexity gets hidden even from the wordsmiths who are trying to carve out new solutions to implacable problems. This is, ultimately, not just about words and ideology, but is fundamentally more about praxis, human agency, and human choice. There are two particular complexities that remain safely cached behind the cultural bunkers of amer-european wordsmithing in Hough's essay:

First, we have not yet paid attention to the symbiosis between that particular strand of amer-european religiosity represented by its various strands of christian (from liberal to fundamentalist) belief and its other major strand of religiosity represented by the american exercise of political and economic power in its desire to globalize capital to its own benefit. Second, and this would be inherently much more difficult for Hough to recognize, Hough's essay continues to perpetuate an antipluralistic imposition of amer-european categories of cognition, for instance, insisting on some implied universality invested in his christian language of "God" and "redemption," which he seems to imply as equally functional in other religious (and, implicitly, cultural) traditions as in his own. It is this combination of unconscious propagation of euro-western categories of cognition and the hidden connection between amer-european Christianity and the globalization of capital that lead repeatedly back to american exceptionalism and the undying sense that Americans have of themselves as God's gift to the world. There is a curious paradox here. While I would expect Hough to want to distance himself from any expression of american exceptionalism, his comfortable use of language does just the opposite.

The collusion of christian churches with the center of politico-economic power is readily apparent historically in the validating and enforcing functions of the church and its missionaries with respect to its involvement in the euro-western colonial invasion and conquest—along with its long and consistent history of lies, theft, murder, and general violence. Hough names a piece of the euro-christian history of violence, but he essentially stops with the anti-muslim crusades of medieval Europe and the anti-jewish persecutions, especially during the european Inquisition (under the leadership of Tomás de Torquemada). But this overlooks the viciousness of the extirpations in the Americas pursued by spanish Catholics and avoids completely the religious (christian) foundations of north american violence perpetrated against Native peoples for the sake of securing the land base that made possible the creation and continued maintenance of the United States. Hough's strong language calling for christian repentance must be extended and broadened considerably if it is to effect real change in north America today.

In anglophone christian north America,[15] for instance, this history begins with the Pilgrims pillaging, a week before their arrival at Plymouth, an Indian village at the easternmost tip of Cape Cod—an incident of grand larceny that William Bradford memorialized in his *Plymouth Plantation* as "God's good providence."[16] The enduring american myth, which continues to this day, is that these Pilgrims were fleeing religious persecution (not in England, but in Holland?) rather than engaging in early economic venture capitalism. The north american history continues with the religio-political doctrine of Manifest Destiny, which Americans then extended into latin America with the subterfuge of the Monroe Doctrine early in the nineteenth century and the invasion of missionaries into the colonized southern hemisphere in the later nineteenth century until the present. The emerging literature on the collusion between american christian missionaries and the Rockefeller industrial empire's penetration of the Third World is a more contemporary example of

---

15. The spanish, of course, were already long ensconced in the north american southwest.

16. Neal Salisbury, *Manitou and Providence: Indians, Europeans, and the Making of New England, 1500-1643* (New York: Oxford University Press, 1982), 113; and Dwight B. Heath, *Mourt's Relation: A Journal of the Pilgrims at Plymouth* (New York: Applewood Books, 1963), 26, 37, and 19-37 passim.

the explicit collusion of church with the powerful forces of the political and economic center.[17]

And again the evidence demonstrating the ease with which the Central Intelligence Agency (CIA) recruited american missionaries in the Third World is not merely an indictment of particular individuals.[18] Rather, it is part of a festering systemic whole in which the christian individual is, and christian institutions are, so enmeshed that collusion all too often seems the most christian course of action—not to say the patriotic and right thing to do. Former CIA agent John Stockwell offered this extraordinary insight in a 1989 speech at the University of Colorado:

> The moral in this thing . . . is that we so obviously carefully teach ourselves in our television shows and everywhere that we're the good guys, and that it's the Aryan Gestapo maniacs, that it's the Slavic KGB monsters who are committing the real evils. Now the vogue is sadistic Vietnamese colonels in the Rambo and Missing in Action films that do hideous things to other people. And it's not. . . . It's red-blooded, American, sane, sober decent people who do hideous things to other people if their society rationalizes that it's the proper thing to do, as we have done. Dan Mitrione [CIA field agent who was assassinated] was not a raving psychopath. He was a devout Catholic, a devoted family man, a father of four, and he had devoted his life to torturing people he knew were not guilty of anything because his society had said that there was something so noble about the fight against communism that it was a noble thing for him to do. When he was exposed and killed for his activities, he was brought back to the United States and honored with a hero's burial.[19]

---

17. Gerard Colby, with Charlotte Dennett, *Thy Will Be Done: The Conquest of the Amazon: Nelson Rockefeller and Evangelism in the Age of Oil* (New York: HarperCollins, 1995). See also Marcos Cueto, ed., *Missionaries of Science: The Rockefeller Foundation and Latin America* (Bloomington: University of Indiana Press, 1994). Of course, one should pay attention to the growing literature on the Wycliffe Bible Translators and particularly their secularized persona, the Summer Institute of Linguistics (SIL), which has been the formal arm of Wycliffe for engagement with governmental agencies (both in the United States and in the Two-Thirds World). The SIL and its founder, Cameron Townsend, are an important focus of Colby and Dennett; see also David Stoll, *Fishers of Men or Founders of Empire? The Wycliffe Bible Translators in Latin America* (London: Zed Press, 1982).

18. Colby and Dennett, *Thy Will Be Done*, 564f., 743-59.

19. From John Stockwell, "Teaching Torture: Our Secret Government and Its Covert Agenda," *The Mustard Seed* (1989: a local newsletter produced by the Denver Justice and Peace Committee). For a more accessible description of Dan Mitrione's strong commitment to his church and the inability of that faith connection to impede his CIA work of torture of political prisoners in Uruguay, see A. J. Langguth, *Hidden Terrors* (New York: Pantheon Books, 1978). For a fuller description of the sort of torture engaged in by Mitrione and others on behalf of the United States, read any of the several books by Stockwell or the speeches that are still cir-

This means that Hough's confessive apologetic and argument for a new christian theology, in the final analysis, rings a bit hollow and needs to be drastically revised to speak to the history of christian (euro-western, amer-european) colonialism and violence—beginning with the violence perpetrated on our own continent—if it is to be really helpful either to christian people (meaning euro-Christians) or to those whose commitments lie in faith traditions outside the colonial center of power vested in this postmodern moment of globalized capital with its new and ever more insidious metanarrative structures and exercise of power.[20]

In spite of the new theologies embracing a more pluralistic viewpoint, the mainline churches are still peopled by, and especially funded by, those same captains of industry (from high tech to banking) who are the engineers of colonial globalization, and they use their religious understanding still today to validate and legitimize their economic plundering, even if the thought process has become subliminal over the generations. All too often, denominations whose theologies press them toward identification with the struggles of the poor and oppressed find themselves morally and theologically immobilized by their dependence on sustained funding from those elite denominational members who need the church to identify with and validate their own commitments to growth, development, the maximization of corporate profits, and the globalization of capital as sources of world redemption.

Hough graciously concedes that "God" is working in other religious traditions, in ways we "do not yet even know," to "redeem" the world. Yet if "God is working . . . to redeem the world" then what exactly will this new christian theology do to redeem the world from the vicious poverty created by globalized capital and the politico-economic policies imposed on the world by U.S. power? What will this new theology do to redeem those communities scarred by the violence of massacres—at Mystic (1637); at Sand Creek (1864); at Wounded Knee (1890)? Or for that matter in Rwanda or Bosnia (in the 1990s)?[21] Will

---

culating on the Internet. It should be noted that in response to Mitrione's death the Vatican, "in an unsigned article on the front page of *L'Osservatore Romano*, condemned crimes committed in the name of fanatical ideologies" (Langguth, *Hidden Terrors*, 26). See also Margaret Atwood's poem, "Footnote to the Amnesty Report on Torture," in *Two Headed Poems* (New York: Oxford University Press, 1978).

20. Needless to say, all those postmodernists who would announce the demise of metanarrative need to read the Patriotism Act and listen to the rhetoric of the Bush administration.

21. It should be noted here that the genocide in Rwanda had clear and distinct roots in euro-christian colonial conquest. The so-called rwandan tribes, Hutu and Tutsi, were, after all, colonial inventions of Flemish colonial administration, which also created the imbalance of privileging and dis-privileging. For some of the colonial history, see Gerard Prunier, *The Rwanda Crisis: History of a Genocide* (New York: Columbia University Press, 1995).

this new theology actually participate in redeeming the world, or will it merely continue the euro-christian tradition of individualism, limiting its vision of redemption to the personal salvation of individuals? In the meantime, what happens to those whose dreams of a liberated life are dashed by six-dollar-a-day piece work in Two-Thirds World factories supplying Wal-Mart, Penney's, Liz Claiborne, GM, and IBM with cheap electronic and mechanical parts and cheap finished clothing to satisfy the consumptive habit of northern "saved" Christians? Hough is unclear how God is working to redeem the world and equally unclear whether God will accomplish this in spite of the consumptive habits of God's faithful among amer-european and european Christians of the north. His new theology fails to speak of its role in any redeeming work. This theology seems to be a mere rewording of euro-western hegemony in a way that makes some new room for the other, as long as the other can be understood and described in euro-western terms.

The second concern, the concern for the use of language and the categories we summon so easily in our discourse and so effortlessly apply as universal descriptors of the world, might begin by asking the prior question: What exactly does it mean to say God is redeeming the world? To begin with, "God" is a euro-western quotient, a cultural category of cognition with built-in parameters that may not work for other peoples—and certainly it does not work well for non-theist American Indians whose notion of the Sacred is extraordinarily different. Hence, to say that "God" is working in other religious traditions, in ways we may not know, to "redeem" the world is to presume that whatever other religious traditions have to say, this euro-christian, anthropomorphic "God" figure is still functioning behind the scenes ("to redeem the world," and so on). Thus, the colonial "God" still reigns supreme—as does, one suspects, the colonial or neo-colonial hegemonist.

This objection aside, however, *how* will God, this anthropomorphized and personalized (christian) actor, "redeem" the world? It seems as if Hough has invested not only "God" but the concept of "redemption" with unavoidable euro-christian freight that already biases the answer to his question. Indeed, redemption is a quintessentially euro-christian concept that has no logical place in American Indian cultural systems without some engagement in mental gymnastics to make it fit somehow—as if it were a universal category that God gave to euro-Christians and withheld from others and which we must now make fit into our world. If we were to concede, just for the moment, that we might possibly find some place for the concept in American Indian cultures, then we Indian peoples would also have to argue for a meaning of redemption that does not privilege human beings in the redemption process at all. In fact, if our perception of the world is correct, the "redemption" wrought by that all-encompassing and generative energy we (Osages) would call *wako^{n}da* may work itself out in ways that are quite inimical to the hopes of Amer-europeans. Many Native peoples in the Americas have clear traditional insights that the world we inhabit is not the only "world" that has happened or may yet happen in this place.

As the inhabitants of each successive world violated the principles of harmony and balance in irreparable ways, that world came to an end and gave birth to a new world. Thus, American Indian traditionalists have less of a fear for this earth than White liberal environmentalists who fear the earth's destruction. Yes, the earth may become uninhabitable for human life—and much other life. But our Grandmother will survive just fine without us and will eventually give birth to a new world of life—with or without some humanoid replacement. So what if "God's redeeming" of the world results in removing human beings from the world? That, I suppose, is what most scares our White relatives, who so privilege human beings in their religious (and scientific) philosophies that the rest of the world is reduced to a mere resource to be used to enhance human comfort. A real pluralism must begin to open its ears to a wholly other way of seeing the world—a way of seeing the world that is wholly other than the market economy spirituality of globalized capital and commodified religion that sees the great diversity of life in the world as consisting merely of resources to be used rather than as relatives to be respected and cared for.[22]

A Brand New Evangelism: Be Jesus. Don't Preach Jesus.

Finally, I want to suggest another agenda—related to the one Hough details for us—that might point to a deeper, more intense healing of communities of northern (euro-western) Christians and lead to a more significant transformation and healing of our world and our relationship to it. Like Hough, I want to encourage euro-western Christians to avoid all tendencies toward christian exclusivism or christian uniqueness as a "distortion of Christianity" (Hough's language),[23] and I want to add my voice to his and others' insisting that the

---

22. There are American Indian spiritual elders from a variety of different Indian nations who today foresee the end of this world as we know it—at least, the end of human occupancy of the world. The signs they point to are precisely the increasing lack of mutual respect for one another in the world among the most public global players and the lack of respect that american and european consumption habits allow human beings to show for the rest of the world—that is, the growing evidence of irreversible environmental devastation. The greed of an individualist, competitive, consumptive social whole in north America will continue only at a price.

23. And like Hough, I too want to confront this tendency as it has been recently voiced by the Vatican in "*Dominus Iesus*: On the Unicity and Salvific Universality of Jesus Christ and the Church," a document released by the Vatican Congregation for the Doctrine of the Faith, August 6, 2000.

contemporary christian tradition "must be exposed to serious theological and moral questioning."[24] Ultimately, however, I am calling for a complete rearrangement of euro-western christian priorities and a radically new reinterpretation of both gospel and church, a reimagining of a distinctly postcolonial (that is, anticolonial) sort. I do think that euro-christian theologians such as Hough, Diana Eck, John Hick, John Cobb, and Paul Knitter are headed in the right direction, but I want to push them even further than they have yet gone (even Cobb). The question is how to achieve a more balanced pluralistic world of genuine mutual respect.

While Hough wants to distinguish "faith" and "religion" (a clearly euro-christian move since neither category applies to any American Indian cultural equivalent),[25] both are rooted in (euro-) theological and philosophical discourse, both expressed as constructions of language. The suggestion I want to pursue here is that, in some sense, language be dis-privileged in favor of the action of living a consistent and coherent life rooted deeply in a communal spiritual identity.[26] The problem with language—and to wit with creating a new theology, even a new christian theology of pluralism—is that amereuropean language usage is so bound to its own historical usage, inherently and subconsciously, that it does not seem possible to avoid some expression of colonial hegemony. Thus, a slight shift in theological articulation (however radical it may seem at the moment) is insufficient for addressing contemporary global complexities that include empiric expressions of american hegemony and the globalization of an economic system that continues to create american wealth on the backs of the impoverished in the Two-Thirds World.

My argument is that it is time for amer-european Christians to declare a

---

24. Hough, "Christian Revelation and Religious Pluralism," 8.

25. Osage, like virtually all indigenous languages, lacks any word for "religion" as a category in the euro-western sense. See my encyclopedia entry, "Religion," in *The Encyclopedia of the American Indian*, ed. Frederick E. Hoxie (Boston: Houghton Mifflin, 1996), 537-41. Likewise, the euro-western christian/biblical language of "faith" is something that must be imposed on the Indian context.

26. This is in no way to suggest the facile appropriateness of every shirtsleeve liberal impulsive action—in other words, the Christian do-gooders who act without thinking. Loring Abeyta's gentle objection to my argument raised the following question: "Isn't some degree of reflection and exploring the true history of the situation required? Don't we learn better skills for listening by engaging in some more liberating form of language?" My point is that there are cultures other than the amer-european dominant culture of north America in which doing and living a consistent and coherent value system creatively contributes to a balanced social whole. Amer-european culture is so rooted in discursive thinking that purity of political or theological construct becomes an impediment to building balanced and coherent social wholes. My impetus here is my own cultural attachment to an American Indian value system. For a very fine radical irish catholic take on "christian action," see Carmelite scholar Noel-Dermot O'Donoghue's essay "The Things That Are Caesar's," *The Furrow* 30 (1979): 333-52.

moratorium on twentieth-century style evangelism.[27] To put it bluntly: just say no to preaching Jesus. Instead, amer-european Christians should focus on living the claim that their gospel makes on themselves. That is, Christians who take the gospel seriously should become Jesus to the world. Stop worrying about purity of doctrine—especially other peoples' purity of doctrine—or newness of theology and just concentrate on living the purity of the gospel in relationship with other people. If Jesus is important, then Jesus must first of all be important in how the adherent, the Christian, lives her or his life in relationship with others. If one is justified by the love of God in Christ Jesus, then act it. Be this justifying love to others. Be Jesus quietly and without pontificating, because it is the latter that consistently causes problems of human hegemony.

Any amer-european theological position that continues to think of Jesus in terms of a commodity that the Amer-european has and that unbelievers in the rest of the world need will continue to play the role of global colonizer exporting a product designed to replace goods and services that the colonized already have provided for themselves. This means that such theologies will continue to pursue implicit, if not explicit, othering of those whose relationship with the Sacred is expressed in ways that are quite different from amer-european materialists. In the interests of genuine world peace and a more egalitarian world society, it is time for Euro-christians to give up their modernity-laden notions of evangelism and proclaiming of the gospel. Finally, after some two thousand years, it is time for Christians to follow Jesus—that is, to be Jesus to the world. It is not a matter of finding the correct language. It is a matter of acting and doing a different and more legitimate kind of evangelism. After all, what would Jesus do?

Legitimate evangelization today will require an ongoing critical analysis of power structures in the world. Jesus calls on his followers to be wise as serpents. Being Jesus, then, requires wisdom, not rationalization. Real evangelization will always come with the great cost and risk of critical self-reflection. Repentance, as a euro-christian category of transformation, is much more important for the church, for amer-european Christians, than for those outside of the church for whom the church usually prescribes it—just as it was as much for Jesus as for the samaritan woman (Matthew 15:21-28). Being Jesus means repentance. Real evangelization means an active struggle to facilitate social, economic, and political transformation for justice, peace, and the integrity of creation.

---

27. The implicit point here is that the Reformation traditions have no notion of evangelism in the twentieth-century sense. For better or for worse, Martin Luther, John Calvin, and the others show a total lack of interest in processes of conversion.

Finally, I would add, being Jesus means the church must sacrifice any arrogant ambition of being Herod or Pilate or Caesar or even archbishop. The church (any denomination) is so susceptible to the temptations offered Jesus by the tempter. The power and privilege inherently invested in Whiteness (for the amer-european Christian) always seem to incarnate themselves in a sense of being God's authoritative judging and ruling Christ to the world rather than the caring and loving Jesus who confronts and resists power. Hence, our theologies always tend toward the individually prescriptive rather than the systemically responsive. The powerful find their friends among the powerful, the rich among the rich, the privileged among the privileged. As the powerful continue their exploitation of the weaker today, the churches must decide where they will stand. Will american Christians continue to act both implicitly and explicitly as religious validation for existing power structures, or will they join their voices with Jesus, calling for a real evangelization that recognizes the *basileia* (kingdom, queendom, reign, realm) of God that Jesus proclaimed as near or in your midst?[28] The well-being of the world, the lives of people around the globe, hang in the balance.

---

28. My argument for a radically different interpretation of the *basileia* appears in a couple of essays: George E. Tinker, "Spirituality, Native American Personhood, Sovereignty and Solidarity," in idem, *Spirituality of the Third World: A Cry for Life*. Papers and Reflections from the Third General Assembly of the Ecumenical Association of Third World Theologians, January 1992, Nairobi, Kenya, ed. K. C. Abraham and Bernadette Mbuy-Beya (Maryknoll, N.Y.: Orbis Books, 1994), 119-32; "A Native American Reading of the Bible" in *New Interpreter's Bible*, ed. Leander E. Keck et al. (Nashville: Abingdon Press, 1994), 174-80.

In direct opposition to virtually all euro-western exegetical interpretation of the *basileia*, my American Indian reading of the text treats the *basileia* as a spatial designation and not merely some temporal signifier for a future event that can be experienced proleptically by the christian faithful. Thus the question (contra Johannes Weiss) is *where* is the *basileia*? and not, *when* will it come? The argument I have made at greater length in other venues, is that the *basileia* is here "in our midst" now. In brief, look around yourself. There is the kingdom: in your neighbor, the person on the street, in the squirrel in the park, the buffalo at the zoo, the pigeons fouling the window ledges at Union Theological Seminary, the eagles flying free above my reservation land, the trees in Central Park, and the hills and mountains of Colorado. Christians need to expand their notion of pluralism to include an understanding of the Native American sense of the interrelationship of all creation. See Vine Deloria's analysis of this concept of interrelationship of the created realm in "Kinship with the World," in *Spirit and Reason: The Vine Deloria, Jr., Reader*, ed. Barbara Deloria et al. (Golden, Colo.: Fulcrum, 1999), 223-29.

Chapter 6

American Indian Liberation
Paddling a Canoe Upstream

Some years ago, I made a trip to the site of the 1864 Sand Creek Massacre to help a group of Indians from the Denver metropolitan area. This Indian group, in conversation with Cheyenne people, had agreed to bury the ancestral remains of two Natives who were said to have died in that unprovoked surprise attack. Around midnight, several hours before the ceremony at dawn, two of us walked out from the cottonwoods at the old village site in the hollow at the bend of the creek bed and ventured into the prairie a couple of hundred yards. As we stood under the light of the moon, we were quietly stunned by the sounds of a large and busy village coming from the cottonwoods. In the middle of this semi-arid Colorado ranchland, miles from the nearest town and more than a mile from the closest lone ranch house, we distinctly heard children playing, dogs barking, neighing horses, men singing around a drum, people calling to one another. As we stood still and took it in, I remembered an experience on an earlier visit a couple of years prior.

On that earlier occasion, four of us had trekked to the site for a sunrise prayer ceremony to commemorate the murderous event and to remember those who died there. The temperature was thirty degrees below freezing and there was a fresh four-inch coat of snow on the ground, conditions similar to those reported for the day of the Rev. (Col.) Chivington's preemptive attack on the unsuspecting Cheyenne and Arapaho families who were just beginning to stir for the day.[1] Ours was the only car in the parking area in the early dawn

---

1. It should be clearly noted that the U.S. attack on Iraq in 2003 was certainly not the first time the United States has engaged in preemptive war making. American Indians know this kind of immoral violence all too well. The best book on the Sand Creek Massacre, as just one example of american violence, is still Stan Hoig's *The Sand Creek Massacre* (Norman: University of Oklahoma Press, 1961). For a fuller picture of the persistence of colonial violence in the Americas, see Ward Churchill, *A Little Matter of Genocide: Holocaust and Denial in the Americas, 1492 to the Present* (San Francisco: City Lights Press, 1997); or David E. Stannard, *American Holocaust: Columbus and the Conquest of the New World* (New York: Oxford University Press, 1992). Churchill also has written an outstanding analysis of the failures of con-

darkness and the only tracks in the new snow as we began to walk through the icy cold. By the time the sun had begun to rise above the horizon, we had walked beyond the cottonwoods out into the expanse of the prairie and had filled a *non-ni-on-ba* (a prayer pipe) and sung a ceremonial song to the pipe to ask for its help. Then as we each in turn took the pipe to speak our prayers, I was surprised to see an Indian woman about sixty yards to the south, praying with her face to the sunrise. She was dressed in a black skirt or dress, wrapped in a red shawl, and had long black hair braided down her back. I watched her while we prayed until finally, as we smoked the pipe to finish our prayers, I looked up again and noticed that she was gone just as suddenly as she had appeared.

It took me nine years before I ventured to talk about that woman. I sat over coffee with Leonard Quiver, the person with whose pipe we had prayed that morning. Wanting to confirm what I had seen, I asked him about it. A rational, reasonable man not prone to exaggeration, he replied, "Yeah, I saw her." And then he went on to corroborate exactly what I had seen. "Yeah," he chuckled, "I went over and looked for footprints in the snow, just like you. No footprints; no other cars; no tire tracks. We were alone."

These two stories recall experiences, personal and communal, that have helped to shape my own understanding of the world. As is the case in other liberation theologies, but in a significantly different sense, any American Indian articulation of a theology will necessarily be constructed on the foundation of experience. Thus, I want to use these two narratives as the starting point for my own expression of an American Indian liberation theology—not simply because they happen to have been my personal experiences but rather because they capture something that runs deep in the experience of Indian communities—both in terms of our awareness of our own history as recipients of injustice and violence and the experience of the sacred. As Indian liberation must, the stories combine spiritual experience and political sensibilities.

The classic liberation theologies have always been explicitly political. The

---

temporary scholarly literature (since Hoig) about Sand Creek; see his "It Did Happen Here: Sand Creek, Scholarship and the American Character," in *Fantasies of the Master Race: Literature, Cinema and the Colonization of American Indians*, 2nd rev. ed. (San Francisco: City Lights Books, 1998), 19-26, where he argues that Hoig remains the most balanced and objective treatment of the travesty. In *A Little Matter of Genocide*, Churchill uses a Chivington quote (from instructions the evening before the attack, urging his men to kill Indian babies) as the title of an important chapter that traces the more general history of euro-western and explicitly amereuropean violence in north America: "Nits Make Lice: The Extermination of North American Indians, 1492-1992," 129-288. It should also be remembered that one of Chivington's company commanders, Silas Soule, when he found out the night before exactly what Chivington's vicious strategy was, refused to join in the attack and held his entire company back. For his demonstration of conscience, Soule was assassinated by some of Chivington's men in downtown Denver some months later.

liberation of oppressed and poor people must struggle with the role that political systems play in maintaining oppression. So too, American Indian perspectives on liberation must be nothing short of explicitly political. American Indians are the poorest of the poor in north America, consistently oppressed and suppressed politically, socially, psychologically, economically—with ramifications that manifest themselves in our physical and mental health and in our spiritual well-being as well.

Yet, an American Indian liberation theology must necessarily have a different starting point than many of these other liberation theologies. Both the cultural particularities of American Indian communities (and indeed those of any indigenous community) and the particularities of Indian experiences of colonization and conquest mandate a different approach. Indeed, American Indians represent cultures and communities that predate by thousands of generations the euro-western invasion of the Americas. We were people who knew the spiritual side of all life, who had firm experiential connections with the Creator, who had well-developed ceremonies to help us maintain harmony and balance in the life of our communities and the world around us. We were communities of peace, most of whom did not even have words for war.[2] Thus any Indian liberation theology must take these ceremonies and spiritual traditions seriously. It must begin with the specifics of Indian cultures and cultural values.

The "classic" liberation theologies read in north America almost always

---

2. I realize this seems preposterous to those whose knowledge of Indian history has been finely honed by Hollywood extravaganzas. Yet it is an important aspect of American Indian liberation that we Indians liberate ourselves from the self-serving colonizer histories of Indians, which are filled with fabricated myths and lies that seem solely intended to justify the conquest and validate the amer-european occupation of the north american land base. See M. Annette Jaimes and Theresa Halsey, "American Indian Women: At the Center of Indigenous Resistance in North America," in *The State of Native America: Genocide, Colonization and Resistance*, ed. M. Annette Jaimes (Boston: South End Press, 1992), 311-44; and also in the same volume, Tom Holm, "Patriots and Pawns: State Use of American Indians in the Military and the Process of Nativization in the Untied States," 345-70. See also Holm's more extensive analysis of Indian war modalities in *Strong Hearts, Wounded Souls: Native American Veterans for the Vietnam War* (Austin: University of Texas Press, 1996). I am currently working on a chapter that will be titled "War and Peace in Native North America," in which I will unpack some of the evidence that refutes the Hollywood—and even professional historian—portrayal.

On the use of lies and illegalities to secure the amer-european theft of lands, see Ward Churchill, *Struggle for the Land: Indigenous Resistance to Genocide, Ecocide and Expropriation in Contemporary North America* (Monroe, Me.: Common Courage Press, 1993). On the american fabrication of legal pretexts (called "Federal Indian Law"), see David Wilkins, *American Indian Sovereignty and the U.S. Supreme Court: The Masking of Justice* (Austin: University of Texas Press, 1997); and Robert Williams, *The American Indian in Western Legal Thought: The Discourses of Conquest* (New York: Oxford University Press, 1990).

begin with a radical interpretation of Jesus and the gospel. To be absolutely fair, they actually begin with the people—that is, with the "experience" of the poor and oppressed—and then move decidedly toward a people's liberating interpretation of the gospel.

For American Indians, on the contrary, the radical interpretation of Jesus would be an unproductive and even counterproductive starting point for a liberation theology because the first proclamation of Jesus among any Indian community came as the beginning of a colonial conquest that included the total displacing of centuries-old religious traditions and the replacing of those traditions with the imposition of a one-size-fits-all euro-western Jesus. And even the occasional contemporary move to correct Jesus' ethnicity historically to some shade of mediterranean brown helps little to obviate our historical experience of the way the missionary preaching about Jesus was used to destroy our cultures and legitimate the theft of our property.[3] Thus today, even embracing a radical Jesus and a radical interpretation of the gospel means validating to some degree the evil perpetrated against our ancestors by those who first brought Jesus to us and engaged in the colonization and conquest of our peoples and our lands. Moreover, to do so would also necessarily mean a continued disaffirmation of ourselves and the ancient traditional spiritual traditions given to us by the sacred power that Christians call "God."

If Jesus is not to be our starting point, then we must look for another—a more unconventional and much more complex starting point for a Native liberation theology. Let me describe four aspects of the beginnings of an American Indian liberation theology, which must build upon the tensions between Indian peoples and missionary Christianity, on the peculiarities of israelite history with regard to those tensions, on the cultural abrasiveness of colonially imposed categories of cognition that derive from missionizing evangelism (past and present), and on the renaissance of Indian traditional culture and ceremonial life as a source of revivification and uniquely Indian source of liberation.

TENSIONS WITH CHRISTIANITY

The tensions between Christianity and Indian peoples (including christian Indians) derive first of all from notions of amer-european christian triumphalism, christian uniqueness, the proclaimed necessity of salvation according to the european missionary message, and the concomitant sense of euro-western and amer-european superiority.

---

3. See George E. Tinker, *Missionary Conquest: The Gospel and Native American Genocide* (Minneapolis: Fortress Press, 1993).

From the healthy perspective of an Indian, an Indian liberation theology must recognize the source of our bondage and thereby acknowledge a long and tension-filled relationship with Christianity as the religion of our colonizer and with its missionaries imposing themselves on our peoples. Today, all Indian people have been touched in some way by these missionary processes. Many have converted; some out of a genuine desire to be like our White relatives; others out of some perceived necessity to placate the colonizer. For well over a hundred years there have been firmly established missionary outposts in every Indian reservation community, usually providing a variety of denominational choices.[4] What must be acknowledged, however, is that the first euro-western missionary to set up shop on any reservation immediately functioned to divide the community against itself. For the first time, each person was forced to make a choice between participating in the life of the community (that is, particularly in the ceremonial and religious life of the community) and the newly introduced missionary church with its proclamation of salvation in Jesus alone. While this may have been a useful political function in terms of the conquest, it had devastating social consequences for which Indian people are still paying. Before long, there were other choices that could be made for a variety of denominational mission churches. This scenario works in a heavily individuated culture but was and is wholly destructive to the communitarian cultures of Native America. It becomes a cultural conquest, converting our communities to euro-western individualism and ripping our community structures asunder. Thus, it must be explicitly said that in the missionary mandate, the absolute necessity for confessing Jesus as a means for accessing (individual) salvation meant the unequivocal disavowal of the beliefs, experiences, ceremonies, community connectivity, and religious traditions of one's own culture. In this regard, it should be remembered that there is no Indian religion (in the euro-western sense of the word) but that the spiritual traditions of any Indian community are invariably deeply embedded in the whole of the culture and the whole of the day-to-day life of the community.

At the same time, it should be noted that the crucial issue is not Jesus per se. While many traditional spiritual leaders on our reservations today are quick to affirm Jesus as a deeply spiritual person historically—one with continuing relevance and even continuing spiritual presence in our world (though they would not use language of "resurrected one" and, even less, "lord")—they are

---

4. The government-missionary alliance was established at the beginning of the U.S. republic in the form of federal funding allocated as a "Civilization Fund" for mission schools in the annual "Trade and Intercourse Acts." The alliance became more pronounced after 1869 when the "Peace Policy" initiated by the administration of President Grant allocated control of reservation Indian agencies among the various mainline denominations. See chapter 5 in Tinker, *Missionary Conquest.*

also apt to denounce the historical and contemporary function of the churches as key participants in the devastation of their own communities. The problem is not Jesus but, rather, the particularity of the missionary preaching of Jesus. To this extent, missionaries worked through the institutional structures that promoted a singular brand of Christianity, and were thus always a part of the genocide of Indian peoples in one way or another. Whether Indian people find liberation through accepting and adapting some version of Christianity or rejecting it outright, the issues of religious conquest and religious colonialism must be acknowledged.

Exchanging Histories: Canaanites, Cowboys, and Indians[5]

In constructing any "christian" liberation theology for American Indians, one must reconcile the claims that two conflicting histories make on Indian peoples' lives. One of the curious oddities of euro-Christianity relates to its canonical inclusion of the hebrew Bible, which results in necessarily forcing all adherents to embrace a history that is not the natural or actual history of the persons or peoples who become adherents—unless they are "Jews for Jesus." That is, all converts and their succeeding generations are expected to embrace the history of one small, relatively insignificant asian country, ancient Israel (and then Judea), as their own history, investing their lives with meaning and identity rooted in the historical experiences of a people distant from their own both in terms of culture and time. This business of appropriating a foreign history as one's own means, in some regard (more for some than for others), the denial of one's own proper history. For American Indians, it means, for instance, the denial of important aspects of our own history in order to affirm not only israelite history but ultimately also euro-christian history, including amer-euro-christian history. This is particularly evident, for instance, in any intellectual understanding of the history of christian doctrine, which is inevitably a european history—something to which we will return.

More significantly, for American Indians, affirming israelite history means ultimately affirming precisely the historical narrative that has been used consistently by our euro-western colonizers to validate their theft of our property and murder of our ancestors. As Robert Warrior has demonstrated, the seventeenth-century puritan use of the Exodus narrative of Israel's escape from slavery and conquest of the land of Canaan empowered their colonial invasion of Indian lands and justified in their minds the murder of Indian peo-

---

5. This heading is borrowed from Robert Warrior's 1989 essay "Canaanites, Cowboys, and Indians: Deliverance, Conquest, and Liberation Theology Today," *Christianity and Crisis* 49, no. 12 (1989): 261-65.

ple in New England. Eventually, it is the same narrative that gives birth to the religio-political doctrine of Manifest Destiny (and eventually the absurdity of the Monroe Doctrine) and all contemporary religious and political forms of american exceptionalism. As a narrative about escape from slavery, it has proven a powerful liberating story for african Americans. Yet for American Indians, Warrior reminds us forcefully, the conquest narrative is one in which we always discover ourselves to be the Canaanites, the conquered, and never the Israelites.[6]

The result of this process is self-disavowal and even subtle forms of self-hatred on the part of American Indian peoples who are converted. It must lead the perceptive and sensitive observer to wonder whether any appropriation of the euro-christian gospel can be liberative for American Indians. It is curious that Christians are led logically to believe that "God," until the birth of Jesus, cared only for one small people on the face of the earth, leaving all others to ignorance, "sin," idolatry, self-destruction, and eternal damnation. For Indian peoples, the message only becomes more difficult because it is conveyed through the clear inference that "God's" love (in the Jesus event) was denied Indian peoples until God, in God's graciousness, sent White people to kill us, lie to us, steal our land, and proclaim the saving gospel to us.

Imposition of the Colonizer's Categories of Cognition

Any Indian notion of liberation must attempt to break away from the way language is used so easily and comfortably by our colonizer. Euro-western categories are infused throughout the colonizer's language, from religious and theological categories to political ones to the simplest categories of everyday life—from individualism to images of the Sacred Other that the colonizer calls "God" with a capital G and then invests with particular anthropomorphic characteristics.

The problem is that missionary and government boarding schools have

---

6. Robert Warrior, "Canaanites, Cowboys, and Indians." Warrior's essay has been reprinted at least twice: in *Voices from the Margins: Interpreting the Bible in the Third World*, ed. R. S. Sujirtharajah (Maryknoll, N.Y.: Orbis Books, 1989), 287-95; and in *Native and Christian: Indigenous Voices on Religious Identity in the United States and Canada*, ed. James Treat (New York: Routledge, 1996), 93-100. One should note Norman K. Gottwald's groundbreaking work in his *Tribes of Yahweh: A Sociology of the Religion of Liberated Israel, 1250-1050 B.C.E.* (Maryknoll, N.Y.: Orbis Books, 1979), in which he argues for a "peasant revolt" model—as opposed to the traditional (nineteenth-century) model—of conquest underlying the material in the books of Exodus and Judges. Yet, for American Indians, the narrative problems remain. Whatever the actual occurrence might have been, it is the historical uses of the conquest narrative that have fueled euro-western colonial projects and have served to justify their conquests—politically, militarily, religiously, theologically, morally, and even legally.

thoroughly inculcated colonial thinking in our minds over generations making it more and more difficult for us to make the break. Even my own essay is only a beginning in this regard. I realize that it, too, is rooted too deeply in those euro-western cognitional categories.

The cover art on a recent book of which I was a coauthor can serve as a prime example of imposed categories of thought. The cover is a reproduction of a famous American Indian painting done by Dick West many years prior, depicting Jesus as an Indian man praying in the garden of Gethsemane.[7] At a recent conference a Mohawk critic, Chris Jocks, pointedly noticed that the image, even as it clearly depicts Jesus as an Indian, is still euro-western. Jesus is kneeling in prayer with his hands reverently folded just like every other euro-western depiction of Jesus in Gethsemane, a fine summoning of pious emotion for all euro-western peoples but a posture of prayer that is just as decidedly *not* Indian, even as it plays on Indian themes and tries to lend a sense of cultural comfort to Indian converts.[8] Kneeling and folding hands are not Indian postures of prayer, any more than bowing the head. So when the missionary says, "Let us bow our heads and pray," Indians have to wonder what the biblical injunction is that demands bowing of heads, kneeling, or folding the hands, and whether that has now become the only way to pray. Obviously, I am eager to distance myself from the decision to use that painting for the cover of our book.

Categories of discourse run far deeper than postures of prayer, however, and affect thinking processes from the mundane to the explicitly theoretical. We have space to point only to a few examples here.

1. We have already noted individualism, which, as is well known, explodes into euro-western critical consciousness with the beginnings of modernity, the Renaissance, and René Descartes—although Martin Luther seems to me to be another overlooked progenitor, with his teaching about individual salvation invested in the great Reformation doctrine of "justification by faith." In any event, teaching American Indians to value the private ownership of property as a means of inculcating individualism became a battle cry, repeated in speech after speech, for those american religious and political leaders who would "civilize" Indians in the late nineteenth century.[9] We, whose cultural

---

7. Homer Noley, Clara Sue Kidwell, and George E. Tinker, *A Native American Theology* (Maryknoll, N.Y.: Orbis Books, 2001).

8. It makes no difference that the image was created by an Indian artist. The colonized is capable of, and to wit has been trained to, recreate colonial imagery as our own. Ngugi Wa Thiongo, like Franz Fanon and Albert Memmi before him, describes the process as the colonization of the indigenous mind itself: *Decolonizing the Mind: The Politics of Language in African Literature* (London: Heinemann, 1986).

9. Francis Paul Prucha, *Americanizing the American Indian: Writings of the "Friends of the Indian," 1880-1900* (Cambridge, Mass.: Harvard University Press, 1973).

values are based on community, were explicitly taught to say "mine" instead of "ours" and "me" instead of "us."

2. The traditional ecumenical creeds of euro-western Christianity are deeply rooted in the categories of late classical (hellenistic) greek philosophy, of stoicism and middle platonism, and all euro-christian theology since has built implicitly or explicitly on these categorical distinctions. Christian seminaries still dutifully teach the complexity of early christian debates dealing with the essence or substance of deity as if these greek christian decisions describe something that was actually real rather than a cultural metaphor for the real. What does it mean that the Father and the Son are of the same substance rather than of a similar substance?[10] To an American Indian the words have little meaning within our cultural frame of reference—unless we purposefully distance ourselves from our own worlds and intentionally immerse ourselves in the intellectual substance of the world of the euro-west. Spirit and substance are antithetical notions for Indian peoples to the extent that a spirit cannot be conceived of as having substance. These are different realms of existence that require a careful differentiating. *Wako^{n}da*, the Sacred Other, the primordial creative force, or god—whatever this thing is, Indians conceive of it as spirit or energy. This means that to talk about "God" as having "substance" is, for us, bizarre at best. Hence, to engage in christian theology and christian history once again requires that we engage in wholehearted denial of our own world of knowledge and experience in order to affirm the colonizer's (greek/hellenistic) understanding of the world.

3. Another aspect of missionary Christianity that is destined to be forever difficult for Indian people is the euro-western religious language of fall and redemption—as we have already indicated in chapter 2. Sin is the universal starting point in the euro-christian religious proclamation, with salvation in Jesus posited in some form as the answer to the problem of sin and fall.[11] This functions as an additional factor of stress in American Indian communities where people continue to suffer from the effects of conquest by european immigrants over the past five centuries. We live with the ongoing stigma of defeated peoples who have endured genocide, the intentional dismantling of cultural values, forced confinement on less desirable lands called "reservations," intentionally nurtured dependency on the federal government; and conversion by missionaries who imposed a new culture on us as readily as they preached the gospel. All this has resulted in a current situation marked by a dreadful pov-

---

10. *Homoousios* rather than *homoiousios* is the greek-language distinction played out in early christian history and reflected in the Nicene Creed; it means "same substance" rather than "similar substance."

11. See my argument in more detail in George E. Tinker, "The Integrity of Creation: Restoring Trinitarian Balance," *Ecumenical Review* 41 (1989): 527-36.

erty and community distress not usually associated with the United States in the minds of the international community.

More to the point, the pervasive result is a depreciated level of self-esteem which all too readily internalizes any missionary preaching that intends first to convict people of their sin. Needless to say, this internalized self-depreciation is filtered through a lens of racial inferiority imposed by generations of conquest. White Christians see the inferiority of Indian peoples through one lens, while Indian peoples internalize this idea of racial inferiority through another lens. The end result is that for both groups, Indian "sinfulness" is seen as somehow connected to their racial/ethnic identity.

Unfortunately by the time the preacher gets to the "good news" of the gospel, people are so bogged down in their experience and internalization of brokenness and lack of self-worth that too often they never quite hear the proclamation of good news in any actualized, existential sense. Both in terms of intrinsic Native American values, then, and in terms of Indian sociological and psychological realities, a fall/redemption starting point is singularly unhelpful and even destructive. To the contrary, any Indian theoretical notion of the world and the role of human beings in it would begin with the creation of the whole as a gift, which means a first-article/creation starting point would form a natural bond with indigenous cultural roots. While the ecumenical creeds all include creation as the first article, they also commonly place excess weight on the second article, a tendency that has been exacerbated in modern euro-western ecclesial life.

4. If the convert is required to adopt israelite history, it becomes an important part of the conversion experience for Indian people to adopt european history as well—at least, to a certain extent. If one is to become a "theologian" in my institution, it is expected that one will have studied the full history of european theological development, even if one intends to pursue an indigenous theology. In other words, it is not enough to know indigenous theology, but one must be at least well-enough versed to put it into the framework of nineteenth- and twentieth-century european thinkers, from Friedrich Schleiermacher and G. W. F. Hegel, to Søren Kierkegaard and Karl Barth. In designing a course on "western science and indigenous knowledges" I was chastised because I failed to include Alfred North Whitehead in the discussion—not to mention other western philosophers and theologians. In this way our own traditions are rejected out of hand as having any possible credibility as sources of knowledge (science)—unless they can be measured against the presumed normativity of euro-western theology, science, and philosophy.

In this regard, Indian Christians, and other indigenous Christians, are destined to be forever "one down" because they are not native speakers of or educated in the technical languages of Christianity—greek, hebrew, german, latin, italian, and so on—and neither are they as comfortably conversant in the cultural-linguistic concepts almost automatically presumed by euro-western Christians. Thus, christian Indians must rely on "professional" interpretations of their christian faith (in other words, euro-western interpretations) from the missionaries that the denominations have sent us. Even when we do learn greek and hebrew, we learn it from the same professional euro-western interpreters and, thus, we merely learn to mimic the colonizer who always knows more greek and hebrew than we seem to learn. And if an Indian becomes a scholar with intense language skills and resources, it always seems as if we lose that person to a deeply acculturated and possibly assimilated status within the White church or White society and mimicry becomes even more enhanced. That is, in our mimicry, we always learn the technical language and concepts through those euro-western lenses of concepts such as individualism.

5. Even traditional liberation theologies' radical resistance language— such as the "preferential option for the poor"—can become just another example of imposed language. This is a laudable and liberative notion within the christian tradition, yet it does not immediately speak to Indian peoples as it speaks to so many others in the Two-Thirds World or to those ethnic minorities in the United States. While the concept is attractive in one sense, for Indians it represents too neat a packaging of things in a traditional christian language category. It sets priorities that are not ours but are priorities imposed by others—however well meaning.

Indian people are the poorest ethnic community in north America. Yet the language of "option for the poor" is nearly meaningless language for Indians. "The poor" as a category presumes a radically non-Indian world of social hierarchy, socioeconomic organization, and social class structure that are all foreign to traditional Indian communities. Furthermore, it implies a socialist (if not outright marxist) analysis and proposed solution that are completely at odds with American Indian aspirations. As I have argued in an earlier essay, Indian people want affirmation not as "persons" (the language of Gustavo Gutiérrez) or as individuals but rather as national communities with discrete cultures, discrete languages, discrete value systems, and our own governments and territories.[12] To put it in straightforward language, Indian people do not aspire to be recognized in terms of class structure as workers, the proletariat, peasants, or even as ethnic minorities, but rather as peoples. We should add that "production," the marxist category, is of little interest to Indians for whom

---

12. George E. Tinker, "Spirituality, Native American Personhood, Sovereignty and Solidarity," in *Spirituality of the Third World: A Cry for Life*, Papers and Reflections from the Third General Assembly of the Ecumenical Association of Third World Theologians, January 1992, Nairobi, ed. K. C. Abraham and M. Bernadette Mbuy-Beya (Maryknoll, N.Y.: Orbis Books, 1994), 119-32.

the land is primary. As we have suggested, should the workers of the world finally unite and take control of the means of production, then Indian people will still be in the same bind they find themselves in today. The only change is that the means of production—and the control of Indian land—will shift from the upper (capitalist) class to a new class structure that must assimilate all cultures into itself and work to destroy Indian particularity and difference. The results will be no different than the imposition of the Christianity brought by the missionaries, as siberian indigenous communities in the former Soviet Union can attest.

If the legitimate Indian aspiration is to be recognized as peoples, as distinct communities living distinct cultures, then cultural alterity or difference becomes far more important for any indigenous community than euro-western (marxist) categories of class analysis. While indigenous peoples would form a more or less united front of resistance against capitalism, euro-western notions of representative democracy, the forces of globalization, and amereuropean hegemony in general, there has never been an indigenous rush to marxist-style class analysis or political notions of socialism. The goal of every indigenous community is to be recognized as a community, as a cultural whole distinct from the colonial settler hordes who have surrounded us, murdered our ancestors, stolen our property, forced their education on our peoples, and made every attempt to deny us the cultural continuity of language and community solidarity. Socialism provides no real solace for those who have suffered thus. Indeed, it intends the destruction of cultural difference just as much—even if for different reasons—as democratic capitalism.

For American Indians the problem with this theological/hermeneutic procedure is that it continues to presume the universality of the colonizer's religious foundations—even as it radically reinterprets those foundations against the colonizer's self. In sum, while the claim for liberation can play on christian and biblical themes, these are not *our* themes or *our* language. We will have to look elsewhere for freedom.

Liberating Renaissance of Indian Traditional Religious Structures

We are left with some choices. The liberation track for which I will argue here is one that affirms the "old covenant" promises that the Creator has given Indian peoples and presumes that those promises are still good and appropriate for Indian peoples—even if they dissolve into new-age pablum (i.e., pabulum) when appropriated or misappropriated by our non-Native relatives. When my brother, Larry Sellers, decided some years ago to bring the Sun Dance back to the Osage people after a seventy-seven year absence, that was a clear liberative act with deep theological implications for the Osage Nation. The revival of the Sun Dance in so many plains and prairie Indian communities over the past twenty-five years is indicative of a larger movement among Indian peoples to reclaim the religious traditions and ceremonies that were denied us by the missionaries and even by federal policy and actual legal interdiction.

More than two decades ago, I suggested that christian Indians (and colonial settler Christians) need to think of our traditional Indian cultures—with their rich stories and powerful ceremonies—as part of an "old testament" tradition that might become for christian Indians the only appropriate foundation for affirming Jesus and expressing a christian commitment.[13] Why adopt someone else's "testament" when we have had our own all along? The hundreds of traditional stories told and dozens of ceremonies observed in each of our different Indian cultures are indeed more than mere pagan superstitions made up by human beings to satisfy the needs of communities at given points in time.[14] Rather, these traditions need to be respected as gifts from the Creator, gifts that were given to the people to help them achieve balance and harmony in the world. Instead of thinking of our traditions as somehow diametrically opposed in spirit and substance to the traditions of ancient Israel and Christianity, we think it is time to recognize that this thing that our christian relatives call "God" has and has had historically multiple relationships in the world with huge varieties of peoples and cultures all over the world, even at that moment when the Jesus event was emerging in Palestine two millennia ago.

One possible Indian response, then, that would take christian conversion and commitments seriously would be to insist that Indians who have converted to the colonizer's religion must be free to interpret the gospel for themselves, even constructing an interpretation of Jesus on the "old testament" foundation of ancient tribal traditions. That, of course, is a difficult thing to achieve, given

---

13. This idea was picked up by Steve Charleston (Choctaw), then on the faculty at Luther Theological Seminary in St. Paul, Minnesota. See his essay "The Old Testament of Native America," in *Lift Every Voice: Constructing Christian Theologies from the Underside*, ed. Susan Brooks Thistlethwaite and Mary Potter Engle (San Francisco: Harper & Row, 1990), 49-61. An African theologian, Kwame Bediako, has made a similar argument that "ancestor worship" should serve as preparatory for the advent of Christianity in Africa; see his *Christianity in Africa: The Renewal of a Non-Western Religion* (Maryknoll, N.Y.: Orbis Books, 1995). Kwasikwakye-Nuako, a Ghanaian scholar, has critiqued Bediako as not being bold enough, and implicitly his critique would apply to Charleston. See Kwasikwakye-Nuako, "The Akan People, Ancestors and Christmas: Toward Indigenizing Christianity in Africa," *Voices from the Third World* 25 (December, 2002): 175-204: "Important as Bediako's arguments are, I regard his reflections to be triumphal; a characteristic of what I consider as bourgeois theology, in which Christianity remains the only true religion [to which] all others must succumb" (194).

14. The latter, of course, is only one of the traditional missionary arguments—the more liberal and generous argument. Others straightforwardly asserted that the stories and ceremonies derived directly from Satan and characterized them as elements of devil worship.

the deep roots of colonization—physically, emotionally, intellectually, and spiritually. The controlling impetus of every denomination is loath to allow Indians to move very far away from the denomination's central doctrinal focus in their own attempts to reinterpret.

We could argue that an interpretation of Galatians 5:1 gives christian Indians the freedom "in Christ" to continue to practice their ancient and traditional ceremonies and rites alongside a new religious commitment to Christianity. "For Christ has made you free. . ." ought to allow for a great variety of religious experience and not merely cute liturgical inventions to "make" the gospel or worship "more relevant." We could ask missionaries and bishops alike, exactly how free are christian Indians to pray the way they want or have for generations?

Yet, the internalization of colonialism in our personal and communal psyche, quite apart from denominations' continuing colonial control mechanisms, means that many christian Indians are already so deeply inculcated in the act of disavowing their own traditions that they reject the very freedom that the gospel seems to preach. They have been taught that our own spiritual traditions and ceremonies are actually dangerous things to be avoided, that they can cause harm, that the spirits that are summoned can hurt people, that those who practice them will surely go to hell.

There is, however, a corollary argument for the continuing validity of our traditions that would allow Indians to choose another path. Especially since World War II, most euro-western and amer-european Christians have finally begun to concede that God's promises (old testament) with the Jews must still be good, that God will not have summarily reneged on God's promise to them. Otherwise, there is a logical problem that would necessarily leave Christians with a sense of God's capriciousness that would allow them little faith in God's intention to keep the new promise in Jesus as the Christ. If God can renege on one promise, what makes us so sure that God will not change God's mind with regard to the new promise? In the same way, Indian people need to argue that the Creator's promises to each of our tribes, invested in our traditional stories and traditional ceremonies, are still valid and still a source of life and liberation for Indian peoples. We need to find the courage and strength to insist as whole communities that our traditional perspectives of and experiences of the Sacred are just as valid as the perspectives of the colonial Christianity imposed on our ancestors by colonizing missionaries and enforced to this day by strict control of denominational mission dollars.

Thus, I want to argue that Indian people who are serious about liberation—about freedom and independence—must commit themselves to the renewal and revival of their tribal ceremonial life, bringing their ancient ceremonies back to the center of their community's political existence. More to the point, it may be important to live these traditions quite apart from any attempt to force them into some indigenous pattern of Christianity. While there are numerous examples of small groups within nearly every reservation community who have made the move back to their ancient traditions, seldom has this movement embraced the whole of a national community in such a way that the ceremonies have become once again the spiritual base for the political cohesiveness of an independent nation. To make this move requires a boldness that is able to say clearly that "Jesus" is not the answer for Indians who hope to rebuild their own cultures and set of indigenous values.

To say "Jesus is the answer" is to assume a euro-western question to begin with—to say nothing of the hegemony of the amer-european denominational structures that direct mission activities on reservations. How can Jesus be the answer to the question of Indian genocide or, say, to the massacre of several hundred people at Sand Creek? How is Jesus the answer to the intentional destruction of our Indian cultures and languages—perpetrated by White missionaries, first of all, and in the name of Jesus? More to the point, if we can successfully argue the continuing validity of God's promises to us in our traditional ceremonial prayer life, what is it that Jesus might offer our peoples in addition to the life promised in the regular completion of certain ceremonies? And what compromises must Indians make in order to affirm Jesus as their own? Will they have to concede the intrinsic goodness of their colonial invaders, and finally concede as legitimate the historical thefts of Indian properties?

While our traditional ceremonies do not address the trauma of Indian historical losses directly, they were also not participatory in causing those losses in the same way that Christianity and the missionaries were. After five hundred years of conquest and missionary imposition, it seems time for Indian communities to resuscitate their old, communal ways of relating to the Sacred, to find life for the peoples in those ceremonial ways and cultural values. Thus, the ceremonies in which I participated at the Sand Creek massacre site are representative of a widespread revival of traditional Indian cultures and religious traditions. And the experiences I shared on those two occasions are also representative of the deep spiritual power we know are an everyday part of our world. To buy into colonial Christianity means that Indians have to shut their ears to the chatter of spirits and close their eyes to the blessing presence of Sacred Energy like the woman spirit that came to us that day.

CEREMONIAL REVIVIFICATION AND NEW-AGE COLONIALISTS

While the revivification of Indian tribal ceremonies must be seen as a source of healing and liberation for Indian peoples, these traditions must be understood within the parameters of tribal cultures and dare not be suddenly understood within the context of the colonizers' cultural traditions and values. Even as I write this book, the cultural values inherent in ceremonial traditions such as the Sun Dance are shifting noticeably away from the communitarian values of "dancing for the people," "that the people might live." As more and more non-Indian relatives invade our ceremonies as the newest and hottest exotic playground, the values have shifted to address the needs and cultural values of these tourists. The Sun Dance is increasingly danced for the purpose of personal (individual) achievement, a new and exotic source of individual salvation and personal empowerment.

I would encourage our amer-european relatives to find another way to find their own center of balance rather than invading our ceremonies and imposing their presence on Indian communities at moments of ceremonial intimacy. Indeed, there is unfinished business that deeply affects the spiritual well-being of our White relatives that cries out for attention today.

AN INDIAN CHALLENGE TO OUR AMER-EUROPEAN COLONIZER RELATIVES

For American Indians, our struggle for liberation must go one step further in order to deal constructively with contemporary realities. At our best, we understand that our liberation is not possible without the liberation of our White relatives who share this continent with us. We American Indians realize that our continued existence represents something of an embarrassment for White America because we serve as a constant reminder of America's history of violence. Yet the guilt will not simply evaporate with the final death of Indian people. We stand as a source of judgment over against the continued amer-european occupancy of north America and will always present amer-european folk with a choice: Either confess and acknowledge that history and move beyond it in a constructive healing way, or engage the addict's device of denial and keep those memories deeply suppressed and repressed where they will continue to fester and disrupt all of american life and well-being.

An American Indian theology of liberation, then, will hold the colonizer to his and her own best spiritual and moral imperatives:

- Thus, in the name of their own Jesus we call on all White Christians to confess—to acknowledge the american history of violence: violence as military genocide, as political genocide, as cultural genocide, and particularly as the spiritual genocide of missionary conquest.
- And in the name of their Jesus we call on all White Christians to cease and desist from any attempts to impose their beliefs on others. Especially, we

call on them to resist the temptation to attempt to convert tribal peoples from their ancient and God-given spiritual and religious traditions. It is not too late at this global moment to call on Christians to cease all conversion-oriented missionary outreach.[15]

- In the name of their Jesus, we call on our White relatives to resist judgment of our religious and ceremonial traditions. The ways in which these traditions have been interpreted by missionaries, government officials, professional academics, and Hollywood are not the ways in which our ancestors actually lived them. Nor do they accord with our contemporary experience of our own world. Allow us to interpret our own traditions and cultures for ourselves—without judgmental second-guessing. After all, the vast majority of White interpretations of our religious traditions have been self-serving validations for euro-western and amer-european conquest. Christians have typically conceived of their religion as being so much better than what indigenous people anywhere in the colonized world practiced that in their minds as superior colonizers they could not and cannot do anything but justify all the killing that has happened in Jesus' name and the destruction of the cultures and the histories of those conceived of as inherently less-than.[16]

- Instead, we call on our White relatives to reflect deeply and honestly on their own history and its contemporary manifestations in the form of mass consumption, commodification, the globalization of capital, and the establishment of a new world empire predicated on White american hegemony.

CHALLENGES FOR INDIAN PEOPLE

Even as I call on our amer-european (White) relatives to engage me and other Indian people in dialogue about the struggle for Indian freedom, I also want

---

15. At the same time, it is important that the mainline denominations not use this appeal as an excuse to abandon those indigenous communities in which they have been historically involved. Having already imposed their theological beliefs on these communities, they would commit a far worse sin to leave them now. Those historical missionary commitments must now be honored, especially at a time when their price tag seems to be increasing.

16. See, for instance, the critique of euro-western (including amer-european) academic interpretations of the Indian world voiced by indigenous scholars such as Barbara A. Mann, *Iroquoian Women: The* Gantowisas (New York: Peter Lang, 2000); George E. Sioui, *Huron-Wendat: The Heritage of the Circle*, rev. ed., trans. Jane Brierley (Vancouver: University of British Columbia Press and Michigan State Press, 1999). For an incisive critique from an indigenous scholar from another part of the globe, see Linda Tuhiwai Smith, *Decolonizing Methodologies: Research and Indigenous Peoples* (London: Zed Books; Dunedin, New Zealand: University of Otago, 1999).

to end this essay by calling on Indian people to take their cultures and traditions seriously. If we want to be free and want our grandchildren to be free, then there are things we need to do in order to secure a liberated future and to break away from the bondage we have experienced under the tutelage of amereuropean values, education, economics, and politics.

- Culture is lived by people and is not something preserved in museums. Therefore, we Indian peoples must live the traditional cultural values of our peoples as faithfully as we can.
- Our movement for liberation must be a spiritual movement as much as it is political. We must relearn that spirituality and politics are not separate but go together and need each other.
- Our traditional spirituality and cultural values must become a real part of everything we do as Indian persons, in political action groups, in our ceremonies, and especially as Indian communities.
- Liberation is freedom to practice, recover, restore, and reinvent whatever tribal/indigenous practices and life ways are enriching, healing, and life-sustaining.
- Each one of us should strive to be personally in balance. It is important that we live spiritually every day and every moment in balance within ourselves and with the people around us, in harmony with the ceremonies we so affirm, in harmony with our tribal communities and their aspirations, and in balance with all our relations in this world, including our non-human relations—the two-leggeds, the four-leggeds, the winged, and all the living-moving things, from rocks and trees to mountains and fish.
- Affirmation of our own cultural values must accompany a commitment to live those values in the face of forces that insist on an increasingly globalized culture of commodification and consumption. We must, then, join our voices in solidarity with all those in the world today who are engaged in overt resistance to amer-european hegemony and the globalization of capital.

These are the commitments to liberation we owe to the memory of those ancestors who gave so much in the colonial contest that resulted in the loss of our lands and the loss of so many lives for more than five hundred years.

Chapter 7

Culture and Domination

A "Postcolonial" Quandary[1]

From this distant point we watch our bones
auctioned with our careful beadwork.
Our quilled medicine bundles, even the bridles
of our shot-down horses. You: who have
priced us, you who have removed us: at what cost?
What price the pits where our bones share
a single bit of memory, how one century
turns our dead into specimens, our history
into dust, our survivors into clowns.

Wendy Rose (Hopi), "Three Thousand
Dollar Death Song"

Wendy Rose reminds us pointedly that after Indian people survived the initial holocaust of colonialism and conquest, of terrorism and massacres, we then became fair game for commodification in the settlers' economic scheme for generating excess wealth. After they took the land, they then began collecting our ancestors' bones as a fetish for dominance and control of the land and our natural resources. Collecting our spiritual scalps as new-age White "individuals" flood into our most private and intimate "community" ceremonies then becomes the newest fetish for conquest and commodity value—even in some of the most well-meaning of our White friends. The freedom imposed on American Indians by the colonial power center is freedom to forget our past, our traditional values, our community bondedness; freedom to forget that we were once peoples; and freedom at last to enter the White economy and generate our own personal wealth—by selling our most sacred traditions.

Yet, Indian peoples in the Americas are survivors—perhaps even "post-

---

1. The first draft of this essay was delivered as a public lecture on the occasion of my installation as Professor of American Indian Cultures and Religious Traditions at Iliff School of Theology in February 1998.

Indian warriors of survivance" (Gerald Vizenor's term[2]), and in our deepest hopes we want the survivance of all our relatives in this hemisphere and in the world. This is a very difficult proposition because the cultures of colonizer and colonized, of dominance and survivance, have been and seem perpetually headed toward tensive conflict with each other. The metanarrative of european and amer-european superiority and conquest began with violence—for instance, the violence of the first evangelical Pilgrims who parked the Mayflower off of the coast of Cape Cod days before their famous Plymouth landing and proceeded to steal the entire winter corn supply from an Indian village. Having never yet seen an Indian, they were already sure that this crime of theft was "God's good providence" toward a superior and divinely chosen race.[3]

While this marks the beginning of the violence that is America, the metanarrative continued its violence in the imposition of a metaculture on the conquered that has had genocidal consequences that have not let up over the years in spite of amer-european notions of *progress* and *development*. America's history of violence, like the violence of an abusive parent or spouse, stands hidden behind a facade of american self-righteousness and denial which functions to continue the violence and breed ever new forms of it that will not stop until the past has been acknowledged and denial has been overcome. There is a metaculture in north America today that dominates and imposes itself, but there is no "common culture" that actually includes all of us in its american story, and there cannot be until the moral coherence of indigenous cultures is acknowledged and validated as a viable worldview in its own right, and the western colonizer culture of abuse and violence is finally exposed for all of us—as it is exposed in the everyday realities of contemporary Indian peoples. To illustrate this point let me offer you a vignette.

I saw the man in the back of a city parking lot with two Whites, all of them equally dirty from living on the streets and, obviously, several days of inebriation. The Indian, I knew, was going to cost me a couple of dollars. More than that, it was going to take a little time to hear the brother's story. It seems that no Indian wants to take another Indian's money without some explanation. He had been drinking about two weeks straight, he said, and he certainly smelled

---

2. Gerald Viznor, *Manifest Manners: Postindian Warriors of Survivance* (Middletown, Conn.: Wesleyan University Press, 1994).

3. Neal Emerson Salisbury, *Manitou and Providence: Indians, Europeans and the Making of New England: 1500-1643* (New York: Oxford University Press, 1982), 113; William Bradford, *Of Plymouth Plantation*, ed. Samuel Eliot Morrison (New York: Knopf, 1952); and Dwight B. Heath, *Mourt's Relation: A Journal of the Pilgrims at Plymouth* (New York: Applewood Books, 1963), 26, 37, and 19-37 passim: ". . . a spetiall providence of God, and a great mercie. . . ." To which Bradford added: "the Lord is never wanting unto his in their greatest needs; let his holy name have all ye praise."

like one of those bars "down the line" in Leslie Silko's novel *Ceremony*. He had just arrived in town from another city not too far away having worn out his welcome there. He was "just an alcoholic," he assured me with typical Indian honesty, and he intended to buy a drink with the money put in his hand. It had not always been that way. At one time, he said, he had been a college graduate and an officer and platoon commander in the U.S. Army.

Inconceivable. So few of our people make it through the basic levels of the education establishment, yet here was one who had made it a long way up the ladder before taking a deep fall. With obvious surprise I joked with the man in an Indian way: "Brother, what happened? You look like you got run over by a bar." After he finished his inebriated laugh, the man became serious, and with growing sadness, and eventually tears, he told of his experience in Vietnam. The following poem captures his story better than it could be retold. I wrote it in 1991, the night after I met this honorable wreck. I title the poem "Mai Lai Is Not Alone" because it catalogues a massacre on an occasion similar to the infamous 1972 Mai Lai event. The man's story also demonstrates a different experience of life and a very different sensitivity to life.

Mai Lai Is Not Alone

367 children. Murdered.
367 children. Forgotten by all but one lone Indian soldier.
367 children. Remembered only in the pain of nightly jungle dreams
    and daily drunken stupor.

He smelled of alcohol—yesterday's drink and the day before.
Deep sadness poured out of his gaze
A college degree and military commission
the elite of American Indian peoples
The hope for the future
a role model for a new generation.

But the living memory of brutal death killed the hope.
Life itself becomes untenable without dulling the senses with daily dosages.

Meanwhile, Lt. Calley rests in peace;
the walking dead driving a Mercedes Benz and selling apartheid diamonds
    in the Alabama South.

It was just a war, and "we were under orders"—
like Chivington at Sand Creek, Mason at Mystic or the Seventh Cavalry
*   at Wounded Knee.*
Children were unfortunate but necessary victims.
It couldn't be helped.
America, sleep well and safe!

But the Indian doesn't sleep.
Just following orders won't work
when the sacredness of life lives buried in the heart.

Savages with a history, we are used to the violence of death.
Yet our history is not one of killing but rather of being killed.

To Calley and to Chivington they were just dark-skinned nits
—red and yellow and black and brown
Gooks and Charlies, not real human beings.
That is their history.

But the Indian knows and must live with the horror.
The sacredness of life violated in senseless killing he could not prevent.
Bullets and bayonets, soldiers and anger with no ears for compassion,
a platoon lusting for action and medals, living the power of America
*   strong. . . .*
367 children. Remembered only by a lone Indian vet.
Remembered when he wants to forget.

This final chapter is an attempt to share something of the intellectual and social core of my own theological existence, sharing with a readership that I presume already has long developed social commitments rooted in their own intellectuality. I initially wrote this chapter, in the spirit of collegiality, as a response to my colleague William Dean, continuing a conversation that began when he first arrived at Iliff School of Theology as professor of theology in 1997. Dean argues in his book *The American Spiritual Culture* that creating stability in the United States today requires establishing a common culture, a shared cultural narrative, that is rooted in a common spiritual tradition. Along the way he explicitly identifies the social movement of multiculturalism of the past twenty years or so as a major impediment to his goal of creating this common culture. He is a liberal theologian searching for the unifying factors of american life and deeply fearing that disintegration will replace integration in the social fabric of our continent.[4]

Dean's notion is certainly not a new one. Rather, it has a very self-conscious precedent that goes back at least to the New England idea of a "city on a hill" and the puritan notion of creating a "new Israel" in a new promised land, Indian land but land given to the Puritans, they said, by their God. This is an idea that continued to have vibrant roots in the early notions of Manifest Destiny, the idea that somehow "God" wanted White people to conquer the entire continent for euro-western cultural and religious development.[5] But it has particularly vibrant roots in the speech delivered at the American Historical Association in Chicago in 1893, a meeting scheduled to coincide with the Chicago World's Fair, the World Columbian Exhibition. The foremost american historian of the day, Frederick Jackson Turner, delivered his famous (for some of us, infamous) "frontier thesis" paper, an essay that continues to have a formative influence on our own day. Turner identified the american common culture of his day, but did so with explicit disregard for the aboriginal inhabitants of the continent. His concern at that time was that the closing of the frontier and the final military conquest of the continent would leave the United States with a significant problem of identity—precisely Dean's concern more than a century later. The last of the "battles" with the aboriginal owners of the land had just occurred two and a half years earlier with the massacre (not Turner's term) of the Lakotas at Wounded Knee (December 29, 1890), which brought a whole era of american adventurism to a close. What now, asked Turner, would replace the necessity of conquest and bring cohesion (Dean's common culture) to the resulting national whole?[6] After all, argued Turner, it was the frontier experience, its hardship, the contest with savages—whom the settlers both defeated and from whom they learned how to live on this continent—that had transformed these Europeans into Americans. Identity was at stake and, as Dean would insist, a common culture.

---

4. William Dean, *The American Spiritual Culture: The Invention of Jazz, Football, and the Movies* (New York: Continuum, 2002), 12, 46-50.

5. See *Manifest Destiny and Empire: American Antebellum Expansionism* (Walter Prescott Webb Memorial Lectures), ed. Sam W. Haynes, Christopher Morris, and Robert Walter Johannsen (College Station: Texas A&M University Press, 1997).

6. Frederick Jackson Turner: "The Significance of the Frontier in American History," 1893: http://www.fordham.edu/halsall/mod/1893turner.html; also recently republished in Frederick Jackson Turner and John Mack Faragher, *Rereading Frederick Jackson Turner: "The Significance of the Frontier in American History" and Other Essays* (New Haven, Conn.: Yale University Press, 1999). And see the discussion of Turner in Shari M. Huhndorf, *Going Native: Indians in the American Cultural Imagination* (Ithaca, N.Y.: Cornell University Press, 2001).

My response to this neoconservative/neoliberal[7] argument for a common culture or a color-blind society is the same as my response to marxist/socialist fantasies of a redemptive future based on class analysis. The marxists have an equal antipathy to culture as a mode of differentiation, something that defined communities as different. The aspirations of Indian people have never merely hoped that we could be included somehow—either in Dean's common culture or in latin american liberation theology's preferential option for the poor. Indians have never wanted inclusion in some class of people, whether workers, the proletariat, or the poor. Rather, what Indian peoples want most is the freedom to exercise their peopleness as discrete political (national?) entities with their own unique sets of cultural values, a distinctive spirituality, and their own economic bases. The greatest fear of Indian traditional folk is the imposition of something like Dean's common culture.

I should add that my concern is not just for foregrounding the genocidal displacement of American Indian peoples historically in the thinking of White Americans or even for emphasizing the continuing residual of poverty and ill-health among Indians that has resulted from centuries of colonial conquest. Rather, I have an equal concern for the wholeness and well-being of those who have formed this continent of "displaced persons" (Dean's term)[8] or what Churchill would refer to as this "outlaw settler state"[9]—and all those who have become attached to it whether through choice or by force. Thus, I believe that I share deeply some of the same concerns as Dean, even if I come to radically different conclusions, especially as I refuse to concede that America is a "nation of immigrants," the all-too-popular aphorism that he perpetuates.[10] Like him, I too hope for some new vision of wholeness that can begin to ground our being together on this continent and create some notion of american solidarity. But my vision of wholeness calls for a mutual respect for cultural differentness and not the imposition of sameness. Yet the spiritual and emotional well-being of all Americans may depend on how White Americans finally decide to confront

---

7. I use neoconservative/neoliberal here as two very closely related categories, with aims that are not terribly distanced from each other—even as the proponents vociferously debate their differences. See the discussion of these categories in Howard Winant, "United States: The End of the Innocence," chap. 7 in *The World Is a Ghetto: Race and Democracy Since World War II* (New York: Basic Books, 2001), 147-76.

8. Dean, *The American Spiritual Culture*, 46.

9. Ward Churchill, *From a Native Son: Essays in Indigenism* (Littleton, Colo.: Aigis Press, 1996); idem, *A Small Matter of Genocide Holocaust and Denial in the Americas, 1492 to the Present* (San Francisco: City Lights Press, 1998).

10. Dean, *American Spiritual Culture*, 49: "Thus, America remains a nation of immigrants with, as Higham says, its 'memory of displacement from somewhere else.'" While this is certainly true for most Americans, it overlooks those most negatively affected by that immigration, who are after all not immigrants but the aboriginal owners of the land.

and deal with their own history of violence. White american Christians need a liberation theology of their own to free them from the denial of their own past, which has grown along with history.

Ten years ago I would have argued that a Native American theology must be a liberation theology if it is to speak to American Indian people effectively, and that a liberation theology must be deeply rooted both in context and in praxis. But even then my conception of liberation was entwined with the experience of freedom Indian people had before the european invasion began. My conviction back then was that liberation theology would need to speak out of Indian traditions and cultural values first of all, and not out of the historic accumulation of european theological doctrines of god, salvation, sanctification, or the like. We Indian peoples already had and continue to have a relationship with the spirit world. Our theologies need to find ways to honor that and summon the power that is inherent in our traditional ceremonial life. Moreover, an American Indian theology must speak to the tragedy of Native life today in the Americas. I am less enamored today with the language of liberation, but notions of freedom have become a burning postcolonial concern for survival. A White critic (immigrant german-jewish) writing forty years ago put it rather starkly. Hannah Arendt called freedom in the United States, her adopted country, no more than the freedom to vote and the freedom to pursue economic gain. For us today, both for Indian and non-Indian alike, freedom must come to mean much more than that.[11]

This volume has been an attempt to describe both the foundational context and the pragmatics of my attempts at speaking a Native American theology. In this last chapter, I want to give some idea of what it is I deal with as a Native

---

11. "It may be a truism to say that liberation and freedom are not the same," says Arendt, "that liberation may be the condition of freedom but by no means leads automatically to it; that the notion of liberty implied in liberation can only be negative, and hence, that even the intention of liberating is not identical with the desire for freedom." See Hannah Arendt, *On Revolution* (New York: Viking, 1963), 29. Arendt argues that the founding fathers of the United States indeed had a useful ideal of freedom in mind but that they ultimately failed to sustain their ideals as they became immersed in the politics of state. As David Scott puts it (arguing from Arendt), "Their failure was a failure "to establish the cognitive conditions of 'remembrance' of what they were originally seeking to do." As a result, argues Scott, "Freedom in America became merely freedom from politics; freedom to pursue economic gain." David Scott, *Conscripts of Modernity: The Tragedy of Colonial Enlightenment* (Durham, N.C.: Duke University Press, 2004), 216. On an American Indian ideal of freedom, note Taiaiakai Alfred (Kahnawá:ke Mohawk), *Wasáse: Indigenous Pathways of Action and Freedom* (Peterborough, Ont.: Broadview, 2005). Alfred describes the colonizing reality, and lack of freedom inherent, in native "self-government" and points to a genuinely liberating struggle predicated on Indian independence.

American theologian on a day-to-day basis. Indeed, I am a theological being to my core in that my deepest and most intense reflective action is focused on the holistic well-being of my community in a social, emotional, political, and economic sense—all rooted in a package of community spiritual well-being. This requires a deeper commitment to the praxis of the community's spirituality than most people in America's settler class realize. In full ceremonial and spiritual participation with the community, I engage a praxis-oriented reflection on the community's well-being, critiquing where necessary and affirming the contextuality of our ceremonial life where it is strong and appropriate and always trying to speak some healing/salvific word to the contextual disruption of Indian community well-being.

Moreover, I need to remind the reader that my community lives today in continual pain from generations of severe abuse—abuse from a dominating colonial power that enters our world from outside our natural borders but continues to live among us and around us in a context that anthropologist Robert Thomas would call "internal colonialism."[12] American Indians thus live in a continuing close relationship with the perpetrator of our historical and contemporary abuse. We live today with the continuing results of America's history of violence in ways that have a particularity that is distinctly different from ways experienced by other marginalized communities of color in the United States. Our relationship with our perpetrator is perhaps most similar to the context of aboriginal Australians, Maoris in Aotearoa, or other indigenous peoples in settler colonies around the globe. At the same time, we must not forget that any Indian theological vision must—for reasons of Indian wholeness and genuine freedom—also include all Americans and indeed all our *relations* in this world. The colonizers, the traditional perpetrators of the abuse and violence, are also in need of freedom and healing.[13] Nevertheless, the pain

---

12. At its naïve surface level, the language of postcolonialism is, of course, entirely too hopeful, especially in the case of American Indians. The colonization of American Indian peoples has yet to end; it continues in the present as "internal colonialism," a distinction first articulated by Cherokee anthropologist Robert Thomas, "Colonialism: Internal and Classic," *New University Thought* 4, no. 4 (1966-67); see also Ward Churchill, "Remembering Bob Thomas: His Influence on the American Indian Liberation Struggle," in *Since Predator Came: Notes from the Struggle for American Indian Liberation* (Oakland, Ca.: AK Press, 2005), 1-10; and M. Annette Jaimes, "La Raza and Indigenism: Alternatives to Autogenocide in Native North America," *Global Justice* 3, nos. 2 and 3 (July/October 1992).

13. I make this claim in spite of the usual american insistence that freedom is the essential characteristic of the american political landscape. We only need to remember the political usage that President George Bush has put the word freedom to in the past seven years since the moment of violence wrought on the United States in 2001. In one version or another, the illusion of freedom is summoned in his speeches: "We stand for freedom. That's why they hate

of Indian folk, as the conquered on this continent, continues in a particularly virulent form.

As a few close friends and colleagues know well, the death of my brother more than a decade ago dealt me an emotional blow from which I have not yet and probably will never quite recover. To be quite clear in this transcultural setting of settler north America, he was *closer* than flesh and blood. In an ancient and honored Indian way, we were "adopted" brothers, sharing a *huⁿka* relationship in an irrevocable and responsibility-encumbered kinship association that made it difficult to ever conceive of saying no to him or him to me.[14] Once, during a period of alcoholic recovery, he took three weeks to completely rebuild the engine of my truck (spreading the parts all over my garage) simply because he knew that I used that old, two-hundred-thousand-mile pony as an urban Indian community vehicle, lending it to anyone who asked. That was a community act that he considered culturally important. Moreover, I should acknowledge that he was the real genius behind what started as Living Waters Indian Ministry and went through a cultural transformation into Four Winds American Indian Council. He was the genius, and not always democratic about it; I was merely the public "front" man. One day, when it was still Living Waters, I showed up late for a Saturday clean-up day to discover that the fine old pulpit of our turn-of-the-century Denver church had been taken apart at my brother's direction and split into kindling for a sweat lodge fire. We had not used the pulpit at Living Waters, of course, having preferred to arrange the former sanctuary into a circle of chairs around a makeshift, more "Indian"-style altar, yet it seemed a bit presumptuous to me at the time to merely destroy it. He retorted simply and matter-of-factly, "You were never going to use that pulpit. It'll do us more good on the *inipi* fire." So that evening we prayed with rocks that had been cooked red hot with the last sacred hellfire of that old pulpit, and thus we were freed of one more shackle of colonial accommodation and compliance, freed momentarily again from some socially constructed notion of the metaculture of dominance.

That was when he was sober. On the anniversary of the Sand Creek Massacre in 1995, my brother did something that he had been trying to accomplish for a long time. He combined his antidepressant drugs with prodigious amounts of alcohol and quietly left the world of the living. No one really knows

---

us." The word "freedom" (often enough paired with "preemptive strike") appears eighty times in the fifty-seven-page governmental document "The National Security Strategy of the United States of America" (March, 2006).

14. That this was an "adoptive" relationship in no way diminishes the importance of the relationship in an Indian context. Rather, these adoptive relationships in the Indian world are considered closer than blood in terms of their enduring importance. They are only engaged in after deep reflection and commitment.

the full extent of the pain that he carried with him throughout his life, but he shared at least some of that pain with me, sometimes on long journeys across the country to one reservation or another, or sometimes when I would visit him periodically in a hospital psychiatric ward or a county alcohol detoxification unit. What I know for sure is this: by the time he was six years old, he had already been physically and emotionally abused by his parents, themselves already the products of the abuse of colonization. Then at the age of six, he was taken away by Bureau of Indian Affairs police on his reservation to a church mission school. It was soon after his arrival that a priest baptized him, not into the christian faith but into the evil realities of Indian domination by Whites, of child domination by adults, of the domination of individual self-gratification in a White-world way. Having introduced the youngster to a forced intimacy that had been completely unknown to him before, this priest proceeded to demonstrate his extraordinary virility that same night by transferring his affections to his roommate, Clifford. He then left after threatening both boys with physical punishment and eternal perdition should they reveal anything of what had transpired. Then, he said to me, these two little boys were left to wonder aloud about what had happened to them and to ask each other, "Did it hurt?" As is the case with an inordinate number of Indian youth (up to ten times the average for all U.S. teenagers), Clifford committed suicide at age seventeen, leaving my brother with a deep, enduring sense of responsibility not only for his own shame but for the death of his young friend. He always felt, he said, that he should have done *something* to help Clifford, however irrational that may seem to us in hindsight.

I do not share these bits about the life and death of my brother merely in order to share my own pain. His experience of sexual abuse in a mission boarding school is shocking and heart-wrenching, yet the real shock is in discovering how pervasive his experience is in the Indian world. While our women have been more forthcoming in revealing stories of missionary sexual abuse and sexual abuse in general, Indian men my age and older have been increasingly emboldened to reveal their own experiences of the same evil—at the hands of both men and women—ministers, teachers, and guardians. Thus, I am much more interested in using his life as a heuristic device and as a metaphor for all of Indian pain and dysfunctionality. Both my brother and the Indian veteran I encountered on the street are victims of generations of abuse of Indian peoples by the systemic tide of amer-european invasion that has swept American Indian peoples aside in its divinely mandated conquest of our land.[15] If

---

15. To understand Indian peoples as abuse survivors, see the literature on post-traumatic stress disorder, child abuse, and adult survivors of child abuse and their enduring symptomologies. See, for instance, John Briere, *Psychological Assessment of Adult Posttraumatic States* (Washington, D.C.: American Psychological Association, 1997); Carol S. Fullerton and

Amer-europeans see themselves as the "new Israel," as was claimed by amer-european *conquistadores* from John Winthrop to Walt Whitman, following some God-given mandate to steal Indian land, a mandate white-washed as the doctrine of Manifest Destiny, then Indian communities are no more and no less than the Canaanites of the hebrew Bible, as fellow *wazhazhe* Robert Warrior argues.[16] Any attempt to develop a useful theological response, an American Indian theological response, must begin with our experience of abuse and victimization—even if it must also move beyond victimization to a new and inclusive vision of wholeness.

Five hundred years of conquest and domination, the ever-lingering trauma of mass murders, the loss of land, and, thus, of a self-sustaining economic base, and the continuing experience of racism and marginalizing disempowerment, combined with living in rather intimate closeness with our abuser and feeling constantly the colonizers' pressure to accommodate their culture and values has left Indian peoples in a state of chronic poverty and suffering a community-wide dysfunctionality that is similar in many ways to the typical psychological profile of the adult survivor of child abuse so common in north America today. That is to say, Indian people are, as a community, damaged merchandise. Of course, the same history of violence has left amer-european settlers with a different and much more defensive response, one of denial and self-righteous self-justification that all too often hides behind the myth of american exceptionalism, or what psychologist Rollo May called more than thirty years ago "[a]merican pseudo-innocence."[17]

Robert J. Ursano, eds., *Posttraumatic Stress Disorder: Acute and Long-term Responses to Trauma and Disaster* (Washington, D.C.: American Psychiatric Press, 1997); Stephen Joseph, *Understanding Post-traumatic Stress: A Psychosocial Perspective on PTSD and Treatment* (New York: John Wiley, 1997); Steve Trimm, *Walking Wounded: Men's Lives During and Since the Vietnam War* (Norwood, Ont.: Ablex, 1993); Shirley Dicks, *From Vietnam to Hell: Interviews with Victims of Post-traumatic Stress Disorder* (Jefferson, N.C.: McFarland, 1990); Richard A. Kulka et al., *Trauma and the Vietnam War Generation: Report of the Findings from the National Vietnam Veterans Readjustment Study* (New York: Brunner/Mazel, 1990); Kim Oates, *The Spectrum of Child Abuse: Assessment, Treatment, and Prevention* (New York: Brunner/Mazel, 1996); Alan Sugarman, ed., *Victims of Abuse: The Emotional Impact of Child and Adult Trauma*, Monograph Series of the Ralph R. Greenson Memorial Library of the San Diego Psychoanalytic Society and Institute (Madison, Conn.: International Universities Press, 1994); John Briere, *Therapy for Adults Molested as Children: Beyond Survival*, rev. exp. ed. (New York: Springer, 1996); I. Lisa McCann and Laurie Anne Pearlman, *Psychological Trauma and the Adult Survivor: Theory, Therapy, and Transformation* (New York: Brunner/Mazel, 1990).

16. Robert Warrior, "Canaanites, Cowboys and Indians: Deliverance, Conquest, and Liberation Theology Today," *Christianity and Crisis* 49 (1989): 261-65.

17. Rollo May, *Power and Innocence: A Search for the Sources of Violence* (New York: W.W. Norton, 1972; 1998 reprint). African american philosopher Cornel West once referred to the pathology at stake as "America's ahistoricism."

The history of violence hurts and damages both communities still today and spawns ever more violence.

The resulting poverty of Indian peoples puts us at the bottom of virtually every economic indicator, although any public announcement of statistics usually manages to conceal the enormity of Indian poverty by including Indian statistics in that nebulous category called "other," hiding us among a number of american population sectors that are doing quite well. Indian people are 45 percent below the poverty line, with the lowest per capita income of any American, including new immigrants. Longevity still lags some twenty years behind the average for all Americans, which means that Indians die, on average, in their fifties rather than in their seventies. Unemployment statistics for Indian communities are notoriously difficult to obtain, because the Department of Labor does not include the chronically unemployed in its statistics. Research over the past two decades, however, shows a consistent real unemployment rate among Indian peoples of 40 to 60 percent, with unemployment on some reservations as high as 85 to 92 percent. Disease rates are abnormally high among Indian peoples, with, for instance, tuberculosis occurring seven times the U.S. average and diabetes at 6.8 times the U.S. average. Given the poverty and the long history of community trauma, it should surprise no one that alcoholism also occurs at an abnormally high rate. Teen and young adult suicide ranges from three to ten times the national average with one in six Indian adolescents having attempted suicide. Depression is chronic in every Indian community. And the public school drop-out rate is still nearly half (48 percent) with only 4 percent of our young people managing to complete a college curriculum.[18]

And yet, the real problem in the American Indian community is not the poverty so aptly revealed by these statistics. The real underlying problem is that American Indian poverty is and always has been a necessary condition for american wealth and well-being—both politically and economically! We are, as it were, a "national sacrifice" population that must be kept in veiled suppression in order to continue the validation of U.S. occupancy claims to the north

---

18. Note again the summary of contemporary conditions of Indian communities in Tex G. Hall's op-ed piece, written in the wake of the unfolding Jack Abramoff scandal, cited above in chap. 2: Hall, "American Indians and the Abramoff Scandal: You Don't Know Jack," *San Francisco Chronicle* (January 27, 2006), B-13; http://sfgate.com/cgi-bin/article.cgi?file=/chronicle/archive/2006/01/27/EDGT0GTK471.DTL. See also George Russell, "Contemporary Demographics of the American Indian," in *American Indian Digest* (1995): 49-53. See also George E. Tinker and Loring Bush, "American Indian Unemployment: Statistical Games and Cover-ups," in *Racism and the Underclass in North America*, ed. George Shepherd and David Penna (Westport, Conn.: Greenwood, 1991), 119-44. While these sources are more dated, the statistics are remarkably similar from census to census.

american land mass.[19] Really healthy Indian communities (that is, emotionally, economically, and politically healthy Indian communities) would become entirely too successful in pressing legal and moral claims against the United States and its settler population. The threat is that the reclaiming of significant territories would undermine the economy of the United States and its dominant population, giving an entirely different flavor to the notion of the common good. The further problem, of course, is that Indian peoples in the Americas refuse to die quietly and fade into the museums and annals of history. Indeed, American Indian communities and their discrete set of cultural values seem to have a tenacity for survival and survivance that is extraordinary.

So there have been several, even several dozen, generations of intentional marginalization and overt oppression in north America—and, we should add, not only of Indian peoples. My argument is that this marginalization continues today in spite of more than two centuries of liberalism's promises of individual freedom. The contemporary context of Indian peoples continues to be shackled by economic, political, and cultural desperation and deterioration. This much I think I can and have demonstrated. What can we now conclude from these facts? How can all this begin to inform a new, constructive Native American theological vision?

Unlike Dean and the neoconservative movement in the United States today (strange bedfellows, no doubt), I find *some* version of multiculturalism to be an appealing solution.[20] My vision of multiculturalism, however,

---

19. In this regard, one should note the behavior of the United States in the U.N. Human Rights Commission and particularly in the U.N. Working Group on Indigenous Populations in the long saga of that group's ill-fated process. For an incisive analysis of a small part of this history of injustice and violence, see Ward Churchill, *Struggle for the Land: Indigenous Resistance to Genocide, Ecocide and Expropriation in Contemporary North America* (Monroe, Me.: Common Courage Press, 1993). The language of "national sacrifice areas" seems to have been coined in a study commissioned by the National Academy of Science on resource development on Indian lands. It was submitted to the Nixon administration in 1972 as input toward a national Indian policy. See Thadis Box et al., *Rehabilitation Potential for Western Coal Lands* (Cambridge, Mass.: Ballanger, 1974), for the published version of the study; also Churchill, *Struggle for the Land*, 54, 333, 367; and Russell Means, "The Same Old Song," in *Marxism and Native Americans*, ed. Ward Churchill (Boston: South End Press, 1983), 25; and Churchill and Winona LaDuke, "Native America: The Political Economy of Radioactive Colonialism," in *The State of Native America: Genocide, Colonization and Resistance* (Cambridge, Mass.: South End Press, 1992), 241-66.

20. While Dean is hardly a conservative theologically, his call for establishing a common culture in America sounds strangely concordant with the neoconservative rhetoric calling for a "color-blind society" in a rush to do away with affirmative action or any sort of special set-asides intended to level the playing field for people of color or women. Indeed, Dean's call for a common culture is very much a racist concern for excluding the radically different cultural perspectives of American Indians, for instance. In the final analysis, his common culture is

depends on the societal will to commit itself to the intentional empowerment of the disempowered and even to the self-disempowerment of the dominant sector of north american society. If the truth were known, I, too, have deep reservations about the multicultural movement as we have come to know it in the United States today, but my reservations are predicated on reasons exactly the opposite of most commentators. My concern is that multiculturalism has already been coopted by the systemic forces of the dominant culture in the United States and is in actuality a strong "liberal" move toward precisely the sort of assimilative sameness that Dean and others seem to desire for american unanimity and would describe as a positive.

Contemporary multiculturalism is in keeping with liberal traditions of inclusion, dressing up such inclusion in the modern garb of diversity in skin color or language, all the while maintaining the normativity of Whiteness. Despite such high-sounding aspirations, the driving force of this modern-day multicultural liberalism remains the value system of the dominant White, amer-european culture of this country. What results is a praxis of multicultural inclusivity predicated merely on the basis of skin color or language differentiation with little regard to lived cultural commitments or modes of resistance to systemic domination. Indeed, cultural compliance to the standards of Whiteness is mandated for those marginalized people of color or women who receive affirmative action's gift of inclusion. The underlying hope of this multicultural strategy, it appears, is that the metaculture can establish itself in the hearts of a few chosen individuals of color to the extent that inconsequential surface structure differentiation such as skin color or language can be obviated through a process of assimilation. The fear here is that multiculturalism runs the risk of merely becoming a device to neutralize and depoliticize the resistance of those on the margins. Thus, I would argue that multiculturalism tends too often to be an exercise in monoculturalism! It is merely the newest and most progressive power move of establishment societal forces and the dominant culture. We have consistently engaged, or declined to engage, in exactly this debate among my faculty for several years now with regard to what sort of faculty members of color we should hire.

Yet, the conservative political reactive negation of multiculturalism, affirmative action, and welfare, according to Immanuel Wallerstein, is merely a more reactive form of classic, post–french revolution, european "Enlighten-

---

some amalgam of euro-western Whiteness. For a very useful critique of the inherent racism of neoconservative rhetoric, see Howard Winant, *The New Politics of Race: Globalism, Difference, Justice* (St. Paul: University of Minnesota Press, 2004); idem, "United States: The End of the Innocence," in *The World Is a Ghetto*, 147-76; and Michael Omi and Howard Winant, *Racial Formation in the United States: From the 1960s to the 1990s*, 2nd ed. (New York: Routledge, 1994).

ment" liberalism.[21] It is not really intended as a reaction to the failure to create a common culture but is rather a vindictive and punitive response out of a
distinct fear of achieving this common culture in which all might experience
some sort of personal, individual freedom—in the american dream sort of
way.[22] We might argue explicitly here that any establishing of a common culture works to inhibit or even prohibit any redistribution of power in society.
It is rooted in a fear that the poor might indeed *not* remain poor, that people
of color *might* gain some real sense of political and economic parity. Yet, as I
would argue, neither of these "solutions" are real solutions that take seriously
the humanity of diverse ethnic and cultural communities in north America
and eventually in the world. They are, rather, different versions of the same
imposed liberal ideal.

Establishing some sort of a common culture would require much more than
finding a lowest-common-denominator story that we can all embrace. In fact,
it would require us to mitigate between the different habitual responses to the
world experienced in the widely disparate ethno-cultural groups that share the
U.S. land mass today. Yet, how we might get there from here is a terribly complex
question that involves, ultimately, making choices between sets of cultural values that are diametrically opposed. Will this new "common culture" be *spatially*
based (as is the case with almost all indigenous peoples of the world, including
American Indian communities), or will it succumb to the dominance of linear
temporality and *hierarchy*, which is so characteristic of patriarchal european and
amer-european modernity (and of postmodernism, I might add)?[23] Will this new
common culture continue to promote the radical *individualism* of the west, or
will it recapture the indigenous commitment to *communitarian* values and social
structures?[24] At this point I should add that indigenous communitarianism is

---

21. Wallerstein, *After Liberalism* (New York: New Press, 1995).

22. Whatever one might think either philosophically or morally about abortion, the anti-
abortion ("respect for life"?) movement strongly functions to punish poor women and especially young women of color who do not have access to abortion in the same way that White
middle- to upper-middle-class women do. Rather than being principled, the anti-abortion
stance is too often merely punitive and functions to maintain social structures of racial and
class inequality. I tend toward personal objections to abortion but do not find that personal
decision to be significant in the contemporary political debate. At the same time, I always find
it curious and ironic that a great many of the same radically conservative politicians who support the anti-abortion, right-to-life political position at the same time strongly support the
death penalty. A strange paradox in right-to-life language.

23. Vine Deloria, Jr., *God Is Red* (New York: Grosset & Dunlap, 1973); revised and republished as *God Is Red: A Native View of Religion* (Golden, Colo.: Fulcrum, 1992; 30th anniv. ed.,
Fulcrum, 2002); and several of my own articles.

24. Again, see Deloria, *God Is Red*; also Jace Weaver, *That the People Might Live: Native*

also light worlds away from the socialist/marxian notions of class collectivism that have been such a key component of political and economic discourse for most of the twentieth century. As Brooklyn Rivera, the MISURASATA resistance leader in Nicaragua during the 1980s, said to me some years ago, communism is merely state-run capitalism. It too emerges out of european liberal ideology and was always firmly committed to european culture's affection for temporality, development, and progress.

Regardless of the basic cultural and value choices we might make for some common culture, of course, the most difficult question is how will we impose this sameness on those who would have naturally made different cultural choices based on their historical experience of community culture. Is this at all possible without engaging in yet another exercise of self-righteous violence of a majority on a minority? Like Christianity, both marxism and so-called democratic capitalism have their own sense of universality and moral superiority. As such, all three of these modalities have a strong inclination to insist on a common expression of culture. While the current globalization process is driven by the religious fervor of democratic capitalism, marxist thinkers are certainly not indisposed to the prospects of what they themselves call internationalism.[25]

Against all calls for marxist internationalism or the globalization of capital and the advance of so-called democratic capitalism, I insist that we need to engage a resistance that will allow once again for American Indian independence, for an existence that does not depend on or conform to the dominant culture of the colonizer. Both Indian resistance and enlightened White resistance must combine to make a new social space that encourages indigenous peoples to maintain the integrity of their communities and cultural values, their spiritual connections with what euro-westerners call the Sacred, and their persistent presence as a conscience for our White relatives on this continent.[26] Our resistance and protest may depend on our ability to continue

---

American Literatures and Native American Community (New York: Oxford University Press, 1997).

25. Michael Hardt and Antonio Negri, *Empire* (Cambridge, Mass.: Harvard University Press, 2000), provide a very strong critique of the globalization movement as a movement toward empire. Yet, in their own solution, the second half of the book, they want a marxist international system to take advantage of this globalization of capital in order to impose a new socialist order. The result necessitates imposing some sort of cultural (class?) uniformity on all peoples.

26. Of course, for Indian people the outstanding question remains: Would we be able once again to take responsibility for feeding our people? Can we finally break from the relationship of dependence that has been so carefully constructed by the U.S. government to actually claim our independence?

claiming our cultural differences. But our resistance must be matched with the resistance of our non-Indian relatives for there to be real and creative transformation in our world.

On many occasions, in the classroom or in the Indian community, I have been regularly challenged to do more than just critique the present reality. I have been challenged to offer some version of a constructive vision for social change. Part of the problem in offering my own solution is that any real change in our world must come from a more communally based vision of transformation. Nevertheless, I will conclude this volume by offering some nine steps, described very briefly and sometimes summarized from the text of earlier chapters, that we can begin to take together in order to change our world of violence and to restore the balance of creation.

1. First of all, White Amer-europeans must courageously own their past—*without guilt* but with great intentionality—to change the present and the future. This means Amer-europeans will have to engage in a collective or corporate type of confession and repentance that looks incisively at the systemic and ingrained violence that has been such a consistent part of the american experience—from the massacres of Indians and the kidnapping and enslavement of Africans to our more contemporary insistence on domination in the whole of the world, from El Salvador and Guatemala to Afghanistan and Iraq. I should repeat that this important exercise dare never devolve into a mere personal experience of guilt. As I have too often said, emotions of guilt always fail to achieve any creative good.

2. We must work together to identify the systemic structures of oppression and mark them for genuine deconstruction, that is, for dismantling. This will involve careful and committed critical analysis first of all. If there is to be one mode of being (common culture) that will be crucial for any successful change in our common future, it will require consistent and careful critical analysis. At the same time, our analysis dare not give in to romantic hope, but it must fearlessly confront the present and lay bare the destruction that modernity has wrought.

3. We dare not undertake this task without understanding the severe risks that will necessarily accompany such dismantling or deconstruction. There will be enormous personal risks for all of us—to our lifestyle and to our economic well-being. Indeed, as we struggle successfully for this transformation, the economy of the United States must reduce its levels of consumption in favor of a more equitable distribution of wealth in the rest of the world. Yet we must be willing to take this risk. And we should be clear that any proposed solutions should be interrogated from the grassroots—from the everyday experiences of the marginalized—and not become just a new imposition from above.

4. In this regard, we must get serious about reducing consumption. And what we must get serious about changing is not our personal (individual) consumption practices, even those these must surely change as well. It is critical that we challenge consumption in the United States, with the reigning regime of consumerism, as a broad-based corporate practice as opposed to merely individual practice. It will be constantly necessary to critique new modalities of consumption even as they are created supposedly to solve earlier problems of consumption. Ethanol gives us new and cheaper alternatives to petroleum but at a great cost to the environment. The modern production of corn has created new and serious problems of environmental waste, problems that are threatening portions of the Gulf of Mexico, for instance. At the same time, people around the world still go hungry while we convert our food to gasoline so we can drive more.

5. We must learn to relate across cultural boundaries in ways that are predicated on genuine and mutual respect, that is, respect for boundaries, respect for differentness, and respect for the particularity of wisdom held in disparate communities around us.[27] Instead of imposing our notions of a common culture, we need to make viable spaces for the cultural expressions and values of the other.

6. It will be difficult to learn respect for the cultural other unless each of us gains a proper sense of one's own community in order to avoid new-age encroachment and misappropriation of what belongs to someone else, that is, to another community and its culture. To begin with, White Americans must gain an understanding and appreciation of their Whiteness. This means it will be critical for amer-european people to complete a task largely ignored until now, namely, to identify amer-european (White) culture. And once Whiteness is carefully identified, it then should become a target for deconstruction. Indeed, we could say the same thing with regard to maleness and male privileging in our world.

7. To reiterate discussions in earlier chapters (especially chapters 2 and 3), our White relatives must begin to learn from indigenous peoples worldwide the importance of respecting all their own relatives in the created world, including trees and rivers, animals and flying things. It is this worldview of the interrelatedness of all on the earth, including the earth itself, that gives us a chance to imagine genuine justice and an authentic peace in the world around us.

8. While it is something of a tautology to say that liberalism is modernism, we need to stretch beyond western liberalism in ways that postmodernism

---

27. Now we have the *Mensaje de conferencia de teologia india* from Indian Christians of latin America calling on the churches to recognize and respect the traditional wisdom of their indigenous communities (Cochabamba, Bolivia, August 26-30, 1997).

has, so far, only imagined. To begin with, it is time that our theological reflection abandon the narrow liberal focus on the individual, seeking to provide answers that respond primarily to the needs of individuals—whether for some sort of salvation or to expand the individual need for knowledge or consumption to a view of reality that foregrounds the corporate whole of community. It will become increasingly important, then, that we find ways to deconstruct the dominance of individualism in our society and to replace individualism with broader ideas of community. This shift will necessarily challenge notions of the centrality of competition for goods and the accumulation of individual wealth as we create persistent images of community well-being in our neighborhoods and reservations, in our cities, in our continental whole. The question is still this: How will we live together, Indian and non-Indian, White and people of color, men and women?

9. Finally, we must begin to dream together, Indian and non-Indian, White and color, to dream a new vision of the world in which domination and privileging lose their seemingly natural prominence in structuring a world society. Yet, we need to reiterate that our visioning, our imagination, dare not collapse into mere romantic dreaming.

* * *

If deeply reflective concern for confession and repentance must today become collective acts that involve the whole of societies and social units and avoid generating mere emotive feelings of individual guilt, then our deepest constructive theological reflection must also become a collective act that speaks insistently and persistently to the well-being of the people as a whole—whether we call it community or society, nation or state. In this, I believe, I do agree wholly with Dean. The question around which he and I would debate is how we will get there and how we will know when we have arrived? A quarter of a century ago, I arrived as a young new faculty member at a school of theology thinking that the largest discrete population sector and best positioned folk in north America for affecting real social change were those people attached to churches and synagogues, especially those who professed some relationship with the Creator, whether through faith in Jesus as the Christ of God or through some similar religious faith commitment.

I am a characteristically optimistic sort of person, always hopeful that the future holds something better than the Indian experience of the past five hundred years. As I get older, however, I am forced to wonder more and more how warranted that optimism has been.[28] My fear today is that the large insti-

---

28. See the historiographic analysis offered by David Scott, *Conscripts of Modernity*.

tutional denominations that make up most of the religious landscape in the United States are entirely too entwined in the very structures of oppression (structures of *sin*, to use the language of the churches) to be of much help in dreaming a new way of being together in the world. All I can really cling to is that vague oxymoronic hope voiced so long ago now by Martin King, a widely spoken african american aphorism that says, "God makes a way out of no way!" And to a hope that in increasing numbers we will find one another and stand together to dream a new dream of a just society living in balance with all our relations. While that dream must be a postmodern one in some respect, I believe that it must be heavily endowed with insights from the value system of indigenous premodernity.

Yet, if we cannot rally the moral judgment of religious peoples in the United States I suspect there can be no grassroots movement toward any creative transformation of our society. Religious communities in the United States, not the institutional structures that organize them but the communities themselves, are the critical mass necessary for generating a movement toward lasting change. That is where our movement for transformation must begin, with you and me. If we dream of peace, of course, we need to work for justice, as the old saying goes. And if we imagine together justice and peace, the material reality can begin to emerge in the generations that come. Dream, then. Dream a new dream. Imagine a new world, and struggle to give it birth.

Suggestions for Further Reading

All of these authors are American Indian. The list is heavily weighted with titles by Vine Deloria, Jr., simply because he was the foremost American Indian intellectual writing about Indian people in our contemporary world. He wrote with equal fluency about law, history, political theory, philosophy, and religion. I have included books here that might be of interest to readers of my own volume. Anyone interested in furthering their understanding of American Indians should read Deloria.

Alfred, Taiaiake (Kahnawá:ke Mohawk). *Wasáse: Indigenous Pathways of Action and Freedom*. Peterborough, Ont.: Broadview Press, 2005.

Churchill, Ward (Cherokee). *Kill the Indian, Save the Man: The Genocidal Impact of American Indian Residential Schools*. San Francisco: City Lights Press, 2004.

Deloria, Jr., Vine (Standing Rock Dakota/Lakota). *Behind the Trail of Broken Treaties: An Indian Declaration of Independence*. New York: Delacorte Press, 1974.

———. *Custer Died For Your Sins: An Indian Manifesto*. New York: Avon Books, 1969; reprinted University of Oklahoma Press, 1988.

———. *Evolution, Creationism and Other Modern Myths: A Critical Inquiry*. Golden, Colo.: Fulcrum, 2002.

———. *For This Land: Writings on Religion in America*. Edited by James Treat. New York: Routledge, 1998.

———. *God Is Red*. New York: Grosset & Dunlap, 1973; rev. and republished as *God Is Red: A Native View of Religion*. Golden, Colo.: Fulcrum, 1992; 30th anniversary edition, 2002.

———. *The Metaphysics of Modern Existence*. New York: Harper & Row, 1979.

———. *Red Earth, White Lies: Native Americans and the Myth of Scientific Fact*. Golden, Colo.: Fulcrum, 1995.

———. *Spirit and Reason: The Vine Deloria, Jr., Reader*. Edited by Barbara Deloria and Sam Scinta. Golden, Colo.: Fulcrum, 1999.

———. *We Talk, You Listen: New Tribes, New Turf*. New York: Macmillan, 1970; Winnipeg: Bison Books, reprinted 2007.

———. *The World We Used to Live In: Remembering the Powers of the Medicine Men*. Golden, Colo.: Fulcrum, 2006.

Grounds, Richard (Yuchi), David Wilkins (Lumbee), and Tink Tinker (Osage). *Native Voices: American Indian Identity and Resistance.* Lawrence: University of Kansas Press, 2001.

Huhndorf, Shari M. (Native Alaskan). *Going Native: Indians in the American Cultural Imagination.* Ithaca, N.Y.: Cornell University Press, 2001.

LaDuke, Winona (White Earth Anishinaabe). *All Our Relations: Native Struggles for Land and Life.* Cambridge, Mass.: South End Press, 1999.

————. *Recovering the Sacred: The Power of Naming and Claiming.* Cambridge, Mass.: South End Press, 2005.

Mann, Barbara Alice (Wendat/Seneca). *Iroquoian Women: The Gantowisas.* New York: Peter Lang, 2000.

Newcomb, Steve (Shawnee). *Pagans in the Promised Land: Decoding the Doctrine of Christian Discovery.* Golden, Colo.: Fulcrum, 2008.

Smith, Andrea (Cherokee). *Conquest: Sexual Violence and American Indian Genocide.* Cambridge, Mass.: South End Press, 2005.

————. *Native Americans and the Christian Right: The Gendered Politics of Unlikely Alliances.* Durham, N.C.: Duke University Press, 2008.

Tinker, George E. "Tink" (Osage). *Missionary Conquest: The Gospel and Native American Cultural Genocide.* Minneapolis: Fortress Press, 1993.

————. *Spirit and Resistance: Political Theology and American Indian Liberation* Minneapolis: Fortress Press, 2004.

Weaver, Jace (Cherokee), ed. *Native American Religious Identity: Unforgotten Gods.* Maryknoll, N.Y.: Orbis Books, 1998.

Williams, Jr., Robert A. (Lumbee). *The American Indian in Western Legal Thought: The Discourses of Conquest.* New York: Oxford University Press, 1990.

Index